THE
Wildlife
Garden

von Sue & John April 99

THE

Wildlife Garden

PLANNING BACKYARD HABITATS

Charlotte Seidenberg

Drawings by Jean Seidenberg

UNIVERSITY PRESS OF MISSISSIPPI·JACKSON

Frontispiece illustration: Maypop or passionflower vine, red morning glory, northern mocking-bird, ruby-throated hummingbird, gulf fritillary butterflies (larva and chrysalis)

Book and cover design by John William Costa

Manufactured in the United States of America

98 97 96 95   4 3 2 1

The paper in this book meets the guidelines for permanence
and durability of the Committee on Production Guidelines for
Book Longevity of the Council on Library Resources.

Library of Congress Cataloging-in-Publication Data

Seidenberg, Charlotte.
    The wildlife garden : planning backyard habitats / Charlotte
Seidenberg.
      p.   cm.
    Includes bibliographical references (p.   ) and index.
    ISBN 0-87805-808-7 (cloth : alk. paper)—ISBN 0-87805-
835-4 (pbk. : alk. paper)
    1. Gardening to attract wildlife.   I. Title.
QL59.S45   1995
639.9'2—dc20   95-22161
                                                  CIP

British Library Cataloging-in-Publication data available

To my daughter, Dara Rosenzweig,

my son, David Alexander Rosenzweig,

and my grandson, Zev Rael MacGregor.

They will cultivate the

wildlife gardens of the future.

Contents

S HE'LL OUTGROW THIS when she has children!" my father told my mother when she reported a surge in the numbers of wild things living with me after my marriage at age twenty-one. Was he wrong! My love of plants and animals is even stronger now that the children have grown up and left home. My entire property is a childhood wild-place fantasy, lush with flowers and shrubs and ponds for attracting, feeding, sheltering, and nurturing little creatures: birds, bees, butterflies and bugs; frogs, toads, lizards, turtles and snakes.

I'm not alone. I have found many friends who share my interests, and who, as adults, developed their own backyard wilderness. There is even a name for who we are and what we do. We are wildlife gardeners, and we create our different versions of a wildlife garden.

My father, now in his seventies and living outside Pittsburgh in a house bordering a wildlife refuge, eventually admitted to the obsession and even acknowledged that I probably got it from him. His letters detail his latest plans for attracting and defending against the creatures that come from the forest-garden at his doorstep into his world: sunflower seed feeders (with baffles to keep the squirrels out) that draw purple finches, sparrows, cardinals, and mourning doves; thistle holders for siskins, goldfinches, and redpolls; suet for downy, hairy, and red-bellied woodpeckers, titmice, and nuthatches; safflower for cardinals.

Raccoons visit at dusk or nighttime—two mothers and six cubs at one time—and a skunk! In icy November chipmunks and chickadees drink from the birdbath, thankful for the immersion heater. Late February brings skunks and raccoons, grouchy from interrupted hibernation and squabbling on the back porch, and the first robins of spring. And grackles, juncos, cottontail bunnies, deer, bats . . .

This book presents a plan for developing a wildlife garden based partly on my own experience and that of gardening and birdwatching friends and also containing much information from authorities in various fields of the natural sciences and horticulture that I collected in conversations, on field trips, listening to lectures and reading literature. I plan this book as a starting point and hope the material on these pages will lure you further into this new world of gardening!

The part of me that felt compelled to defend my obsession was quieted when I found an explanation in *Biophilia: The Human Bond with Other Species,* a book written in 1984 by evolutionary biologist E. O. Wilson. In his essay on the need to preserve organic biodiversity, Wilson argues that biophilia, our drive to explore and affiliate with life, is instinctive. He says: "To the extent that each person can feel like a naturalist, the old excitement of the untrammeled world will be regained. I offer this as a formula of reenchantment to invigorate poetry and myth: mysterious and little known organisms live within walking distance of where you sit. Splendor awaits in minute proportions."

What better place to look for excitement, to discover mysterious and little-known organisms, to find splendor in any proportion, than in your own backyard—than in a wildlife garden!

Acknowledgments

M ANY PEOPLE HAVE HELPED, directly or indirectly, with this project. I offer thanks to all of them. To my husband, Jean Seidenberg, of course, for his drawings, his encouragement, and his cooking and the other maintenance chores he performed so that I would have time to look at flowers, bugs, and birds, and to write. To my daughter, Dara, who listened to the stories first.

To JoAnne Prichard at University Press of Mississippi. A book on wildlife gardening was her idea. To Carol Cox for her editorial assistance. To Anne Bradburn who fit a quick read-through into her Christmas season so I could send the manuscript off in time! To Robert F. Brzuszek for his evaluation, all his useful feedback, his enthusiasm, and for the bog tour he led at the Crosby Arboretum last June. To Latimore Smith of Louisiana's Natural Heritage Program and The Nature Conservancy, Southeastern Region.

To all the scientists to whom we owe our knowledge of the natural world. To the organizations in each region of our country, like the Louisiana Nature and Science Center in New Orleans and the Lafayette Natural History Museum, who interpret science to the general public. To the Crosby Arboretum in Picayune, Mississippi, especially.

To John O'Neill, Tom Sherry, and Tracey Sherry for technical assistance with the birds and Vernon Brou with the moths and butterflies in the cover painting. For assistance with drawings, I thank Susan Palm, whose turtle, Magnolia the Magnificent, posed and Leslee Reed, whose bullfrog Jeremiah lives on in our art if not in her pond.

To all my birdwatching friends who didn't mind my "botanizing" on our birding trips in Louisiana, Texas, Alabama, Mississippi, Bolivia and Peru over the past year and a half: Leslee Reed, Jacqueline Bishop, Denise Schoen, Gloria McKinnon, Mary Joe Krieger, Kay Siebel, Helen Landry, Susan Palm, Margie Baldwin, Ed Guillot, Bill Hemeter, Bob Eble, Joan and George Sladovich. To Nancy Newfield for shared information on hummingbirds and hummer plants and for telling me about Richard Dufresne's lecture and salvia sale at Lydia's Audubon Shoppe in Waveland, Mississippi. To Gary Ross, the first scientist to document the trans-gulf migration of monarch butterflies!

To plant people, generous with networking time: John Mayronne, from whom I learned about Bill Fontenot's *Native Gardening in the South* and Brenda Brown, who told me about Sally Wasowski; Rosemary Sims of the New Orleans Old Rose Society who pointed out *Gaura* in Allen Lacy's *The Garden in Autumn*; Vaughn Banting; Karl and Gretchen Becnel and The Garden Trellis; Melinda Taylor; Teresa Forrest; Charlene Quinlan; and Elizabeth Register (who buys all those native perennials for Guillot's Nursery).

To those who unknowingly contributed stories that enlivened my text: Fred Crane, Susan Davidson, Pat Henican, Leticia Alamía and John O'Neill, Judy Burks, Liz Bennett, Leslee Reed, and Denise Schoen.

THE

Wildlife
Garden

CHAPTER ONE

What Is Wildlife Gardening?

Lions and tigers and bears? Oh, my!
—Dorothy in *The Wizard of Oz*

THE ONLY LIONS AND TIGERS AND BEARS you're likely to find in a wildlife garden are lion's ear (a mint family plant with velvety orange flowers attractive to hummingbirds), tiger swallowtail butterflies on the spicebush, or woolly bear caterpillars—the fuzzy, black larval form of the giant

Illustration: Spanish moss, bald cypress tree, red bat,
cypress sphinx and angle-winged emerald moths

leopard moth—on the sunflowers or in the willow tree. Wild
things they are, but hardly dangerous!

According to *Webster's*, wildlife is "living things that are neither human nor domesticated; *esp*: mammals, birds and fishes. . ."
By that definition, we can include fauna such as earthworms,
snails, spiders, butterflies and other insects, reptiles and amphibians; we can say wildlife is found in every garden. Wild creatures
are so prevalent that some lurk in even the most barren city lot
waiting to be drawn out from hiding: squatty toads that hop
from under houses toward puddles after rain to sing songs of love
and lay long strings of eggs, little brown snakes that coil in dark
places, eastern box turtles like the one that crawled out of the
ferns to cross the brick walkway to my front door in the fifth
year of my wildlife garden. Who knows where he had been
hiding all those years!

Disgusting, you say? But you probably love birds. Few people
can resist birds. Consider my neighbor who surrounded her
house with page fences, concrete walks, and lawns of St.
Augustine grass kept plush and green through the use of chemicals and meticulously mowed and edged—she calls it low maintenance. She grows nothing else, not flowers, not shrubs, certainly not trees! Too messy! But I've seen her spread bread
crumbs on the concrete landing to draw house sparrows close to
her doorway. I wonder if she notices that mockingbirds sing on
the roof overlooking the yard with elderberry trees but do not
come to hers; that night melodies of toads and green tree frogs
and spring peepers come from the four gardens on the block
with ponds and lots of vegetation and insects, but not from her
yard; and that butterflies avoid her neat but poisonous lawn to
seek the passionvine and milkweed around the corner and down
the way?

Any garden, even a midcity one, will attract some birds year-round: cardinals, blue jays, mockingbirds and the alien house sparrows in the Southeast. Most people do not look beyond the birds unless it's to react negatively to creatures such as slugs and bugs that are considered pests. But a garden full of the other life forms will have more birds, too.

The difference between a wildlife garden and other types is that the wildlife gardener has taken deliberate steps to make the land appealing to native creatures, either using limited measures such as hanging bird or squirrel feeders or growing the flowering plants that will draw hummingbirds and butterflies, or through more extensive efforts aimed at re-creating a favorite piece of wilderness that will entice all its forms of life.

One of my favorite "natural" places is the Indian mound at Dauphin Island, Alabama. I remember birding there one October weekend with the Crescent Bird Club.

It had rained early Saturday morning. Moisture was hanging in the warm air that formed a stationary cushion between two warring fronts. The group gathered at the front of the mound before heading into its series of raised areas and depressions, of grassy paths and clearings in thickets of magnolias, hackberries, mulberries and ancient spreading oaks draped with Spanish moss and the orange blooms of trumpet vines or muscadine grapes. We found hawthornes, red cedars, toothache-trees, berried yaupons and smilax in the midstory and edge. A sumac here and there and occasional Chinese tallows offered autumn reds. As the last person arrived, we birders headed up a gentle slope toward edges formed by shrubs and trees, with someone complaining that "the mowed paths are good for strolling, but the grasses sure could be good bird habitat if they weren't cut back."

"Why don't we head for that depression at the west side of the mound. I always see ovenbirds there."

"It'll be wet after the rain . . ."

"Lots of toads . . ."

". . . and a bee's nest in the big oak tree with overhanging limbs. We'll have to be careful!"

"I saw a summer tanager there, once, snapping up bees as they came out of the nest. They eat bees and wasps, you know!"

"This place is crawling with mockingbirds and cardinals," someone said with dissatisfaction just as movement high in the canopy signaled something else. Binoculars were aimed skyward on the tiny blue-gray gnatcatcher flitting like the insects it pursued. Then came the warblers, yellow-throated and Wilson's, and the day had begun!

It was hard to know whether to look up at the birds or down at the astounding numbers of butterflies and other insects visiting the banks of flowers. The butterfly people in the group named species:

"Monarchs, lots of gulf fritillaries..."

"The aquamarine-colored one with a long tail and wings edged with yellow is a skipper. The yellows are sulphurs."

There were giant bumblebees and honeybees. "What's this blue fly with white spots and a red-tipped tail?" someone called to an expert.

"A polka dot wasp moth!" she responded, excitedly. "Its larva is the oleander caterpillar. They're neotropicals found in Florida. And, I guess, Dauphin Island!"

"There is a hedge of oleanders by the building on the other side of the mound."

Along the shaded pathways grew orange-berried yaupon, red-flowered tropical sage and a white fuzzy-bloomed plant we looked up in a field guide to identify as boneset, a *Eupatorium.* In the sunny spots the display was almost gaudy: golden-orange lantana and goldenrod hillocks with pale yellow Japanese honeysuckle vines intertwined, brilliant blue spiderwort protruding and light blue wild ageratum peeking out at ground level.

On Sunday, the front had moved on, bringing the first coolness of autumn. We returned to the mound for more birding. I found a tiny clearing where the entrance was blocked by a great felled oak spongy with rot. I spread my poncho over the green moss cushion on the log and sat, soon feeling the coolness of the old wood penetrate my jeans. I listened to the constant blow of the wind in the distance and to the near and far sounds of rustling leaves. I felt puffs of coolness and watched the vines sway and the leaves in the upper parts of tree branches move. Was the clearing created when this tree fell? I wondered. I studied the surrounding growth: sweet gum, maple, Chinese tallows, oaks with branches lined with resurrection fern unfurling in the moisture of the morning. Vines, some dead, some living, hung in such great masses from high above as to give the appearance of being freestanding trunks themselves. Palmettos and a spongy carpet of leaves, fresh over decayed, covered the ground.

I watched a squirrel bounding along a branch, a nut between his teeth, plume-like tail waving behind. I sat so very still that birds came close, two catbirds nearest, peering at me to see if I'd move. I didn't. I spotted a yellow-billed cuckoo, eyes closed, its soft brown body all puffed out and soaking up warmth from a sunny site in a tree crown. Birds moved through the trees and vines and across the ground looking for bugs or berries: a white-eyed vireo, a black-and-white warbler running upside down at the underside of a tree trunk, American redstarts and hooded warblers.

I heard voices and occasionally saw the bright color of an

adventure pack through the tree trunks, but I didn't call out to anyone. How nice, I sighed.

Luckily, there are things I can do to draw species of wildlife to my backyard short of transporting the mound there—it wouldn't fit, anyway, and because of soil and regional climatic and exposure differences, it might not thrive. Our favorite natural settings can show us the way. All the necessary elements—food, cover, reproductive space, and water—are there, in trees and shrubs and brambles with limbs and leaves that provide shelter and nesting spots, with blossoms that offer nectar and pollen, then fruit, in wildflower meadows, puddles, ponds, or streams.

When I imagine my rural estate, I see natural plant communities enhanced to draw even more of my favorite creatures: salvias, turk's cap, buckeye, mamou, and swathes of coral honeysuckle and cross vine on the tree limbs to draw hummingbirds, rubythroated in the spring, and rufous, black-chinned, and buff-bellied in the winter; red mulberry trees to lure migratory tanagers and grosbeaks; three species of hawthornes draped with red-berried moonseed vine to send birds and mammals into ecstasy; fields of wildflowers buzzing with insects near a pond so full of fish and frogs that flocks of great blue herons, black-crowned night herons and snowy egrets gorging to their hearts' content wouldn't make a dent in their numbers or decrease the night chorus of amphibians!

City dwellers must fantasize on a smaller scale. Providing the variety of habitats, plentiful food and nectar sources important for lots of wildlife is more of a challenge on a small lot than on a large. But you can do it! Even if all you plan to do is hang bird feeders, knowing some secrets can help you attract more birds and attract birds more selectively. I hope the information in this book will give you ideas and inspiration and will help you devise a plan for attracting wildlife to fit the size of your lot and of your dreams.

Wildlife gardening is a way of thinking. My first thought after developing the plan presented in this book was how far my own garden comes from the ideal! With more research, I became conscious of how many plants in my garden are not native to my area. I realized that some of the native ones grew from seeds collected over fifty miles from my home and that some of my native trees came from a nursery over one hundred miles away. I felt relieved that we had cut down our huge, aged and decaying Chinese tallow tree once I found out what a threat the species is to native plant communities, yet guilty when I realized how much I had appreciated that tree.

Why didn't we leave the tallow trunk standing as a snag? Because my neighbor, who is in the landscaping business, gave us a large dawn redwood to plant in its place as a beautiful back-drop to his garden. Why not a bald cypress, indigenous to the spot? Its knees would grow through the brick sidewalk in such a narrow yard, he said. He's probably right, but will cypress sphinx and angle-winged emerald moths lay their eggs on a dawn redwood the way they would a cypress? The Spanish moss I draped on its limbs seems to be taking—maybe red bats will roost within its clumps—and the orange-crowned and yellow-rumped warblers perch there, anyway, on their way to the bird-bath. It is pretty.

Gardening is for fun. Pick what appeals to you from the infor-mation in the pages that follow. This is not a book of rules but of ideas. You may choose some and discard others. You may have lots of your own to add.

But no matter how involved you've been with plants from

faraway times and places, I defy you not to become as intrigued as I with indigenous plants and animals once you've grown passionflower and become accustomed to fritillaries frolicking through your composites, or grown milkweeds and observed the life cycle of the monarch. I defy you not to be as fascinated as I with the complexity and beauty of our native insect life once you've lived close to blooming goldenrod, mistflower and horsemint, or as enthralled as I with hummers once you've lured your first to a hummingbird-adapted plant, or with amphibians once you've spotlighted a green tree frog, throat inflated with song, on the pickerel weed by your pond.

My garden is becoming a place for learning about the natural world. And the more I know the more I want to know. I hope you'll join me!

CHAPTER TWO

How to Make a Wildlife Garden

OU CAN ENTICE SOME WILDLIFE to a "garden" that's little more than a concrete slab. You can fasten a bird feeder to a pole in the middle and install a birdbath and birdhouse; you can grow some of the vines suggested in chapter 7 up the fence at the edge; you can cultivate in containers flowers that will attract hummingbirds or butterflies (see appendix). The more you do to provide for the basic needs of wildlife—food, water, and cover—the more creatures will call.

The most successful wildlife gardens—the ones that attract

Illustration: House sparrows, blue jay

the greatest numbers and species of fauna from the geographic area—are more than gardens. They are woodlands, meadows, prairies and wetlands, populated with plants from the surrounding ecological region and supplemented with fruit- or nectar-producing exotics. Impossible on a standard city lot? Not if you consider the clumps of copper iris and swamp lilies, Virginia willow, buttonbush and palmetto growing in that low spot on the left side of your house where runoff from your gutters pools to be a wetland. Not if you grow pitcher plants, yellow-eyed grass, meadow beauties, blazing stars, broom sedge and joint-grass in the poorly drained area between your slash pines and call it a savannah. Not if you think of the narrow strip of goldenrod, ironweed, horsemint, spider flower, milkweed and selected grasses along the sunny side of your house as a "prairie." Not if you place dominant forest trees and shrubs from the region along your back property line, plant shrubs under shorter trees under taller trees and call them canopied woods and understory, then border them with irregular paths instead of straight ones to increase the forest edge!

Even if you start with less severe physical limitations than those imposed by a concrete slab, other strictures—a landlord's rules, time, money, an existing garden of nonindigenous ornamentals, and your own set ideas about the way a garden should look—will affect how close your garden comes to the ideal. The "wild" appearance of loosely ordered, natural habitats so attractive to wildlife may not appeal to you. Plan and manage your landscape to meet your tastes. Keep in mind that when you choose simplicity of number and arrangement of species over complexity, or symmetry of design over irregularity, you decrease diversity and, therefore, numbers of creatures that may visit. But you can devise ways to keep your garden looking neat and still attract lots of fauna.

How does one go about creating an ideal tame/wild setting? Transporting a wild place in toto to a city lot wouldn't work. Even if we could move a fragment of forest in its entirety to a garden, it would no longer be a forest. But it wouldn't be a garden, either. The secret is to duplicate certain aspects of local natural habitats—those most significant in terms of attracting wildlife—then to go a step beyond nature and create an unnatural abundance of ornamental and useful plants.

Plants make up the natural environments where animals live; they are habitats in and of themselves. In the words of Bill Fontenot: "Plants (not bird feeders, birdbaths, and birdhouses) comprise the backbone of 99.99% of all wild habitats. Plants produce food in the form of fruits and seeds, harbor food in the form of insects and other animals, and hold water in the form of dew and raindrops. They provide shade, protection from wind and rain, and nesting sites and materials."[1] Obviously, plants growing in original environments were natives; dominant vegetation in the most effective wildlife garden will be indigenous to the ecological region of the garden. But plants are not the whole story.

Professional forest manager Paul Hamel analyzed the components of forest habitat, naming four vegetation layers: herbaceous (plants such as grasses, sedges, rushes and composites), shrub, midstory, and overstory. Within those layers, he identified certain habitat elements important to birds for their life activities: perching (while singing, roosting, preening, or sleeping), nesting and foraging. Within the midstory and overstory are dead trees (snags) of different dimensions, living cavity trees, and big trees, which, depending on patterns of growth, will form closed or open canopy with grassy areas underneath. Soil on the forest floor may be bare or covered with leaf litter and downed logs. There may be rocky places and earth banks and aquatic environments of flowing or still water. In *The Land Manager's Guide to the Birds of the South*, Hamel tells us that "each bird species is adapted to certain successional conditions of certain forest vegetation types, and . . . where those conditions are present within the species' range the birds will be too. . . . Experience in game management demonstrates that specific habitat elements can be produced by purposeful manipulations."[2]

Even if we cannot use Hamel's analysis to predict wildlife in a city garden, we can use it as a guide for improving habitat in a backyard wilderness, both in terms of selection of plant species and in their placement and overall design. When you read the suggestions that follow, you'll see parallels to Hamel's recommendations for a managed forest. In both cases, specific habitat elements are produced by purposeful manipulation. The habitat suitable for birds will meet the needs of other wildlife, too: mammals, reptiles, amphibians, insects, spiders and other invertebrates.

Identifying Your Habitats

Before indulging your dreams of the wild things you'll find in your garden—lacewings and ladybugs, tree frogs, buntings and grosbeaks—and before the fun of designing your overall garden and picking the plants—sassafras and mayhaw, elm-leafed goldenrod and butterfly weed—you must address basic gardening reality. Otherwise, the dreams will never come true!

Examine conditions on the site where the plants will grow. Healthy plants make more food and cover for wildlife; plants are more likely to thrive if planted in suitable conditions. Whether you live in an urban or suburban setting, your first steps will be the same: (1) identify different habitats on your property;

(2) devise a plan incorporating existing plants you want to keep and including new plants adapted to the specific conditions in each habitat—the right plant in the right place.

Each area, with its distinct combination of soil makeup, moisture, exposure, and light conditions, is a separate habitat, suitable for different plants. You'll probably find more than one in even the tiniest yard. I found a wetland of *Sagittaria*, or bulltongue, growing and blooming in miniature in a tire-rut habitat in a grassy field near my home.

Make a map of your site. You don't have to be a cartographer to do this, for even a simple drawing will be useful when you work out a planting plan. Sketch existing buildings and paved areas. Fill in the trees and other elements of the landscape. Then begin your analysis. The lines on your map may show precise divisions, but, in reality, you'll find transition zones where one habitat blends into another.

Start with light, the easiest element to observe. Record areas where the sun is harsh and full, where there is only morning sun, dappled shade or "filtered light," zones of deep shade. Notice the places protected from or exposed to wind with its drying effects. If conditions in one spot are noticeably harsher than in surrounding areas, outline it and label it as another habitat.

Next, look for the different soil types and moisture levels within each of the sectors you have already defined. On porches and patios where you garden in containers, exposure and light are the only factors to consider; you provide whatever growing medium your plants need. In the ground, however, you must determine what conditions exist, and, since soil in its natural state is rare, you must also assess what damage has been done by human disruption of the natural scheme of things.

Play detective! Vegetation is one of the best clues to soil

A Backyard Habitat Plan

The plan on the facing page is keyed with letters to show the various plant habitats found in one backyard wildlife garden and with numbers to suggest plants suitable to those habitats. Two sets of numbers indicate how this plan may be adapted by gardeners who wish to duplicate Bottomland Forest or Mixed Hardwood-Loblolly Forest Communitites.

Plant Habitats in an Established Wildlife Garden

A. higher, very well-drained soil; shady

B. well-drained soil; sunny, warm

C. plantings close to house: drier soil, morning sun only

D. north side of house: swale, lower area draining to front of lot; shady, cooler

E. south side of house: swale, lower area draining to front of lot; part shade

F. western exposure, drier soil, afternoon sun only in planting near house

G. lower area, western exposure, sunny, sun harsh on summer afternoons

Suggested plants for gardens in regions of Bottomland Forest Community

1. Nuttall Oak
2. red mulberry
3. winged elm
4. wax myrtle
5. live oak
6. trellis with vines: trumpet creeper, peppervine, native grapes
7. swamp dogwood, rough leaved dogwood
8. dwarf palmetto
9. swamp red maple
10. Virginia willow
11. green ash
12. red bay
13. sycamore
14. black gum
15. hawthorn
16. honey locust
17. hackberry
18. bald cypress
19. buttonbush
20. dwarf palmetto
21. deciduous holly
22. elderberry
23. pokeweed
24. sweet gum
25. red buckeye (not found naturally in these communities)

Suggested plants for gardens in regions of Mixed Hardwood-Loblolly Forest Community

1. loblolly pine
2. crab apple
3. flowering dogwood
4. wax myrtle
5. southern magnolia
6. trellis with vines: yellow jessamine, blackberries, dewberries
7. sourwood
8. male winged sumac
9. red maple
10. female yaupon (fruit-bearing)
11. sassafras
12. male yaupon (pollen-bearing)
13. southern red oak
14. black gum
15. hawthorn
16. American elm
17. tulip poplar
18. pignut hickory
19. female winged sumac
20. blueberries, huckleberries (*Vaccinium* species)
21. deciduous holly
22. French mulberry
23. pokeweed
24. sweet gum
25. devil's walkingstick

This design is based on the one by Jody Walthall in *Planting a Refuge for Wildlife: How to Create a Backyard Habitat for Florida's Birds and Beasts* by Susan Cerulean, Celeste Botha, and Donna Legare, which suggests plants for gardens in north and south Florida.

Other sources of ideas for design and planting of wildlife/native plant gardens are: Brooklyn Botanical Garden Plants and Gardens handbooks: *The Environmental Gardener. Going Native: Biodiversity in Our Own Backyards*; *Nature's Design, A Practical Guide to Natural Landscaping* by Carol Smyser and the editors of Rodale Press Books; and *Native Gardening in the South* by William R. Fontenot.

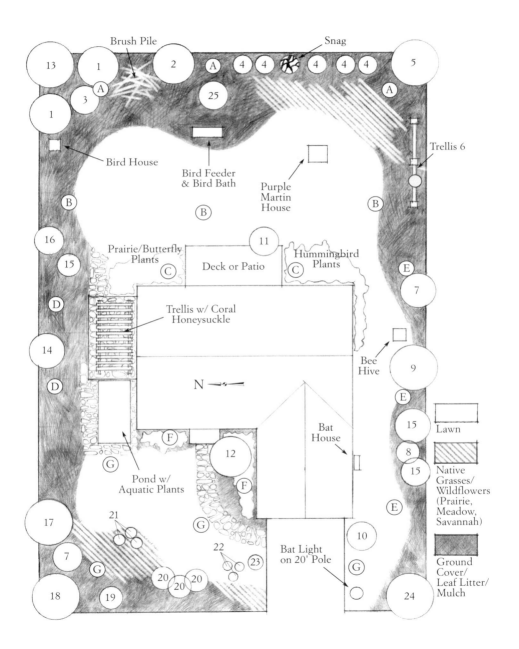

Brush Pile

Snag

13   1   A   2   A   4   4   4   4   4   5

3

1

25

A

Trellis 6

Bird House

Bird Feeder & Bird Bath

Purple Martin House

B

B

B

16

15

Prairie/Butterfly Plants

11

Deck or Patio

Hummingbird Plants

C

C

E

7

D

Trellis w/ Coral Honeysuckle

14

Bee Hive

9

D

E

N

15

Lawn

8

F

15

G

Pond w/ Aquatic Plants

12

F

Native Grasses/ Wildflowers (Prairie, Meadow, Savannah)

Bat House

E

17

21

G

10

Ground Cover/ Leaf Litter/ Mulch

7

22

23

Bat Light on 20' Pole

G

18

19

20

20

20

24

variations. The weeds that quickly invade a disturbed area are indicators of growing conditions. Unless you have just covered your entire lot with a layer of homogeneous fill, you will find that soil will vary from spot to spot, with each site supporting different species. A field guide can help you determine the identity of those ubiquitous weeds, but the difference is the important factor. Weeds are nature's soil improvers. Different species evolved to correct problems in the soil. Through the process of growth and death, they enrich the soil and prepare it for succeeding species. Chickweed, daisy, dock, plantain, and sorrel? Your soil is acid! Lamb's-quarters and mustard family plants? Alkaline! Beggarticks, curly dock, joe-pye weed and smartweed in the low spot in the back? They thrive in poorly drained soil. And legumes, such as clover, vetch and lupines, have evolved to grow in nitrogen-deficient soil.

Make an inventory of cultivated plants that are thriving and research their requirements.

Dig in different spots and examine the composition of the soil. How deep is it? Is it compacted? Fill some holes with water to check drainage. Let them drain overnight, then refill them and observe how fast the water level drops. If it's slower than a fourth of an inch per hour, you have poor drainage.

Study maps and surveys prepared by the Soil Conservation Service of the U. S. Department of Agriculture for an overview of characteristic soils of your entire geographical region and, except to the extent that it has been covered by fill of unknown origin or modified by use, of the soil on your property.

Once you've isolated the different soil types, you can verify your observations and evaluate each area further by testing for pH, porosity, texture (proportion of sand, silt, clay), structure, water, and available nutrients with a soil-testing kit from a garden center, or, for greater accuracy, you can arrange professional soil testing. Find out how from your local county extension agent.

Now, sort all the information you've collected and use it to further subdivide your map. Label the low and high areas, the wet and the dry, the shady and the sunny, the hot and cool. You know where the soil has been abused through human use—where it has been stripped or compacted, thus becoming heavy and draining poorly or being inclined to drain too rapidly and losing original organic matter, or where foreign objects left on the site have disturbed acid-base balance.

Before you plant in areas where the soil is badly damaged, you should improve drainage or texture or pH. How? If professionals analyzed your soil, they will make specific suggestions. (Never add chemicals to change pH without first testing the soil.) But the best improvement is one most gardeners know already: mulch with organic matter. A continuous layer of leaves or bark mulch will help loosen compacted soil, correct improper pH, improve topsoil, prevent crusting, balance soil with too much sand or clay, restore proper nutrients, and feed important organisms that live in the soil. There will be more on mulching in chapter 6.

Now you know the plant habitats on your property. But there is more information to consider before you select your plants.

The Basic Rules

DIVERSITY OF PLANTS

Banks of the same species of oriental azaleas or flowerbeds solidly planted with marigolds and edged with blue torenia are dramatic. But the wildlife gardener achieves drama through diversity. Plant a variety of species, with indigenous plants being predominant. Each native tree will host larvae of particular butterflies and moths; each native flowering plant will draw specific organisms that have evolved as its associates. Use both seed- and fruit-bearing trees and shrubs; those that produce cones, catkins, or seed pods will attract some birds and those with berries or fruit, others. Identify native trees growing in your neighborhood; if you choose different species for your garden, you'll increase diversity in your immediate region. Grow flowering or fruiting vines up your trees. Cultivate an assortment of flowers that will provide continuous bloom and a constant source of pollen and nectar for bees, butterflies, parasitic wasps, syrphid flies, lacewings, lady beetles and hummingbirds, as well as seeds for other birds. Choose plants that will yield food throughout the seasons of the year. Include some evergreen species for cover during winter months.

Diversity of Habitats

An immaculately cropped and groomed lawn edged with straight rows of sheared hedges may be neat, but it does not appeal to wildlife. Keep Paul Hamel's vegetation layers and elements in mind as you lay out your plans. Birds, amphibians, reptiles and mammals will prefer the garden edged with shrubs that have been selected to offer fruit or berries or seeds each season and ground-level growth for critical cover when a cat comes. Wildlife will hide or forage in the patches of herbaceous ground cover. Birds will perch in trees edging the part of lawn given over to wildflowers, waiting to pick off insects visiting the blossoms. Many creatures will love the "ungarden"—the habitat at the back of the yard that has been let go so that "weeds" can materialize. Let fallen leaves remain under deciduous trees as mulch and to lure snails, slugs, and insects, which will in turn become dinner for ground-foraging birds, lizards and toads. Leave dead trees standing to attract insects and their larvae and to make nesting and foraging sites for woodpeckers and other birds. Trim them for safety, of course! Build rock and brush piles in addition to or instead of ground cover in some spots to serve as hiding places for small mammals, reptiles and amphibians and as hibernation spots for butterflies. Wooden fenceposts and rocks in sunny places can serve as basking perches for butterflies and lizards. Leave a patch of sand or bare earth for dust-bathing or foraging birds; moisten it to draw puddling butterflies. Leave feathers, bark, grass clippings, moss and bits of fur on your property for birds and native mice to use as nesting materials.

Shade and Light

Balance shady places with open spaces where grasses or flowers will flourish. Create irregular borders around wooded areas to maximize the sunny edge. Understory trees and shrubs will flower more heavily and produce more fruit in the sunshine. Consider future light conditions when you plant trees—your sunny sideyard will no longer be a meadow when the sapling planted there matures into a densely crowned shade tree. That's the nature of succession. However, in the garden you're in control.

Water

Create aquatic environments. Provide steady sources of fresh water as small as a slow drip into a birdbath or as big as a pond with plants to draw mammals, frogs, turtles, ducks. Place and maintain birdbaths on pedestals or at ground level. Clay saucers or inverted trash-can lids can be makeshift baths and provide permanent puddles.

ELIMINATION OF CHEMICALS

Herbicides (except glycophosphates, essential in the battle against certain invasive alien plants), fungicides, pesticides, and even fertilizers can be deadly to wildlife. Curtail or eliminate the use of chemicals on your lawn or in your garden. Investigate alternatives such as mechanical and biological techniques for pest control, mulch and compost for soil enrichment.

Some Specific Suggestions

IF YOU'RE STARTING FROM SCRATCH

If your property is big enough, edge it, sides and back, with species of trees that will become very large. They will form the forest canopy and provide cover, nesting sites, and food for small mammals and birds.

Mass small groups of shorter flowering trees near the tall trees and at several other spots on the boundary of your lot to make the mid- and understory. The fruits and seeds that follow the flowers will be a source of food for birds; flowers and fruits will attract butterflies and other useful insects, some of which will become additional food for birds.

Surround the small trees with a blend of tall and low shrubs, dense herbaceous growth or brambles to make homes for mammals and birds and a refuge for ground-feeding creatures threatened by predators. Choose species that offer food in their blooms, berries, and seeds for birds, mammals, and butterflies and other useful insects.

Lay irregular, not straight, paths around your woodland to increase the forest edge.

Plant low herbaceous growth and smaller shrubs around your home. Select plants that will stay small and will not grow large enough to block your view.

Consider constructing a trellis for an assortment of native flowering and fruiting vines as an alternative to trees and shrubs to hide an unsightly shed. Vines will create a thicket for nesting sites and for cover, too.

Use alternatives to a lawn: make pathways, or put sidewalks or stepping stones through wildflower plantings and areas of low herbaceous growth, fallen leaves or brush piles.

For Established Plantings

Evaluate plants in terms of contributions to wildlife. If some do not fit into your total plan, replace them gradually. Think carefully before cutting trees, as new ones are costly and take years to grow. A large tree of any species, native or nonnative, is probably more valuable in terms of benefit to wildlife than a new, small one, which may take several years to become productive.

Reduce the area of your lawn by encircling or interrupting it with small clusters of trees and shrubs—flowering, fruiting species, of course.

Surround solitary trees with small shrubs and low herbaceous plants. Again, choose a variety of species that flower and make fruit.

Allow dead trees to stand; they will provide food, homes and perches for a wide variety of mammals, birds, and insects.

Convert your hedges into hedgerows; don't prune fencerow plantings. If unclipped, they will develop the natural density that makes for good cover and nesting sites. Plant thorny branched shrubs and brambles; they will provide the best nesting spots and cover.

The Small Yard

A tree may some day overshadow smaller plantings. If it provides food, shelter, and nesting sites for birds and mammals or larval food for your favorite butterfly species, it may still, from the point of view of wildlife attractiveness, be a better choice than the shrubs you would put in the same place—even if the tree becomes your whole garden.

Grow a well-behaved vine up the tree.

As an alternative to a tree, a hedge of six or eight shrubs in a sunny site can offer a year-round cafeteria for birds and mammals.

If a sunny patio is all the garden you have, plant your garden in pots. A container garden of profusely flowering plants with supplemental nectar and seed feeders will lure birds, hummingbirds and butterflies. Add a potted pepper plant to drive mockingbirds crazy! A birdbath is a must.

CHAPTER THREE

Native Plants for Native Wildlife

I F YOU REPRODUCE THE COMPONENTS of a forest—
the various vegetation layers, substrates and habitat elements
described by Paul Hamel—in a garden of exotic plants, you
can create a setting that looks perfectly "natural." As a matter of
fact, that is the approach most of us with established gardens will
take. I wouldn't recommend that you cut down your only large
tree just because it's not indigenous. It still offers shelter and
food for fauna, and growing a native replacement can take a long
time. You don't have to give up the beautiful oriental hibiscus

Illustration: Horsemint, common sooty wing butterfly,
dragonfly, anole lizard

with the showy red flowers even if hummingbirds don't visit, but they will. *Buddleia davidii* is not called "butterfly bush" for nothing, but it's not indigenous to the United States. Chinese tallow tree and Chinese privet have become scourges of southern landscapes, spread by the birds that seek their seed. Gardens of these and other alien plants are undeniably attractive to wildlife. So, why bother to use natives in a wildlife garden?

Animals are naturally drawn to the plants that shelter and feed them in the wild settings where they live and breed. With a garden of natives, you should see even more species of native wildlife—ten to fifty times as many species, according to the National Wildlife Federation—as with exotics.[1] Most of these are insects, but insects are the main food for other creatures: birds, mammals, reptiles, amphibians, arachnids, and even other insects! Each indigenous plant has the potential to attract an entire system of creatures, sized micro to macro, with which it has evolved: a whole complex of organisms including pollinators and dispersers of seeds, the creatures and predators that live within its bark or eat its leaves or fruit, and the scavengers and saprophytes that feed on its remains when it dies, returning the nutrients bound up in its tissues to the soil to nourish other plants and animals. The creatures range from those too small to be seen with the naked eye to mammals, birds and butterflies— "real" wildlife.

Introduced species evolved within systems, too; however, microbial and invertebrate associates of the *japonicas* and *chinensis* are not likely to find their way to your American garden. So what? You may not care. Something must pollinate and prey on the garden species that adapt to conditions in this country. It's fine for a gardener to be committed to exotic flora, to be uninterested in minute creepy-crawlies and satisfied with the current level of species diversity in his or her garden.

But there is a point I must raise against certain species of introduced plants. A healthy environment, in or out of the garden, is one with the greatest diversity of plant and animal life according to the habitat. If one plant is too aggressive within your yard, you will cut it back or provide barriers to contain its rhizomes or pull excessive seedlings. When aggressive aliens leave the garden—and if they are attractive to birds, like Chinese tallow trees, Chinese privet and Japanese honeysuckle, they will leave, spread by the birds themselves—there is no one to cut them back or pull them up. They crowd out native species and reduce diversity in our native landscapes. As E. O. Wilson says: "Species are disappearing at an accelerating rate through human action, primarily habitat destruction but also pollution and the introduction of exotic species into residual natural environments. . . .Why should we care? New sources of scientific information will be lost. Vast potential biological wealth will be destroyed. Still undeveloped medicines, crops, pharmaceuticals, timber, fibers, pulp, soil-restoring vegetation, petroleum substitutes, and other products and amenities will never come to light."[2]

People frequently don't know what's native and what isn't. "Why, I grew up with that wonderful, fragrant, yellow honeysuckle," a startled southerner told me. "It's everywhere!" Japanese honeysuckle is not everywhere because it belongs! As I have learned more about biodiversity, I have found myself seeing less of the beauty and more of the aggressive bully in Chinese tallow trees, or Japanese climbing ferns, or Japanese honeysuckle. I don't want them in my garden, even honeysuckle. I know it's not realistic to think that cutting down one tree in my yard or rooting out specimens of one vine will reduce the threat to natural plant communities in my area. One person, one tree, one yard might not matter. But they do all add up.

The environmentally concerned may grow indigenous plants

to save them from extinction as their habitats are destroyed through what is called "progress"—cities and towns sprawling into wooded areas, forests being leveled for industrial development. Some garden clubs promote conservation through a pro-native affirmative action policy encouraging members to include a few indigenous plants along with exotics in beds, borders, and edges. But why should we have to be so dutiful? Gardening is for fun!

I attended a recent lecture where the audience was moved to passionate concern by projected images of lush, colorful, long-blooming salvias becoming endangered as their Central American habitats are developed for agriculture, lumbered, or overgrazed by domestic goats. "We can bring them to our gardens to deliver them from extinction . . . like the ginkgo, alive today only because Buddhist monks nurtured it within their monastery walls!" proposed one listener. "We can use them in roadside plantings all over the state!" proclaimed another. But wouldn't that endanger our own natives that are growing along roadsides now? Why doesn't everybody want to save them? I wanted to ask.

Things have changed some, though, since 1874, when Lamson Scribner wrote: "A prophet is not without honor save in his own country; true is this saying when rendered— A plant is not wanting admiration save in its native land."[3] The European gardeners who grow our natives choose them for reasons other than saving the environment. Native plant societies that promote the use of our indigenous plants promote beauty, not duty! You'll understand once you have seen Florida flame azalea blooming golden with native blue phlox at its base, or the vivid purple berries on a French mulberry-American beautyberry shrub, or the elaborate and beautiful forms of passionflower/may-pop flowers.

Sally Wasowski offers a hypothesis as to why we've overlooked our own lovelies: "The natives, you see, were growing wild and uncared for. Naturally, they didn't look their best. Listen, if you were living out in a field, with no one to look after you, how good would you look?"[4] Natives in a region have developed through millions of years of competition during which the fittest—those best suited to the climate and least susceptible to diseases—have survived. The advantages of being in a garden, including reduced competition with other plants and the result-ing room to grow, water during dry spells, and plentiful mulch or compost, will allow them to flourish!

But what's got me so intrigued with the idea of plants indige-nous to my region, what's made me dissatisfied with my plants from faraway places, what's roused in me a rumbling urge to redo the garden again and make it as native as I can is my dawn-ing awareness of the interconnectedness of things—plants, ani-mals, air, soil, water—right here in my own city and state, not off in a faraway rainforest. It started with the native horsemint I grew from seed collected in a south Louisiana woodland edge. When it bloomed its complicated layers of spotted petals and pink petals, amazing numbers of several orders of insects, with varied colors and shapes, appeared to probe the flowers for nectar and pollen, to prey on the others, to fly, to hover, to climb, to crawl—creatures I'd never seen before! During fall migration, species of birds uncommon on Upperline Street stopped in to glean insects from horsemint foliage or sally forth from a perch in the elderberry to snap them out of the air—common yellowthroats, yellow warblers, eastern phoebes. Biodiversity, I saw, can exist or cease to exist in my own backyard as well as on the Tambopata River in Peru.

Ethnobotanist Mark Plotkin tells us that the focus of the early conservation efforts on the "so-called charismatic megafauna" is ironic because "we cannot save the pandas, unless we save the bamboos on which they feed."[5] Luckily for the wildlife gardener, the big wildlife is usually less picky than pandas. Most vertebrates are mobile, ranging through several habitats, and warm-blooded birds and mammals are even less habitat- and plant-specific than are cold-blooded reptiles and amphibians. Scientists suspect that more research will prove invertebrates to be the ones most restricted to specific communities. But there are vertebrate and invertebrate equivalents to pandas in every part of the world, flora and fauna so interdependent or so dependent on particular habitats that they cannot exist separately. Yuccas, for example, have as their pollinators moths of the genus *Pronuba*—there is a species of moth specific to each species of yucca—and there are butterflies and moths with larvae that feed only on members of one plant family and no others.

Participants in restoration of the original plant communities of the Indian Boundary Prairies near Chicago saw animal associates of the plants return, too, creatures found nowhere else in Illinois and some that were thought to be extinct: leafhoppers, grasshoppers, katydids, butterflies and moths, including nine rare species of the genus *Papaipema*, the larvae of which are root-borers and each of which is dependent on a different prairie plant. Other prairie specialists reappeared, too: birds like bobolinks, eastern meadowlarks, Henslow's sparrows, and the elusive yellow rail; reptiles like the rare, smooth green snake; mammals like the gray fox and Franklin's ground squirrel.[6]

I am not equating wildlife gardening with restoration of native plant communities. You can't really reproduce a complex ecosystem with all its plants, animals, and microflora in an urban or suburban backyard. There is, however, wildlife you've never even imagined living in your geographic region and nowhere else in the world! If you use nature as a model for your wildlife garden, studying the flora in remnants of original habitats of your ecological region at the local arboretum, nature center or native plant society, and creating pocket prairies or mini-meadows—little patches of the way things were—at your doorstep, some of that wildlife could live in your own backyard. Maybe there will just be root borer moths that evolved with the provincial goldenrod or tiny spiders who live and love on a local milkweed. You never know for sure what might appear.

In a garden of plants from faraway places, you can travel vicariously to the ends of the earth. But in a garden of plants from your own region, you can lure a real, living, jumping, singing, breeding world to you. And there's always room between the black-eyed Susans and the horsemint for Mexican salvias saved from the goats.

Succession and the Garden

Nature rules the garden, no matter where it grows or what the origins of its plantings. Plant succession is the governing process, and, though gardeners may not realize it, they have had lots of experience with succession. Awareness of this concept will enable you to see that your garden functions as a part of the natural world beyond and allow you to plan in such a way that nature is an ally in maintaining order in your backyard wilderness.

Succession is the process of development of one plant community into another, the end point of which is a climax community, a mixture of plants and animals that is typical of an area and that remains stable year after year. A plant community is a colony of plants of one species or a number of different species adapted to a common site and to each other and established in that site. Deciduous forest, prairie and desert are larger community units, or biomes. Differing moisture levels and soil composition within a forest or prairie or desert at, say, the top of a ridge, in the depression below, and in gradations in between will result in the development of different plant communities. The Southeastern United States Ecological Community Classification lists 215 specific terrestrial and 117 palustrine (vegetated wetland) communities;[7] each community has passed through different successional stages with distinct assemblages of animals and plants adapted to each stage.

Primary succession is progression from bare rock to climax. Secondary succession occurs as the dominant vegetation, the

Forest succession: *bare ground*   *weeds*   *grasses, forbs*

climax community, reclaims an area after a disturbance—for example, as a forest regrows into a field cleared for farming or into an opening created when a tree falls. Botanists have proposed four stages of succession:

(1) Grass/forb Aggressively spreading annual weeds that produce millions of seeds live and die, making the soil more fertile and appropriate for their successors, grasses and perennial plants—the meadow.

(2) Shrub/seedling As the weeds were crowded out, so are the grasses and perennial plants, by the very shrubs for which they paved the way by stabilizing and further enriching the soil. Shade created by shrubs is just the right environment for the next stage.

shrubs   *woodland*

(3) Sapling/poletimber Seedlings of pioneer species of trees appear and eventually overshadow the shrubs.

(4) Sawtimber, the climax phase In the shade of the sun-loving trees, an understory of shade-tolerant trees sprouts and thrives, ultimately overtopping the pioneers.

In some areas, regularly recurring disturbances prevent the climax community from ever being established. Fires, logging, and other events that maintain pine forests, stopping succession to live oak, laurel, and magnolia forest are an example. In many places, introduced plants invade, displacing indigenous species and permanently interrupting progression to the appropriate climax, creating instead a successional stage called disturbance climax.

Gardens are perfect examples of disturbance! And gardeners are constantly producing forms of disturbance that return portions of their estates to stage one of succession, inviting weeds to colonize. Galloping children and pets and tromping adults compact the soil, wear away its vegetative cover, expose it to sunlight and dry it out, creating conditions too hostile for anything but specially adapted weeds. Frequent close mowing is obvious harassment of the earth, but even acts of gardening like turning the soil for planting and pulling weeds constitute assault, bringing dormant weed seeds to the surface and providing a fertile field in which they can sprout and grow.

Weed seeds lie in wait in the soil, sprouting when conditions of light or moisture, pH or temperature are right, or they float by the thousands in the wind, sprouting only if they chance to come to rest in a suitable spot. The weeds that grow in cultivated fields and gardens are not the ones you'll find in lawns or pastures. Some flourish in compacted soil, others in acid or alkaline conditions, others in poor drainage or saline or dry soils with low humus. In places where succession is allowed to progress without further interruption, weeds stabilize and enrich the soil, making it more suitable for less weedy growth and then disappearing, crowded out by grasses, woody shrubs, and trees.

Disturbance begins the succession to climax, but what ends it? What makes climax ultimate? In a forest, shade maintains the climax phase. In the shady garden, there is less bloom, but there are also fewer weeds. Dominant species of long-lived grasses maintain a climax prairie. They form a thick thatch that covers the soil and keeps seeds of competing species from sprouting. If low maintenance is a concern, the obvious solution is to copy the climax community for your ecological region by establishing a shady backyard forest or a thick-thatched pocket prairie.

In a natural setting, the greatest numbers of fauna are found, not in the mature climax forest itself, but in edge, the transitional zone of shrubs and saplings where grass- and forb-filled meadows blend into surrounding taller forest or where shrubs and trees along rivers or streams blend into prairie. There's more sun, more bloom, more fruit, more access to a variety of habitats—in short, more diversity—in an edge. The sunny edge in your garden will potentially draw more wildlife, too—and more weeds. And, unless you trim your edge on a regular basis, its shrubs and saplings will grow to sawtimber size and you'll wonder where the edge has gone. What's a gardener to do?

We exert some control over succession through our choice of plants and through the gardening process itself—weeding, cultivating, trimming. The following are examples of ways in which we direct or suppress or accelerate succession in the garden. You probably have lots more to add from your own experience.

We may plant perennial herbs and grasses, feeding and protecting them from competition. They will eventually establish the extensive root systems that prevent weed seeds from taking hold and will form a meadow that we can help perpetuate by pulling up sprouts of encroaching pioneer shrubs and trees.

We may combine clumping perennials with lower-growing shade-tolerant ground covers in perennial borders to duplicate the thick thatch of a prairie and shade of later successional stages that will protect the soil from disturbance and keep down weeds.

We may plant trees to make a forest. Through the years, they will grow from seedling to sapling to maturity. As they produce increasing amounts of shade on the ground below, they will change a sunny meadow of flowers and grasses into understory for ferns and low-growing herbs.

We may reverse the trend toward shadiness in a mature back-yard woodland by thinning the trees to allow more light to increase bloom and fruiting on the understory plants below. We may use mulches, allow surface litter and overseed with fast-growing annual flowers to prevent soil disturbance and block weeds.

We may grow pioneer species, naturally adapted to hostile planting sites (hawthornes, honey locust, elderberry), in harsh urban environments such as the strip between a sidewalk and a concrete-paved driveway.

A discussion of succession would be incomplete if it didn't cover animal interrelationships with habitat—animal succession. Charles Wharton describes the fauna associated with stages of succession to a climax community called submesic broadleaf deciduous forest in the Piedmont of Georgia:

> Odum (1971) details old field succession, from fields with crabgrass, horseweed (*Erigeron*), and aster—through a grass-shrub stage beginning with broom sedge (*Andropogon virginicus*) about the third year and through pine forest (25-100 years) to an

oak-hickory climax (150 years plus). The fauna appears in successional stages also, from the insects through the mammals. If the ground stays bare long enough, the beach mouse (*Peromyscus polionotus*) may take up residence (if breeding stocks are nearby), or in the weed stage the seed-eating harvest mouse (*Reithrodontomys*) may predominate. In the grass stage the cotton rat (*Sigmodon hispidus*) moves in, but disappears in the shrub stage as grass cover thins out. If the grass stage is prolonged by pasturage, the cool, moist microenvironment may prove acceptable for meadow mice (*Microtus*) in portions of the Piedmont. As the hardwood understory builds with storable food, such as acorns or nuts, and as leaf litter forms, pine voles and deer mice become dominant small mammals.

Some interesting birds, such as the blue grosbeak, are found only in areas of secondary succession. Quail, doves, rabbits, and foxes appear to be more common in such areas, also.

Johnson and Odum (1956) in a classic paper, documented the breeding passerine birds in the stages of secondary succession in the Piedmont of Georgia. They found two species (grasshopper sparrow and meadow lark) in the first three years (forb-grass stage); five other species were added in 15 years (grass-shrub stage), and new species were added as the community progressed. Maximum species diversity was reached about the 60th year (pine forests and understory of hardwoods); the number of species then held steady around an average of 19 through the oak-hickory climax. Some species were added to the oak-hickory (black and white warbler, Kentucky warbler, Acadian flycatcher), and others were deleted. These authors record the dominant (by density) species for each stage as follows: forb-grass stage, grasshopper sparrow, meadow lark; grass-shrub stage, field sparrow, yellow-throat, meadow lark; young pine forest (25-60 years), pine warbler, towhee, and summer tanager; old pine forest (with well-developed deciduous understory), pine warbler, Carolina wren, hooded warbler, cardinal; oak-hickory climax; red-eyed vireo, wood thrush, and cardinal.[8]

No matter how many groupings of naturally associated indigenous plants we grow or how many niches we create by reproducing habitat elements in little city gardens, and no matter how much fauna we actually lure, our manipulations are unlikely to induce the full succession of animal life that occurs in true wildlands, especially of nonwinged creatures. Even if breeding stock of all the appropriate mammals, reptiles, and amphibians for your region exists nearby, they would have to negotiate sewer systems, walk with winkie, or balance on phone wires to get to your yard. In disturbance climax, both animal and plant succession are disrupted.

What wildlife, I wonder, would roam or crawl or fly back to my property if I could interrupt disturbance climax and send my garden on through natural succession towards climax for the community originally on my site? I can have lots of fun speculating. But, since restoration is not a very realistic goal for most urban and suburban settings like mine, I can only hope that some wild things will accept a well-planned and well-developed wildlife garden as a reasonable substitute.

Using a Wild Model

"There's a catalpa around the corner!" I rushed into the house to share news of my discovery with my husband.

"A what?" he asked.

"I can't believe I've lived here over twenty years and never noticed the catalpa tree right around the corner from my house."

"Oh," he smiled indulgently.

"I wonder what other trees I've missed?" During the years I've spent developing my ornamental garden, I've peeked into yards all over the area, but my focus has been less on trees than on shrubs and herbaceous plants with showy flowers. The first catalpa I saw in bloom was not in my immediate neighborhood. I examined a layer of ruffly bignonia flowers fallen from its canopy and was inspired to look up when I realized there was no other plant nearby that could have produced them. Does everybody take trees for granted the way I have?

I had begun the search for habitat remnants in my neighborhood, wondering what creatures might still be hiding there, waiting to come to my backyard woodland if I enriched it with plants of the communities that existed on the site in 1746, before it became part of the Avart family plantation. It wouldn't be difficult to determine the original herbaceous plants, I speculated. Wouldn't they be what would grow if I let a portion of my garden "go wild"? Not exactly. I knew that some plants that grew on my lot—four-o'clocks, cashmere bouquet, St. Joseph's lilies, Peruvian lilies—were left over from earlier gardens. Of the "wild things" that appeared, some were native: field goldenrod, nut sedge, crabgrass, yellow wood sorrel, shepherd's needle, fleabane, wild morning-glory. But when I took my field guide to weeds into the backyard to identify the ones I didn't know, I found that many—like flax, wild mustards, chickweed and mock-strawberry—were European or Eurasian in origin!

How could that be? I found the answer in the book, *Weeds.*[9] The Europeans who settled this country brought weed seeds, intentionally or not—as contaminants in agricultural seeds, in hay and feedstuffs, in ballast in boats. The seeds from parts of the world that were similar to New World points of introduction multiplied and spread in the areas cleared for farming or building. Those introduced to areas dissimilar or undisturbed failed to sprout or sprouted but did not persist. Weeds from regions of open grassland found the formerly forested cleared areas of the eastern United States easy to conquer; there were few native competitors adapted to the open field environment. And conquer they did! In parts of the United States where the original vegetation was open grassland, plains, or prairie, more native species endured and spread as weeds in clearings.

Shouldn't trees be different? Lots of them are native, I told myself. I knew the Avarts' orchard of oranges, persimmons, plums, and pecans had occupied my property at one time. Were Avart pecans, persimmons, and plums native to the site or nursery-bought like the orange trees? Were Avart pecans parents of the giant pecan tree still growing on the block and of others in the neighborhood? Was the catalpa descended from an original member of the plant community for the site, or was it nursery-bought?

Although the map in my field guide to trees placed the probable original range of the southern catalpa further east than Louisiana, the book also says that because the tree has been so widely planted its original distribution is unknown. Maybe the Avarts grew catalpas to attract the catalpa sphinx moth, whose larva, the catalpa worm, is considered choice fishing bait. My field guide to moths describes the range of catalpa sphinx as being wherever the trees are, but the presence of catalpa moths isn't a clue; they may be in my neighborhood because they've expanded their range with the trees.

Anyway, the catalpa is not native . . . but it *is* native. It's native to the southeastern United States but not to my immediate ecological vicinity. Does that make it a foreign native? If even the native trees aren't native, how will I ever determine what used to grow on my land?

Even the experts are finding it a tough task. Latimore Smith says: "Although much of Louisiana is still covered in native vegetation, undisturbed examples of all natural communities are rare, and many are exceedingly scarce. Essentially no virgin habitat remains."[10] Very few areas anywhere remain untouched by meddling human hands. During all the activity considered "improvement," people have altered landscapes—even the ones in the rural areas we city dwellers call "the country"—with a hodge-podge of introduced "escapees" and foreign natives. The only remaining environments in Georgia thought to be untouched are high mountain forest, coastal salt marsh, and rock outcrops.[11] Participants in the Morton Arboretum prairie restoration project in Illinois hand-collected seeds from four square miles of bits and pieces of tallgrass remnants in pioneer graveyards and along railroad rights-of-way, all that is left of an original forty thousand square miles of tallgrass prairie in north-ern portions of what is called "the Prairie State."[12] Similarly, the approximately 2.5 million acres of coastal prairie once found in southwestern Louisiana exists in very limited parcels frequently found along railroad tracks.[13]

Why is there so much concern? "To protect natural biotic diversity, it is necessary to identify and preserve viable examples of the full spectrum of ecosystems, natural biological communities, and species found within a re-gion," Smith explains.[14] In efforts to identify what was there before it is completely gone and to allow research to determine conservation priorities, most states, through Natural Heritage Programs, are conducting inventories of ecological communities. Important issues. Important work. And, incidentally, a source of clues to the original vegetation of your region and guide to plants for your wildlife garden.

Bill Fontenot suggests a plan to be used by people interested in restoring particular habitats or in further supplementing habitats not completely obliterated. He says: "In most cases, regardless of the degree of previous destruction, the places in which we live have been left with varying amounts of native vegetation, particularly in the case of trees."[15] If you examine the species of trees growing in your neighborhood and on your property and compare them to those listed for each community type in your state inventory, you should be able to narrow down possible communities that naturally occurred on your property to a choice of one to three.

If you then choose plants for your wildlife garden from the components of those communities—overstory and understory trees, shrubs, and ground covers of forests and woodlands and grasses, annuals and herbaceous perennials of edges, prairies and meadows—you'll be selecting the vegetation that best fits into your garden plan and is most attractive to wildlife from the ones that nature intended to be grown there in the first place.

As I continued exploration of my own neighborhood, five blocks away from the black willow-lined Mississippi River, I found hackberries, sycamores, pecans, American elm, live oaks, red mulberries, bald cypress and sweet gum to be the most common indigenous species. Some of these were definitely planted by residents. When I first moved into my house over twenty years ago, a large hackberry dominated the backyard and a large Chinese tallow the front. Elderberries and hackberries have consistently returned from seeds spread by birds in spite of attempts at removal. After study of *Natural Communities of Louisiana*,[16] I decided the original community was probably either hackberry-American elm-green ash bottomland forest or sycamore-sweet gum-American elm bottomland forest with live oak forest possible, too. At the river's edge is batture or riverfront pioneer community. Introduced pests described as "serious invaders of these habitats" are all present in my yard and have been since I moved here: Chinese tallow tree, Japanese honeysuckle, and Japanese climbing fern. Indigenous trumpet creeper's orange blossoms glint in the sunlight at the tip-tops of neighborhood trees. Spanish moss, resurrection fern, and mistletoe persist also. And, as my less-indulgent-than-he-used-to-be husband found out after snatching a specimen of leaves and associated white berries from a tree while helping me acquire more hands-on experience with local vegetation, so is *Rhus radicans*. That's poison ivy!

The first step in designing a backyard habitat is to look outside the confines of your property and your city into the man-made and natural environments beyond. You can observe actual examples of ecological communities typical of your region in Nature Conservancy preserves, arboretums and botanical gardens, state and national parks, national forests, wildlife refuges and game management areas. Find out where they are from your local native plant society and nature center. Buy field guides and learn to identify the trees, shrubs, and wildflowers growing in your region.

The following are descriptions of the major plant components of some common terrestrial and palustrine plant communities of the southeastern United States. My source is Latimore Smith's unpublished report, "The Natural Communities of Louisiana," prepared for the Louisiana Natural Heritage Program and Bill Fontenot.[17] There's lots more information in Smith's full report.

Most of these communities are found in some form in the

southeastern states. Plant communities are generalizations which contain variances based on soil moisture and topography change. Components of the communities listed may vary from one location to another, and lots of plants occur that are not included in this list. I recommend that each wildlife garden planner follow up with his or her own state's Natural Heritage Program to obtain materials specific to each locale.

Natural community inventories are being prepared by Natural Heritage Programs (usually a division of the Department of Wildlife and Fisheries) in most states. Contact your state's NHP. If data on the specific plants of each community found in your state are not available, write to NHPs in neighboring states whose plant communities may be the same ones found in your region. I recommend *The Natural Environments of Georgia* to all southeastern gardeners in addition to their own state inventories. It discusses native fauna and presents a wealth of other information.

Use Bill Fontenot's plan as suggested in *Native Gardening in the South*:

• Examine the species of trees growing in your neighborhood and on your property and compare them to those listed for each community type in the following list (or your own state inventory).

• Narrow down your guesses about the community that naturally occurred on your property to a choice of one to three.

• Choose plants from that list, natural associates, to supplement plants that already grow on your lot. Forbs are non-grass herbaceous plants.

• Even if restoring the original community of your property is not your goal, you can use the following chart to identify natural associates of plants you are considering for backyard habitats.

Profiles of Some Common Southeastern Plant Communities/Wildlife Habitats

GULF COASTAL PRAIRIE
(SOILS NEUTRAL TO ALKALINE, WET IN WINTER, DRY IN SUMMER)

Grasses: paspy grasses (*Paspalum* species), little and slender bluestem (*Schizachyrium scoparium, S. tenerum*), big bluestem (*Andropogon gerardii*), other broom sedges (*A.* species), three-awn grasses (*Aristida stricta, A.* species), lovegrasses (*Eragrostis* species), marsh-hay cordgrass near marshes (*Spartina patens*), switchgrass (*Panicum virgatum*), panic grasses (*Panicum* species), Indian grass (*Sorghastrum nutans*), dropseeds (*Sporobolus* species), purple-top (*Tridens* species).

Sedges: caric sedges (*Carex* species), umbrella sedges (*Cyperus* species), beaked sedges (*Rhynchospora* species), nut-rushes (*Scleria* species).

Forbs: Indian plantain (*Cacalia ovata*), sunflowers (*Helianthus* species), blazing stars (*Liatris* species), milkweeds (*Asclepias* species), rosinweeds (*Silphium* species), prairie clovers (*Petalostemon* species), false indigos (*Baptisia* species), blue star (*Amsonia tabernaemontana*), brown- or black-eyed Susans (*Rudbeckia* species), spurges (*Euphorbia* species), flat-topped goldenrods (*Euthamia* species), bluets *(Hedyotis nigricans)*, wild petunia (*Ruellia humilis*), water primroses (*Ludwigia* species), tickseeds (*Coreopsis* species), goldenrods (*Solidago* species), false foxgloves (*Agalinis* species), thoroughworts (*Eupatorium* species), poppy mallow (*Callirhoe* species), mints (*Physostegia digitalis, Salvia* species, *Monarda* species), mountain mints (*Pycnanthemum* species).

COASTAL PLAIN HILLSIDE HERBACEOUS SEEPAGE BOG
(SOILS SANDY, CONTINUALLY MOIST, ACIDIC)

Grasses: broom sedges (*Andropogon* species), three-awn grasses (*Aristida stricta, A.* species), panic grasses (*Panicum* species), toothache grass (*Ctenium aromaticum*), gulf muhly (*Muhlenbergia expansa*), yellow-eyed grasses (*Xyris* species), pipeworts (*Eriocaulon* species)

Sedges: giant white-topped sedge (*Dichromena latifolia*), nut-rushes (*Scleria* species), umbrella grasses (*Fuirena* species).

Forbs: green pitcher plant (*Sarracenia alata*), meadow beauties (*Rhexia* species), milkworts (*Polygala* species), blazing stars (*Liatris* species), bonesets or thoroughworts (*Eupatorium* species), narrow-leaved tickseed (*Coreopsis linifolia*).

Other: ferns (*Osmunda* species) and club mosses (*Lycopodium* species).

COASTAL PLAIN RIVER EDGE SHRUB WETLAND AKA SCRUB/SHRUB SWAMP
(POORLY DRAINED SOIL USUALLY WET, DRY DURING LATE SUMMER OR DROUGHT)

Shrubs: buttonbush (*Cephalanthus occidentalis*), silverling (*Baccharis halimifolia*), dwarf palmetto (*Sabal minor*), wax myrtle (*Myrica cerifera*), marsh elder (*Iva frutescens*), lead plant (*Amorpha fruticosa*), Drummond red maple (*Acer rubrum* var. *drummondii*). Mayhaw slash: mayhaw (*Crataegus opaca*), willows (*Salix* species), water elm (*Planera aquatica*), swamp privet (*Forestiera acuminata*), wax myrtle (*Myrica cerifera*), buttonbush (*Cephalanthus occidentalis*).

BALD CYPRESS/TUPELO SWAMP

Overstory dominants: bald cypress (*Taxodium distichum*), tupelo gum (*Nyssa aquatica*).

Overstory associates: swamp blackgum (*Nyssa sylvatica* var. *biflora*), Drummond red maple (*Acer rubrum* var. *drummondii*), black willow (*Salix nigra*), pumpkin ash (*Fraxinus profunda*), green ash (*Fraxinus pennsylvanica*), water elm (*Planera aquatica*), water locust (*Gleditsia aquatica*), Virginia willow (*Itea virginica*), buttonbush (*Cephalanthus occidentalis*).

TUPELO/BLACKGUM SWAMP

Overstory dominant: gums (*Nyssa* species).

Overstory associates: bald cypress (*Taxodium distichum*), Drummond red maple (*Acer rubrum* var. *drummondii*), black willow (*Salix nigra*), pumpkin ash (*Fraxinus profunda*), water elm (*Planera aquatica*), water locust (*Gleditsia aquatica*), swamp privet (*Forestiera acuminata*), laurel oak (*Quercus laurifolia*), leucothoe (*Leucothoe racemosa*), swamp cyrilla (*Cyrilla racemiflora*), swamp dogwood (*Cornus foemina*), Virginia willow (*Itea virginica*), buttonbush (*Cephalanthus occidentalis*).

Vines: various woody vines.

WET RIVERFRONT AND STREAM BAR FORESTS
(RIVERFRONT PIONEER, BATTURE)

Overstory dominants: black willow (*Salix nigra*), cottonwood (*Populus deltoides*).

Overstory associates: river birch (*Betula nigra*), green ash (*Fraxinus pennsylvanica*), sycamore (*Platanus occidentalis*), pecan (*Carya illinoensis*), hackberry (*Celtis laevigata*), red maple (*Acer rubrum*), swamp privet (*Forestiera acuminata*), water elm (*Planera aquatica*), American elm (*Ulmus americana*), bald cypress (*Taxodium distichum*), box elder (*Acer negundo*), red mulberry (*Morus rubra*), sandbar willow (*Salix exigua*).

Wet River Floodplain Forests

OVERCUP OAK/WATER HICKORY
BOTTOMLAND FOREST

Overstory dominants: overcup oak (*Quercus lyrata*), water hickory (*Carya aquatica*).

Overstory associates: green ash (*Fraxinus pennsylvanica*), hackberry (*Celtis laevigata*), swamp dogwood (*Cornus foemina* var. *foemina*), swamp privet (*Forestiera acuminata*), water elm (*Planera aquatica*), buttonbush (*Cephalanthus occidentalis*).

Vines: various woody vines.

HACKBERRY/AMERICAN ELM/GREEN ASH

Overstory dominants: hackberry (*Celtis laevigata*), American elm (*Ulmus americana*), green ash (*Fraxinus pennsylvanica*).

Overstory associates: water hickory (*Carya aquatica*), Nuttall oak (*Quercus nuttallii*), willow oak (*Quercus phellos*), water oak (*Quercus nigra*), overcup oak (*Quercus lyrata*), sweet gum (*Liquidambar styraciflua*), box elder (*Acer negundo*), winged elm (*Ulmus alata*), Drummond red maple (*Acer rubrum* var. *drummondii*), water locust (*Gleditsia aquatica*), sycamore (*Platanus occidentalis*).

Understory: swamp dogwood (*Cornus foemina* var. *foemina*), hawthorns (*Crataegus* species), red mulberry (*Morus rubra*).

Vines: many vines.

SYCAMORE/SWEET GUM/AMERICAN ELM
RIVERFRONT FOREST

Overstory dominants: sycamore (*Platanus occidentalis*), sweet gum (*Liquidambar styraciflua*), American elm (*Ulmus americana*).

Overstory associates: pecan (*Carya illinoensis*), swamp blackgum (*Nyssa sylvatica* var. *biflora*), hackberry (*Celtis laevigata*), black willow (*Salix nigra*), cottonwood (*Populus deltoides*), box elder (*Acer negundo*), water oak (*Quercus nigra*).

Understory: giant cane (*Arundinaria gigantea*), deciduous holly (*Ilex decidua*), green hawthorn (*Crataegus viridis*), pokeweed (*Phytolacca americana*).

Vines: many vines.

SWEET GUM/MIXED BOTTOMLAND OAK FOREST

Overstory dominants: sweet gum (*Liquidambar styraciflua*), water oak (*Quercus nigra*).

Overstory associates: hackberry (*Celtis laevigata*), green ash (*Fraxinus pennsylvanica*), American elm (*Ulmus americana*), Nuttall oak (*Quercus nuttallii*), Drummond red maple (*Acer rubrum* var. *drummondii*), red mulberry (*Morus rubra*).

Understory: dwarf palmetto (*Sabal minor*), deciduous holly (*Ilex decidua*), green hawthorn (*Crataegus viridis*).

Vines: greenbriers (*Smilax* species), pepper vine (*Ampelopsis arborea*), trumpet creeper (*Campsis radicans*), poison ivy (*Rhus radicans*).

LIVE OAK RIVERFRONT FOREST

Overstory dominants: live oak (*Quercus virginiana*), water oak (*Quercus nigra*), American elm (*Ulmus americana*), hackberry (*Celtis laevigata*), Drummond red maple (*Acer rubrum* var. *drummondii*), green ash (*Fraxinus pennsylvanica*).

Overstory associates: cherrybark oak (*Quercus falcata* var. *pagodaefolia*), Nuttall oak (*Quercus nuttallii*), honey locust (*Gleditsia triacanthos*), sweet gum (*Liquidambar styraciflua*), box elder (*Acer negundo*); bald cypress (*Taxodium distichum*) and tupelo gum (*Nyssa aquatica*) may occur in wet depressions or edges.

Understory: dwarf palmetto (*Sabal minor*), deciduous holly (*Ilex decidua*), green hawthorn (*Crataegus viridis*), swamp dogwood (*Cornus foemina* var. *foemina*), water elm (*Planera aquatica*), wax myrtle (*Myrica cerifera*), elderberry (*Sambucus canadensis*), red bay (*Persea borbonia*).

Grasses: panic grasses (*Panicum* species), basketgrass (*Oplismenus hirtellus*).

Forbs: spiderworts (*Tradescantia* species), seaside goldenrod (*Solidago sempervirens*), green dragon (*Arisaema dracontium*), baby blue eyes (*Nemophila aphylla*), geum (*Geum canadensis*), pennyworts (*Hydrocotyle* species), bonesets or thoroughworts, (*Eupatorium* species), smartweeds (*Polygonum* species), yellow-top (*Senecio glabellus*).

Vines: climbing hempvine (*Mikania scandens*), Carolina moonseed (*Cocculus carolinus*), trumpet creeper (*Campsis radicans*), poison ivy (*Rhus radicans*), rattan vine (*Berchemia scandens*), common greenbrier (*Smilax rotundifolia*).

Other: maiden ferns (*Thelypteris* species), epiphytes such as Spanish moss (*Tillandsia usneoides*), resurrection fern (*Polypodium polypodioides*), mistletoe (*Phoradendron tomentosum*). Several introduced species have become serious invaders of this habitat, including Japanese climbing fern (*Lygodium japonicum*), Chinese tallow tree (*Sapium sebiferum*), and Japanese honeysuckle (*Lonicera japonica*).

Forested Mountain Seep aka Wooded Seep
(SOILS CONTINUALLY MOIST, SANDY, ACIDIC)

Overstory dominants: sweet bay magnolia (*Magnolia virginiana*), black gum (*Nyssa sylvatica*), red maple (*Acer rubrum*).

Understory: Virginia willow (*Itea virginica*), bigleaf wax myrtle (*Myrica heterophylla*), hazel alder (*Alnus serrulata*), swamp blackhaw (*Viburnum nudum*), red chokeberry (*Aronia arbutifolia*), poison sumac (*Rhus vernix*), fetterbush (*Lyonia ligustrina*), staggerbush (*Lyonia mariana*), baygall blueberry (*Vaccinium fuscatum*), wild azalea (*Rhododendron oblongifolium*), swamp titi (*Cyrilla racemiflora*), sweet gallberry (*Ilex coriacea*), summersweet (*Clethra alnifolia*), summer azalea (*Rhododendron serrulatum*)

Ferns: cinnamon fern (*Osmunda cinnamomea*), royal fern (*Osmunda regalis*), sensitive fern (*Onoclea sensibilis*), net-veined chain fern (*Lorinseria areolata*), Virginia chain fern (*Woodwardia virginica*), southern lady fern (*Athyrium filix-femina*).

BAYHEAD SWAMP
(SOILS CONTINUALLY MOIST, SANDY, ACIDIC)

Overstory dominants: sweetbay magnolia (*Magnolia virginiana*), black gum (*Nyssa sylvatica*).

Overstory associates: laurel oak (*Quercus laurifolia*), red maple (*Acer rubrum*), sweet gum (*Liquidambar styraciflua*), water oak (*Quercus nigra*), bald cypress (*Taxodium distichum*), pond cypress (*Taxodium ascendens*), slash pine (*Pinus elliottii*), longleaf pine (*Pinus palustris*).

Understory: red bay (*Persea borbonia*), swamp cyrilla (*Cyrilla racemiflora*), bigleaf wax myrtle (*Myrica heterophylla*), wax myrtle (*Myrica cerifera*), littleleaf gallberry (*Ilex glabra*), sweet gallberry (*Ilex coriacea*), American holly (*Ilex opaca*), fetterbush (*Lyonia* species), leucothoe (*Leucothoe racemosa, L. axillaris*), Virginia willow (*Itea virginica*), red chokeberry (*Aronia arbutifolia*), possumhaw viburnum (*Viburnum nudum*), poison sumac (*Rhus vernix*), summersweet (*Clethra alnifolia*), hazel alder (*Alnus serrulata*), American snowbell (*Styrax americana*), summer azalea (*Rhododendron serrulatum*), wild azalea (*Rhododendron canescens, R. oblongifolium*).

Forbs: ferns such as net-veined chain fern (*Lorinseria areolata*), sensitive fern (*Onoclea sensibilis*), cinnamon fern (*Osmunda cinnamomea*), royal fern (*Osmunda regalis*).

Vines: bamboo greenbrier (*Smilax laurifolia*), climbing hydrangea (*Decumaria barbara*).

Wᴇᴛ Lᴏɴɢʟᴇᴀꜰ Pɪɴᴇ/Sʟᴀsʜ Pɪɴᴇ Fʟᴀᴛᴡᴏᴏᴅs ᴀᴋᴀ Pɪɴᴇ Fʟᴀᴛᴡᴏᴏᴅs
(SOILS MOIST TO WET EXCEPT DURING SUMMER DROUGHT)

Overstory dominants: longleaf pine (*Pinus palustris*), slash pine (*Pinus elliottii*), loblolly pine (*Pinus taeda*), spruce pine (*Pinus glabra*).

Overstory associates: water oak (*Quercus nigra*), laurel oak (*Quercus laurifolia*), cherrybark oak (*Quercus falcata* var. *pagodaefolia*), sweetbay magnolia (*Magnolia virginiana*), red maple (*Acer rubrum*), sweet gum (*Liquidambar styraciflua*), black gum (*Nyssa sylvatica*), ashes (*Fraxinus* species); bald cypress (*Taxodium distichum*) and pond cypress (*Taxodium ascendens*) may occur in low areas.

Understory: dwarf palmetto (*Sabal minor*), littleleaf gallberry (*Ilex glabra*), sweet gallberry (*Ilex coriacea*), swamp cyrilla (*Cyrilla racemiflora*), fetterbush (*Lyonia* species), wax myrtles (*Myrica* species), summersweet (*Clethra alnifolia*), blueberries (*Vaccinium* species), huckleberries (*Gaylussacia* species), St.-John's-worts (*Hypericum* species).

Grasses: spangle-grasses (*Chasmanthium* species), broom sedges (*Andropogon* species), panic grasses (*Panicum* species).

Forbs: blazing-stars (*Liatris* species).

Vines: blackberries and dewberries (*Rubus* species).

Slash Pine Savannah
(Soils Acid, Poorly Drained, Moist Except During Summer Drought)

Overstory dominants: longleaf pine (*Pinus palustris*), slash pine (*Pinus elliottii*).

Overstory associates: sweetbay magnolia (*Magnolia virginiana*), black gum (*Nyssa sylvatica*), live oak (*Quercus virginiana*), blackjack oak (*Quercus marilandica*), laurel oak (*Quercus laurifolia*), pond cypress (*Taxodium ascendens*).

Understory: swamp cyrilla (*Cyrilla racemiflora*), wax myrtles (*Myrica* species), St.-John's-worts (*Hypericum* species), littleleaf snowbell (*Styrax americana*).

Grasses: broom sedges (*Andropogon* species), little and slender bluestem (*Schizachyrium scoparium, S. tenerum*), panic grasses (*Panicum* species), three-awn grasses (*Aristida* species), toothache grass (*Ctenium aromaticum*), gulf muhly (*Muhlenbergia expansa*), plume grasses (*Erianthus* species), joint grasses (*Coelorachis* species), beak-rushes (*Rhynchospora* species), yellow-eyed grasses (*Xyris* species), umbrella grasses (*Fuirena* species), nut-rushes (*Scleria* species), giant white-top sedge (*Dichromena latifolia*), pipeworts (*Eriocaulon* species).

Forbs: pitcher plants (*Sarracenia* species), gerardias (*Agalinis* species), lobelias (*Lobelia* species), meadow beauties (*Rhexia* species), milkworts (*Polygala* species), blazing-stars (*Liatris* species), rose-gentians (*Sabatia* species), various composite family members.

Coastal Plain Small Stream Swamp Forest
(Riparian Forest) (Soils Silty-Loamy)

Overstory dominants: southern magnolia (*Magnolia grandiflora*), beech (*Fagus grandifolia*), black gum (*Nyssa sylvatica*), swamp white oak (*Quercus michauxii*), white oak (*Quercus alba*), water oak (*Quercus nigra*), laurel oak (*Quercus laurifolia*), cherry-bark oak (*Quercus falcata* var. *pagodaefolia*), sweet gum (*Liquidambar styraciflua*), sycamore (*Platanus occidentalis*), red maple (*Acer rubrum*), river birch (*Betula nigra*), water ash (*Fraxinus caroliniana*), cherry laurel (*Prunus caroliniana*), winged elm (*Ulmus alata*), tulip tree (*Liriodendron tulipifera*).

Overstory associates: spruce pine (*Pinus glabra*), bald cypress (*Taxodium distichum*), loblolly pine (*Pinus taeda*), sweet bay (*Magnolia virginiana*) and bigleaf magnolias (*Magnolia macrophylla*).

Midstory and Understory: silverbell (*Halesia diptera*), iron-wood (*Carpinus caroliniana*), arrowwood (*Viburnum dentatum*), Virginia willow (*Itea virginica*), sweetleaf (*Symplocos tinctoria*), hazel alder (*Alnus serrulata*), wild azalea (*Rhododendron canescens*), bigleaf snowbell (*Styrax grandifolia*), starbush (*Illicium floridanum*), sebastian bush (*Sebastiana fruticosa*), swamp cyrilla (*Cyrilla racemiflora*), fetterbush (*Lyonia lucida*), leucothoes (*Leucothoe axillaris*), winterberry (*Ilex verticillata*).

CALCAREOUS PRAIRIE
(SOILS ARE STIFF, ALKALINE CLAYS)

Grasses: paspy grasses (*Paspalum* species), little bluestem (*Schizachyrium scoparium*), big bluestem (*Andropogon gerardii*), bushy broom sedge, (*Andropogon glomeratus*), three-awn grasses (*Aristida* species), lovegrasses (*Eragrostis* species), panic grasses (*Panicum* species), Indian grass (*Sorghastrum nutans*), dropseeds (*Sporobolus*).

Dominant forbs: Composites and legume family members. Composites: asters (*Aster* species), blazing-stars (*Liatris* species), tickseeds (*Coreopsis* species), goldenrods (*Solidago* species), western ragweed (*Ambrosia psilostachya*), ironweeds (*Vernonia* species), black-eyed Susans (*Rudbeckia* species), bonesets or thoroughworts (*Eupatorium* species), purple coneflower (*Echinacea purpurea*), pale coneflower (*Echinacea pallida*), blanketflower *(Gaillardia aestivalis)*, rosinweeds (*Silphium* species), sneeze-weeds (*Helenium* species). Legumes: prairie acacia (*Acacia angustissima*), false indigos (*Baptisia* species), sensitive plant *(Mimosa strigillosa)*, prairie clovers (*Petalostemon candidum, P. purpureum*).

Associated forbs: milkweeds (*Asclepias* species), poppy mallow (*Callirhoe papaver*), crowfoot (*Ranunculus* species), larkspur (*Delphinium carolinianum*), bluets (*Hedyotis nigricans*), prairie bluets (*Hedyotis purpurea* var. *calycosa*), flax (*Linum* species), Mexican evening primrose (*Oenothera speciosa*), wild petunia (*Ruellia humilis*), blue sage (*Salvia azurea*).

Woody species: hawthorns (*Crataegus* species), persimmon (*Diospyros virginiana*), rough-leaf dogwood (*Cornus drummondii*), eastern red cedar (*Juniperus virginiana*), deciduous holly (*Ilex decidua*), white ash (*Fraxinus americana*), honey locust (*Gleditsia triacanthos*), Osage orange (*Maclura pomifera*).

Vines: rattan vine (*Berchemia scandens*), greenbrier (*Smilax bonanox*).

Maritime Dune Shrub Thicket aka Coastal Dune Shrub Thicket
(DRY TO MODERATELY MOIST, SANDY SOIL)

Shrub dominants: wax myrtle (*Myrica cerifera*), yaupon (*Ilex vomitoria*), marsh elder (*Iva* species), silverling (*Baccharis halimifolia*), acacia (*Acacia smallii*), toothache-tree (*Zanthoxylum clavaherculis*).

Vines: greenbriers (*Smilax* species), wild grape (*Vitis mustangensis*).

Southern Mixed Hardwood Forest aka Southern Mesophytic Forest
(Soil is deep, fertile, neutral to slightly alkaline)

Overstory: beech (*Fagus grandifolia*), shumard oak (*Quercus shumardii*), white oak (*Quercus alba*), chinquapin oak (*Quercus muehlenbergii*), cow oak (*Quercus michauxii*), water oak (*Quercus nigra*), tulip tree (*Liriodendron tulipifera*), southern magnolia (*Magnolia grandiflora*), cucumber magnolia (*Magnolia acuminata*), pyramid magnolia (*Magnolia pyramidata*), American elm (*Ulmus americana*), slippery elm (*Ulmus rubra*), Carolina basswood (*Tilia caroliniana*), red mulberry (*Morus rubra*), Florida sugar maple (*Acer floridanum*), pignut hickory (*Carya glabra*), bitternut hickory (*Carya cordiformis*), white ash (*Fraxinus americana*), hackberry (*Celtis laevigata*), sycamore (*Platanus occidentalis*).

Understory: American holly (*Ilex opaca*), spicebush (*Lindera benzoin*), oak-leaf hydrangea (*Hydrangea quercifolia*), mountain hydrangea (*Hydrangea arborescens*), pawpaw (*Asimina triloba*), strawberry bush (*Euonymus americanus*), silverbell (*Halesia diptera*), redbud (*Cercis canadensis*), elderberry (*Sambucus canadensis*), hop hornbeam (*Ostrya virginiana*).

Grasses: giant cane (*Arundinaria gigantea*).

Forbs: Ferns such as northern maidenhair fern (*Adiantum pedatum*), maiden ferns (*Thelypteris* species), silver glade fern (*Athyrium thelypterioides*), glade fern (*Athyrium pycnocarpon*), southern lady fern (*Athyrium filix-femina*), lowland brittle fern (*Cystopteris protrusa*), Christmas fern (*Polystichum acrostichoides*), rattlesnake fern (*Botrychium virginianum*), southern grape fern (*Botrychium biternatum*), ebony spleenwort (*Asplenium platyneuron*), broad beech fern (*Thelypteris hexagonoptera*). Herbs such as hound's-tongue (*Cynoglossum virginianum*), dutchman's-pipe (*Aristilochia serpentaria*), fetid wake-robin (*Trillium foetidissimum*), mayapple (*Podophyllum peltatum*), tuberous puccoon (*Lithospermum tuberosum*), lobelias (*Lobelia* species), allegheny spurge (*Pachysandra procumbens*), ginseng (*Panax quinquefolius*), Canadian ginger (*Asarum canadensis*).

Vines: smooth woodbine (*Schisandra glabra*), grapes (*Vitis* species), cross vine (*Bignonia capreolata*), climbing dogbane (*Trachelospermum difforme*), Virginia creeper (*Parthenocissum quinque-folia*), climbing bittersweet (*Celastrus scandens*). Japanese honey-suckle (*Lonicera japonica*) has become a serious pest in many places.

COASTAL PLAIN CALCAREOUS MESIC FOREST AKA CALCAREOUS FOREST
(SOILS ARE STIFF, ALKALINE CLAYS)

Overstory: post oak (*Quercus stellata*), shumard oak (*Quercus shumardii*), white oak (*Quercus alba*), chinquapin oak (*Quercus muehlenbergii*), nutmeg hickory (*Carya myristiciformis*), shagbark hickory (*Carya ovata*), mockernut hickory (*Carya tomentosa*), short-leaf pine (*Pinus echinata*), loblolly pine (*Pinus taeda*), white ash (*Fraxinus americana*), persimmon (*Diospyros virginiana*), sweet gum (*Liquidambar styraciflua*), hackberry (*Celtis laevigata*), honey locust (*Gleditsia triacanthos*), red mulberry (*Morus rubra*), beech (*Fagus grandifolia*), slippery elm (*Ulmus rubra*), American elm (*Ulmus americana*), winged elm (*Ulmus alata*), rock elm (*Ulmus crassifolia*), red maple (*Acer rubrum*), Durand oak (*Quercus durandii*), Oglethorpe oak (*Quercus oglethorpensis*).

Midstory and understory shrubs: rusty blackhaw (*Viburnum rufidulum*), hawthorns (*Crataegus* species), Mexican plum (*Prunus mexicana*), redbud (*Cercis canadensis*), fringe tree (*Chionanthus virginicus*), pawpaw (*Asimina triloba*), deciduous holly (*Ilex decidua*), winter huckleberry (*Vaccinium arboreum*), Indian cherry (*Rhamnus caroliniana*), flame leaf sumac (*Rhus copallina*), hop hornbeam (*Ostrya virginiana*), flowering dogwood (*Cornus florida*), red buckeye (*Aesculus pavia*). Osage orange (*Maclura pomifera*) may occur sporadically.

Grasses: spangle grasses (*Chasmanthium* species), brome grasses (*Bromus* species).

Herbs: aster (*Aster drummondii*), goldenrod (*Solidago auriculata*), hound's-tongue (*Cynoglossum virginianum*), plantain-leaf pussy-toes (*Antennaria plantaginifolia*), tuberous puccoon (*Lithospermum tuberosum*), Canadian lousewort (*Pedicularis canadensis*), mayapple (*Podophyllum peltatum*), woodland phlox (*Phlox divaricata*), violets (*Viola* species), golden alexanders (*Zizia aurea*), crane-fly orchid (*Tipularia discolor*), bedstraws (*Galium* species), and others.

BEECH/MAGNOLIA FOREST AKA HARDWOOD SLOPE FOREST
(SOILS ARE MODERATELY MOIST, ACIDIC, VARY FROM SANDY TO CLAYEY)

Overstory dominants: beech (*Fagus grandifolia*), southern magnolia (*Magnolia grandiflora*)

Overstory associates: white oak (*Quercus alba*), shumard oak (*Quercus shumardii*), swamp white oak (*Quercus michauxii*), water oak (*Quercus nigra*), laurel oak (*Quercus laurifolia*), black oak (*Quercus velutina*), cucumber tree (*Magnolia acuminata*), bigleaf magnolia (*Magnolia macrophylla*), pyramid magnolia (*Magnolia pyramidata*), tulip tree (*Liriodendron tulipifera*), sweet gum (*Liquidambar styraciflua*), mockernut hickory (*Carya tomentosa*), bitternut hickory (*Carya cordiformis*), pignut hickory (*Carya glabra*), loblolly pine (*Pinus taeda*), spruce pine (*Pinus glabra*). In some areas, live oak (*Quercus virginiana*) and various elms (*Ulmus* species) may be part of this community.

Midstory and understory: sourwood (*Oxydendrum arboreum*), silverbell (*Halesia diptera*), bigleaf snowbell (*Styrax grandifolia*), flowering dogwood (*Cornus florida*), sweetleaf (*Symplocos tinctoria*), cherry-laurel (*Prunus caroliniana*), silky camellia (*Stewartia malacodendron*), downy serviceberry (*Amelanchier arborea*), holly (*Ilex ambigua*), starbush (*Illicium floridanum*), ironwood (*Carpinus caroliniana*), eastern hop hornbeam (*Ostrya virginiana*), winter huckleberry (*Vaccinium arboreum*), Elliot's blueberry (*Vaccinium elliottii*), eastern coral bean (*Erythrina herbacea*).

Grasses: spangle grasses (*Chasmanthium* species)

Forbs: wild ginger (*Asarum arifolium*), wake-robins (*Trillium* species), violets (*Viola* species), Indian pink (*Spigelia marilandica*), bearsfoot (*Polymnia uvedalia*), smooth Solomon's seal (*Polygonatum biflorum*), mayapple (*Podophyllum peltatum*), jack-in-the-pulpits (*Arisaema* species). Ferns: southern lady fern (*Athyrium filix-femina*), broad beech fern (*Thelypteris hexagonoptera*), Christmas fern (*Polystichum acrostichoides*).

DRY SHORTLEAF PINE/OAK/HICKORY FOREST
(OCCURS ON DRY HILLS)

Overstory dominants: shortleaf pine (*Pinus echinata*), loblolly pine (*Pinus taeda*), southern red oak (*Quercus falcata*), post oak (*Quercus stellata*), blackjack oak (*Quercus marilandica*), black oak (*Quercus velutina*), white oak (*Quercus alba*), cherrybark oak (*Quercus falcata* var. *pagodaefolia*), shumard oak (*Quercus shumardii*), mockernut hickory (*Carya tomentosa*), black hickory (*Carya texana*), bitternut hickory (*Carya cordiformis*), winged elm (*Ulmus alata*), white ash (*Fraxinus americana*), black gum (*Nyssa sylvatica*), sweet gum (*Liquidambar styraciflua*), red maple (*Acer rubrum*).

Midstory and understory: winter huckleberry (*Vaccinium arboreum*), bunch blueberry (*Vaccinium amoenum*), fringe tree (*Chionanthus virginicus*), French mulberry (*Callicarpa americana*), rusty blackhaw (*Viburnum rufidulum*), deciduous holly (*Ilex decidua*), hawthorns (*Crataegus* species), Mexican plum (*Prunus mexicana*).

Grasses: panic grasses (*Panicum* species), spangle grasses (*Chasmanthium* species).

Forbs: asters (*Aster* species), goldenrods (*Solidago* species), pussy-toes (*Antennaria* species), wake-robins (*Trillium* species), violets (*Viola* species), partridgeberry (*Mitchella repens*), sunflowers (*Helianthus* species), blazing-stars (*Liatris* species).

MIXED HARDWOOD/LOBLOLLY FOREST

Overstory dominant: loblolly pine (*Pinus taeda*)

Overstory associates: On moist sites: sweet gum (*Liquidambar styraciflua*), beech (*Fagus grandifolia*), water oak (*Quercus nigra*), cherrybark oak (*Quercus falcata* var. *pagodaefolia*), swamp white oak (*Quercus michauxii*), white oak (*Quercus alba*), tulip tree (*Liriodendron tulipifera*), American elm (*Ulmus americana*), southern magnolia (*Magnolia grandiflora*), red maple (*Acer rubrum*), pignut hickory (*Carya glabra*). On dryer, upland sites: southern red oak (*Quercus falcata*), post oak (*Quercus stellata*), water oak (*Quercus nigra*), blackjack oak (*Quercus marilandica*), black gum (*Nyssa sylvatica*), red maple (*Acer rubrum*), mockernut hickory (*Carya tomentosa*), sassafras (*Sassafras albidum*). On sandy, very dry sites: bluejack oak (*Quercus incana*), upland laurel oak (*Quercus hemispherica*).

Understory: Varies with moisture: French mulberry (*Callicarpa americana*), flowering dogwood (*Cornus florida*), hawthorns (*Crataegus* species), sourwood (*Oxydendrum arboreum*), winter huckleberry (*Vaccinium arboreum*), Elliot's blueberry (*V. elliottii*), winged sumac (*Rhus copallina*), wax myrtle (*Myrica cerifera*), yaupon (*Ilex vomitoria*), devil's walkingstick (*Aralia spinosa*), deciduous holly (*Ilex decidua*), crab apple (*Malus angustifolia*).

Grasses: spangle grasses (*Chasmanthium* species), broom sedges (*Andropogon* species).

Forbs: violets (*Viola* species), partridgeberry (*Mitchella repens*).

Vines: yellow jessamine (*Gelsemium sempervirens*), blackberries (*Rubus* species), poison ivy (*Rhus radicans*).

GULF COAST MARITIME FOREST AKA LIVE OAK/PINE/MAGNOLIA FOREST
(SANDY SOILS, MOISTURE LEVEL VARIES)

Overstory dominants: live oak (*Quercus virginiana*), longleaf pine (*Pinus palustris*), slash pine (*Pinus elliottii*), loblolly pine (*Pinus taeda*), southern magnolia (*Magnolia grandiflora*).

Overstory associates: water oak (*Quercus nigra*), white oak (*Quercus alba*), swamp white oak (*Quercus michauxii*), laurel oak (*Quercus laurifolia*), cherrybark oak (*Quercus falcata* var. *pagodaefolia*), sweet gum (*Liquidambar styraciflua*), ashes (*Fraxinus* species), red maple (*Acer rubrum)*, sweet bay magnolia (*Magnolia virginiana*), hackberry (*Celtis laevigata*), black gum (*Nyssa sylvatica*).

Midstory and understory: dwarf palmetto (*Sabal minor*), American holly (*Ilex opaca*), yaupon (*Ilex vomitoria*), blueberries (*Vaccinium* species), American olive (*Osmanthus americanus*), ironwood (*Carpinus caroliniana*), eastern hop hornbeam (*Ostrya virginiana*), sweetleaf (*Symplocos tinctoria*), dwarf pawpaw (*Asimina parviflora*), sourwood (*Oxydendrum arboreum*), devil's walkingstick (*Aralia spinosa*), red bay (*Persea borbonia*), winged sumac (*Rhus copallina*), wax myrtle (*Myrica cerifera*), French mulberry (*Callicarpa americana*), sassafras (*Sassafras albidum*).

Forbs: southern marsh fern (*Thelypteris palustris*), cinnamon fern (*Osmunda cinnamomea*), net-veined chain fern (*Lorinseria areolata*).

Vines: many species

Southeastern Coastal Plain Xeric Sandhill aka Sandy Woodland

Overstory dominants: shortleaf pine (*Pinus echinata*), loblolly pine (*Pinus taeda*), post oak (*Quercus stellata*), blackjack oak (*Quercus marilandica*), bluejack oak (*Quercus incana*), sand post oak (*Quercus stellata* var. *margaretta*), upland laurel oak (*Quercus hemispherica*), longleaf pine (*Pinus palustris*), turkey oak (*Quercus laevis*).

Understory: dwarf pawpaw (*Asimina parviflora*), winter huckleberry (*Vaccinium arboreum*), yaupon (*Ilex vomitoria*), fringe tree (*Chionanthus virginicus*), Indian cherry (*Rhamnus caroliniana*), witch hazel (*Hamamelis virginiana*), sandhill plum (*Prunus gracilis*).

Grasses: broom sedges (*Andropogon* species), three-awn grasses (*Aristida* species).

Forbs: prickly pear cactus (*Opuntia humifusa*), milkweeds (*Asclepias* species), spiderworts (*Tradescantia* species), cupleaf beardtongue (*Penstemon murrayanus*), wild buckwheats (*Eriogonum* species), scarlet catchfly (*Silene subcilliata*).

Vines: sarsaparilla vine (*Smilax pumila*).

CHAPTER FOUR

Backyard Habitats for Birds of the Southeast

S OMETHING WILD'S GOING ON with migration this weekend," Denise Schoen called me from work to say. "I saw a worm-eating warbler, a flock of eastern kingbirds and a yellow-breasted chat in my yard! And you know where they were? In that overgrown area on the side—where the elderberries and mulberries are! I just had to call to tell someone!"

Illustration: Cedar, brown thrashers

"I'm glad you did! I've had birds I've never before seen in my garden this weekend, too," I returned. "Several common yellowthroats, orange-crowned warblers, and a swamp sparrow in the brushy clumps of sunflowers, *Eupatoriums*, and mallows and more in the raised bed of salvias I've let cypress vine and orange morning glory overgrow; an eastern phoebe flycatching over the goldenrod; yellow warblers in the birdbath."

"And hummingbirds everywhere!" we said in unison.

"I signed up for a gardening course at the cooperative extension service. I was going for ideas on how to fix up my yard. I was going to cut back that overgrown area, but not now. No way!!!"

I know that lots of people think unmanicured is un-American, but you don't have to be a birdwatcher to see the payoff for a more casual look. One friend's aging, ailing mother refuses to move from a little suburban house engulfed in a garden or to let her children "help out" by cutting back the growth and making a lawn. "There are box turtles under that ivy, and lizards crawling everywhere, and hummingbirds visiting all those flowers!" she protests.

You really can meet the needs of wildlife in a proprietary way. It's a matter of architecture. Organize your brambles and thickets. Let your wildflowers flop and run riot within the bounds of edging plants. Lay neat paths among exuberant floral and fruiting shrubs. Grow the "messy" trees and vines in spots where their fruit, resin or other debris the fastidious call "litter" can drop without causing problems.

Following are some of the species of birds that may be seen regularly in residential areas in parts of the Southeast, either while breeding or wintering or both. The ones labeled "neotropical migrants" are considered so by the Southeastern Working

Group of the Neotropical Migratory Bird Conservation Program. Check a field guide for specific distribution information. During migration, anything goes! Which feathered beauties drop in depends on how tantalizing you can make your garden.

Read through the habitat descriptions below for ideas about how to design your wildlife garden. Note which elements exist or can be duplicated in your yard. Be aware of the great variety of different habitats used by birds, the importance of snags, and the numbers of species of birds that eat insects. Again, my resource is Paul Hamel's *The Land Manager's Guide to the Birds of the South*.

You may wonder what you can do to encourage insect-eating birds, especially aerial insectivores like nighthawks and swifts, to visit your yard. I don't know if you can really affect the numbers of insects in the airspace *over* your garden, but you can certainly influence what happens on the ground. Birds will feast on butterflies, moths, and their larvae as well as on other insects spared when you curtail or eliminate the use of pesticides in your lawn and garden.

Urban Habitat, Food and Nesting Habits

American kestral (*Falco sparverius*) Winter and breed in parts of the South in open areas—grassy fields, pastures—with scattered trees, telephone wires. Perch in high places, then drop to ground to prey on insects, small mammals, birds. Nest in cavities such as old woodpecker nests in dead trees, holes in telephone poles, crevices in buildings, birdhouses.

Killdeer (*Charadrius vociferus*) In the South year-round though more widespread in winter. Glean small insects and other invertebrates from areas with bare ground or short grass, large lawns. May nest on gravel rooftops.

Rock dove, pigeon (*Columba livia*) Introduced pests and year-round city dwellers; forage on ground in open places, gleaning seeds and grain; eat occasional insects and berries. Also feed on concrete and other man-made surfaces. Nest on ledges of buildings.

White-winged dove (*Zenaida asiatica*) Neotropical migrant. Forage on ground in open places, gleaning seeds of shrubs, grasses, grains, and weeds, and some fruits and insects from open places near shrubby thickets and shade trees. Winter regularly along the western Gulf Coast.

Mourning dove (*Zenaida macroura*) Found year-round in the South. Forage for seeds or other grain in short grass, bare ground, sidewalks edged with seed-producing plants. Nest in shrubs, low in trees along edges, on window ledges, in hanging baskets of flowers.

Eastern screech owl (*Otus asio*) Nonmigratory. Like open to medium-growth woods, clearings, and edges in residential areas. Nocturnal carnivores who watch from perches for potential food—insects and other invertebrates, rodents, reptiles, amphibians, and birds—then drop to ground and pounce. Nest in tree cavities, may use a birdhouse.

Common nighthawk (*Chordeiles minor*) Neotropical migrant. Seen in open airspace above cities and towns in the South where they forage for insects April/May to mid-October. Winter south of the United States. Nocturnal but also forage during daylight. Sleep during daytime on telephone wires, ledges on buildings, trees. Nest on flat-topped gravel roofs.

Chimney swift (*Chaetura pelagica*) Neotropical migrant. Present mid-March to October, then migrate south for the winter. Feed on insects gleaned during sustained flight over different habitats; favor open country and residential regions. Build nests of sticks glued by saliva to insides of structures like chimneys, sometimes in hollow trees.

Buff-bellied hummingbird (*Amazilia yucatanensis*) Neotropical migrant. A few winter in Gulf Coast gardens that offer evergreen thickets and food in the form of insects and nectar in ornamental flowers and in hummingbird feeders.

Ruby-throated hummingbird (*Archilochus colubris*) Neotropical migrant. Live and breed in the southeast United States in moist woodlands, thickets and tangles near tubular flowers from March until October when most migrate south for the winter. Eat insects and flower nectar while hovering; will visit hummingbird feeders.

Black-chinned hummingbird (*Archilochus alexandri*) Neotropical migrant. A few winter along the Gulf Coast in evergreen thickets and gardens with insects, ornamental flowers and hummingbird feeders.

Rufous hummingbird (*Selasphorus rufus*) Neotropical migrant. A few winter along the Gulf Coast in evergreen thickets and gardens with insects, ornamental flowers and hummingbird feeders.

Red-headed woodpecker (*Melanerpes erythrocephalus*) Year-round in open, mature woods with dead trees or stubs (fence posts or telephone poles) where they excavate cavities for nesting. Dig for insects and larvae in tree bark, in the ground; flycatch for flying insects. Also eat berries and nuts.

Red-bellied woodpecker (*Melanerpes carolinus*) Year-round in mature woodlands with dead trees or stubs for nesting cavities. Feed on insects and larvae on tree bark, and on fruits, nuts, and berries. Prefer hardwoods to conifers. Sometimes feed on the ground.

Yellow-bellied sapsucker (*Sphyrapicus varius*) Winter in open deciduous woods in parks and residential areas where they eat insects and larvae in tree bark, pick berries and nuts. Also drill holes in bark and feed on cambium and sap. Rarely feed on the ground.

Downy woodpecker (*Picoides pubescens*) Common year-round in middle-aged and mature woodlands in residential areas. Nest in dead trees or stubs, prefer hardwoods. Feed in conifers and hardwoods, probing for insects and larvae, occasionally eating nuts and berries. Will feed in smaller trees than other woodpeckers.

Northern flicker (Yellow-shafted flicker) (*Colaptes auratus*) Year-round in wooded areas, woodland margins; prefer hardwoods to conifers. Nest in cavities in dead trees or poles. Eat ants and other insects gleaned from tree trunks and limbs; spend much time ground-feeding on ants. May eat berries and seeds during winter.

Eastern wood pewee (*Contopus virens*) Neotropical migrant. Open to medium-growth wooded residential areas, April to October; winter south of the United States. Nest in hardwoods and conifers fifteen to fifty feet from the ground. Diet is flying insects, caught in sallies from perches high in the canopy or gleaned from leaves while hovering. Feed significantly on butterflies, moths, and their larvae.

Eastern phoebe (*Phoebe Sayornis*) Winter in open habitats, including residential areas. Diet is insects captured in sallies from perches like bare twigs or phone wires. Also feed on insects on the ground. Feed significantly on butterflies, moths, and their larvae.

Great crested flycatcher (*Myiarchus crinitus*) Neotropical migrant. Nest in natural cavities, old woodpecker nests, birdhouses, mailboxes in wooded residential areas. Diet is flying insects captured during sallies from the canopy; caterpillars and insects snatched while hovering at vegetation. Sometimes eat fruit and berries. Winter in lower Florida and south of the United States.

Purple martin (*Progne subis*) Neotropical migrant. Live and breed in the United States between February and early October in residential areas where properly built multicellular houses have been mounted; sometimes nest in other cavities. They feed on insects captured during sustained flight over ponds and other open areas. Winter south of the United States.

Barn swallow (*Hirundo rustica*) Neotropical migrant. Breed in the South near and over water; eat insects captured during sustained flight over water, fields, and other open habitat. Nest under bridges and docks, also under barns and other structures usually, but not necessarily, in the vicinity of water. May build their cup-nests in shelf-style birdhouses.

Blue jay (*Cyanocitta cristata*) Live year-round and nest in middle-aged to mature trees, especially oaks, in open woodlands, forests, and residential areas. Eat insects and other invertebrates gleaned from vegetation in summer. May eat the eggs and young of other species of birds. In winter eat mainly nuts and seeds; acorns are their favorites.

American crow (*Corvus brachyrhynchos*) Woods with tall trees for roosting, open areas for foraging. Feed on the ground. Diet is insects and other small animals during warm months, also grain and berries during winter.

Carolina chickadee (*Parus carolinensis*) Wooded residential areas. Favor mixed pine hardwood forests or pure pine. Breed in cavities, usually in dead trees, or in birdhouses. Glean insects from tree foliage or trees in summer; in winter eat insect larvae and eggs, berries and seeds.

Tufted titmouse (*Parus bicolor*) Wooded areas, woodlands; prefer deciduous trees to pines. Nest in cavities in dead trees or birdhouses. Eat insects gleaned from twigs or foliage of trees in summer; in winter eat insect eggs, larvae, seeds, nuts. Will eat sunflower seeds and suet from feeders.

Red-breasted nuthatch (*Sitta canadensis*) Winter in saplings or mature trees, especially conifers, prefer dense stands; regularly found in residential woodlands. Eat insect larvae or eggs, nuts and pine seeds.

White-breasted nuthatch (*Sitta carolinensis*) Frequent in residential areas with mature trees. Prefer hardwoods to conifers. Nest in knotholes and other cavities in living tree; may use birdhouses. Creep up and down tree trunks probing bark for insects, larvae, and insect eggs. Eat some seeds and nuts in winter.

Brown-headed nuthatch (*Sitta pusilla*) Widespread in residential woodlands, open stands of mature pine trees. Nest in cavities in stumps, posts, dead trees, or stubs; may use birdhouses. Glean insects, larvae and eggs from foliage and bark of trees; also eat nuts and seeds.

Carolina wren (*Thryothorus ludovicianus*) Brushy, tangled areas in or near woods. Feed at or near ground, gleaning insects, larvae and other invertebrates from shrubs, herbs, and soil. Build nests in crannies in a variety of spots from ground level to higher up, from natural cavities and depressions to man-made ones, such as birdhouses, building ledges, old hats and coat pockets.

Eastern bluebird (*Sialia sialis*) Open residential areas with scattered trees, open woods. Like to perch on telephone wires and other exposed perches, drop to the ground for food including insects and other invertebrates. Nest in cavities in the open and within ten feet of the ground, such as knotholes or old woodpecker holes, bluebird boxes.

Wood thrush (*Hylocichla mustelina*) Neotropical migrant. Deciduous or mixed forests with a well-developed deciduous understory and well-wooded residential areas, March to October. Nest in vegetation within fifteen feet of the ground. Eat insects and other invertebrates gleaned from shrubs and low trees and from among dead leaves on the ground. Winter south of the United States.

American robin (*Turdus migratorius*) Breed where lawns and other areas of short grass are interspersed with shrubs and trees; common near humans. Winter near areas with berry-bearing trees and moist woods. In warmer weather and late winter, forage for earthworms and other invertebrates on the ground; in early winter, eat berries and other fruits.

Gray catbird (*Dumetella carolinensis*) Neotropical migrant. May breed and winter in residential areas offering abundant dense, dark, tangled shrubbery. Glean insects from shrubs or saplings, sometimes on the ground. In winter, eat mostly berries and some seeds.

Northern mockingbird (*Mimus polyglottos*) Found year-round in almost every part of the South. Prefer areas with scattered trees or shrubs and conspicuous perches such as telephone wires, fences, television antennae. Diet is mostly insects in summer, mostly berries and fruits with some insects in winter. Forage on the ground and in shrubs and small trees. Nest is cup shaped, built in dense shrubbery or vines no more than fifteen feet from the ground.

Brown thrasher (*Toxostoma rufum*) Found year-round in the South. Favor moderate-to-dense cover or shrubs, saplings, and other brush. Eat mostly insects in the summer, insects, seeds, nuts and other items in the winter, foraging in low vegetation or on the ground. Nest is built in thickets or hedgerows within ten feet of the ground.

Cedar waxwing (*Bombycilla cedrorum*) In winter, wander about in large flocks, visiting residential areas with open woods and thickets near berry-bearing trees or shrubs. Nest in high elevations in mature conifers in areas with scattered trees. During summer, primary diet is insects gleaned from tree foliage.

European starling (*Sturnus vulgaris*) An introduced pest. Abundant in open areas near humans, less common in wooded residential areas. Nest in cavities, ledges, crannies in open areas. Probe the soil for insects during summer; during winter, eat insects, berries, fruits; eat human garbage all year round.

Orange-crowned warbler (*Vermivora celata*) Neotropical migrant. Winter in the lower South in various types of thickets or brush, especially wax myrtle thickets. Glean insects and berries from leaves or twigs of shrubs and saplings (preferred to trees), or herbaceous vegetation. Will take nectar from hummingbird feeders.

Yellow-rumped (myrtle) warbler, "butterbutt" (*Dendroica coronata*) Neotropical migrant. Winter in the South in woodland borders, pinewoods, thickets, especially wax myrtle thickets; eat berries, seeds and large numbers of insects, insect eggs, and larvae gleaned from leaves and twigs in the canopy of mature trees or in shrubs and saplings, occasionally on the ground. Also do some flycatching.

Pine warbler (*Dendroica pinus*) Winter and/or breed in parts of the South in middle-aged-to-mature pine forest, open pinewoods and residential pinewoods. Nests are built in pine trees at medium height from the ground. Summer diet is insects; winter diet includes insects and berries gleaned from twigs and pine needles, seeds and insects found on the ground. Most foraging occurs in the crowns of pine trees.

Palm warbler (*Dendroica palmarum*) Neotropical migrant.

Winter in parts of the South in shrubbery, thickets, and open woods. Diet is mainly insects, smaller amounts of berries and seeds gleaned from herbs, bushes, or the ground.

Prothonotary warbler (*Protonotaria citrea*) Neotropical migrant. Breed in the Southeast in swamps, bottomland forests, willow thickets near lakes or ponds; almost always found by water. Food is insects and other small invertebrates gleaned from bushes within fifteen feet of the ground or water surface. Nest in cavities in dead trees, stubs, cypress knees; may use birdhouses.

Summer tanager (*Piranga rubra*) Neotropical migrant. Present in the South late March to October in wooded residential areas. Diet consists of insects, especially bees, wasps, and other flying forms gleaned and hawked in tree canopies.

Northern cardinal (*Cardinalis cardinalis*) Year-round resident of the South, most common in wooded residential areas with plentiful shrubs. Build nests in varied settings, usually under ten feet from the ground. Forage most often on the ground, also in shrubs and understory. Warm weather diet is insects, seeds, berries; in winter, mostly vegetable matter.

Black-headed grosbeak (*Pheucticus melanocephalus*) Neotropical migrant. Occasionally seen at feeders in residential areas during winter in Louisiana, Mississippi, Arkansas, Alabama, Tennessee. Favored winter habitat is evergreen woodlands; cold-weather diet, fruit (especially cherries) and grains; summer food, insects.

Painted bunting (*Passerina ciris*) Neotropical migrant. Winter in parts of the South. Favored residential habitat is dense shrubbery. Nest in thick cover close to the ground. Diet is insects and seeds gleaned from shrubs, saplings, and herbaceous vegetation in summer; insects and a variety of plant food in winter.

Dickcissel (*Spiza americana*) Neotropical migrant. Breed in parts of the South. In winter, may visit feeders in open residential areas edged with thickets or weedy cover. May forage for seeds in shrubs, saplings, or tall forbs (such as composites).

Rufous-sided towhee (*Pipilo erythrophthalmus*) Winter and breed throughout most of the South. Found in brushy places, residential areas where shrubbery abounds. Diet is insects, seeds, and fruit uncovered by scratching in leaf litter on the ground or while foraging in shrubs. Winter diet is more vegetarian.

Chipping sparrow (*Spizella passerina*) Neotropical migrant. Winter and/or breed in parts of the South. Nest in trees in wooded residential areas overlooking lawns or short grasses. Winter in more open areas. Forage in short grasses for insects and seeds in summer, seeds in winter.

Song sparrow (*Melospiza melodia*) Winter in much of the South, breed in some parts. Favor shrubbery and brush in residential areas; like moist habitats. Nest on the ground or in shrubs or saplings. Diet is insects and seeds in summer; mainly weed seeds in winter. Foraging is primarily on the ground.

White-throated sparrow (*Zonotrichia albicollis*) Winter throughout the South in open woods, edges, thickets, and shrubbery in residential areas. Forage on the ground, especially in dead leaves, for seeds; also glean berries and buds from shrubs and trees.

Dark-eyed junco (*Junco hyemalis*) Winter in wooded residential areas and wood margins throughout the South. Forage on the ground for seeds, often scratching in leaf litter.

Red-winged blackbird (*Agelaius phoeniceus*) Found year-round throughout the South in freshwater marshes, ponds and lakes, swamp edges, woodlands; may visit nearby gardens with feeders or low vegetation and lawns where they glean insects and small invertebrates in the summer; grain and weed seeds in the winter.

Common grackle (*Quiscalus quiscula*) Year-round southern resident. Nest in groves of pines in residential areas. May forage on lawns all seasons; for insects and other animal food in summer, grain and other seeds in winter.

Brown-headed cowbird (*Molothrus ater*) Found throughout the year all over the South where they may visit feeders; forage in lawns and gardens for insects, invertebrates, seeds, grain, and berries in the summer; seeds and grain in the winter. Nest parasites, they lay eggs in the nests of other species.

Northern (Baltimore) oriole (*Icterus galbula*) Neotropical migrant. Winter and/or breed in many parts of the South. In summer, glean insects from canopies of hardwood trees. In winter, will visit gardens with a good cover of evergreen shrubs and a scattering of hardwood trees where they eat berries and insects. Will visit feeders stocked with suet, fruits, and nuts and drink nectar from hummingbird feeders and from specially-designed oriole feeders.

Orchard oriole (*Icterus spurius*) Neotropical migrant. Live and breed in the South April to September; small numbers winter along the Gulf Coast. Like scattered hardwood trees in open areas, old orchards, roadside or creekside trees. Glean insects and other small invertebrates from leaves and twigs at middle canopy levels of trees, eat berries and flower nectar, will visit hummer or oriole nectar feeders in gardens.

Purple finch (*Carpodacus purpureus*) Winter throughout the South in wooded residential areas with hardwoods and conifers offering winter fruits, buds, or seeds.

House finch (*Carpodacus mexicanus*) Winter throughout the South, breed in northern parts of the region. Breed near homes in urban/suburban areas in thickets, shrubbery, and dense trees. Nest in cedars or broadleaf evergreens at different heights.

Forage in shrubs, small trees, or herbaceous vegetation, gleaning insects, seeds, berries in summer, seeds and berries in winter.

Pine siskin (*Carduelis pinus*) Winter in moist hardwood forests, conifers, thickets (especially *Alnus*, alders), residential areas and weedy fields. Winter diet is seeds and other plant material gleaned at various heights from branches, cones, and foliage of shrubs and trees. Visit feeders.

American goldfinch (*Carduelis tristis*) Winter throughout the South, breed upper South. Winter diet is seeds gleaned from all heights in weedy places, thickets, open woods, gardens. Will visit thistle feeders; will also eat hulled sunflower seeds.

Evening grosbeak (*Hesperiphona vespertina*) Winter in low numbers in the South, glean seeds and buds from trees or forage on the ground in coniferous woods, hardwoods; in residential areas will visit feeders with sunflower seeds. Strong mandibles allow them to eat hard seeds such as cherry, plum, and peach.

House or English sparrow (*Passer domesticus*) An introduced pest. Widespread in cities, towns, open residential areas, and farms of the South, though scarce in wooded residential areas. Forage on the ground or in low vegetation for seed, grains, table-scraps, other vegetable matter, and insects. Nest in cavities or on ledges.

CHAPTER FIVE

Attracting Wildlife with Wildlife

Y OU MEAN YOU WANT INSECTS in your garden?" my daughter asked.

"Of course! They're wildlife, too."

She thought before continuing. "I guess butterflies are insects.
They're beautiful. So are dragonflies. Cicadas are okay because
they make nice summer noises. And bees pollinate flowers!
And . . ." A frown appeared on her face. "I don't like roaches. Or
flies. I don't know what use they are. Wasps sting. Mosquitoes
bite, and caterpillars . . . they grow into butterflies—but only

*Illustration: Goldenrod, goldenrod gall, Carolina chickadee, monarch butterfly,
ladybird beetle, ambush bug, lacewing*

some of them." Then she smiled. "Ladybugs are insects. Anyone would love to have a garden full of ladybugs!"

"What about a garden full of aphids?"

"Aphids! Aren't they bad?"

"They're pests," I confirmed. "They eat plants and transmit plant diseases. They secrete something called honeydew that encourages mold to grow on plants and attracts ants. They reproduce really rapidly. If I plant milkweed and sunflowers, I can attract them to my garden."

She looked at me, incredulous. "Why on earth would you want a garden full of aphids?"

"What do you think ladybugs eat?" I asked her.

"Aphids? You mean the way to have lots of ladybugs is to have lots of aphids for them to eat?" She smiled as she caught on.

"If you think of creatures in terms of who they eat or who eats them, you see them differently."

"In other words, aphids aren't pests, they're ladybug food?"

"You've got it."

"And caterpillars?"

"Bird food."

"And mosquitoes?"

"Their larvae are fish food."

"Flies?"

"Food for frogs, lizards, and birds. Why do you think they call them flycatchers?"

"Wasps?"

"They eat tent caterpillars. There's even a species of wasp that's parasitic on the egg cases of cockroaches."

Changing the subject to molluscs and arachnids, she said, "I'll bet you don't want slugs and spiders in your garden!"

"Slugs are toad and turtle food. Spiders eat all kinds of insects, good and bad."

"Okay, okay. But I don't think people are going to want a wildlife garden full of pests!"

My daughter is probably right. Most people, even avowed nature lovers, would rather deal with the prettier representatives of the food chain: birds, butterflies, even pesky squirrels. They may endorse biodiversity in the abstract but feel that rejoicing at the presence of bugs and slugs, gnats or bats is going beyond the fringe.

The wildlife gardener can learn from organic gardeners. Rhonda Hart, in *Bugs, Slugs & Other Thugs: Controlling Garden Pests Organically*,[1] sees the complex web of living creatures on earth as consisting of interactions among three components: plants, plant eaters, and plant eater-eaters. She observes that there is little insect infestation in a natural setting because of the balance among the three groups; that is, there are enough plant eater-eaters or "beneficials" so that, through predation or parasitism, populations of the bad guys, or "pests," are kept in line. To organic gardeners, "pest-free" becomes an undesirable goal, because it also means predator-free. Understanding this thinking will enable you to share my excitement about milkweeds drawing such great numbers of aphids (plant eaters), because aphids attract ladybugs and lacewings (plant eater-eaters) and about willow trees hosting so many species of caterpillars (plant eaters), which makes them wonderful sources of food for caterpillar-eating birds (plant eater-eaters).

There's always someone eating someone in the wildlife garden! This diversity of creatures devouring other creatures provides a bonus to the gardener: a balance and a degree of pest control achieved much more easily and safely than by pouring on pesticides. By learning to accept insect pests as wildlife and tolerating some of their mischief—chewed or discolored foliage or blossoms—we allow buildup of their predators and limit their damage. The flower garden becomes alive with activity and even more beautiful with the addition of multicolored insects to flower hues—creatures like predatory dragonflies whose bodies of blue or gold or green or black or scarlet are carried on etched crystal wings that shimmer in the rays of the sun!

Of course, all the "beneficials" aren't as beautiful or innocuous as dragonflies and lacewings. The day tent caterpillars appeared in my newly planted elderberries, my usually tolerant husband was alarmed. "You'd better do something, quick! They'll defoliate that whole tree, and then they'll go after my figs!"

I knew that during some years tent caterpillars do defoliate trees. Even in a natural setting, pest populations fluctuate. But in a diversified environment where no pesticides are used, numbers of predators should rise in response to the increase of the creatures they eat. I also knew that caterpillars are usually host-specific and that although the eastern tent caterpillar feeds on many trees and shrubs, it favors rose family species, like elderberry. So, I told my husband, "This is a wildlife garden. I want to wait and see what happens. Elderberries are natives, and tough, pioneer species at that. They'll certainly come back without any trouble. And, besides, the tents are pretty when they're new. It's when they lose their freshness and become dusty with age that they're less interesting."

For three days, we watched the tents increase in size, encompassing one, then two, then three branch tip leaf clusters. Wasps began circling. On the fourth day, the tents stopped growing. Did the caterpillars complete their cycle and fly away as moths that fast? More likely, they were eaten by the beneficials: predatory wasps.

My favorite beneficial is the homely toad. You can lure him with snails, slugs, sowbugs, cutworms. "Ughhh! They're even more disgusting than toads!" the squeamish will say. If you consider the toad's role in the greater scheme of things, you'll agree "pretty is as pretty does" and rejoice that he's there to balance things out.

A recent visitor to my garden asked my husband, "Why don't the slugs eat up your plants the way they eat my impatiens?"

Even without coaching from me, he observed, "Toads eat the slugs before they can do too much damage."

Why are there so many toads in my garden? Is it the pond? The ground-cover plants and mulch that give them places to hide? Or is it the slugs?

Three rules for sustaining the predators that live in your garden now and for attracting new species are the same as the ones for designing a wildlife garden in general:

- Hold the Raid! Provide a pesticide-free environment.
- Provide water, shelter, reproductive space and food.
- Provide a diversity of plants and habitats.

Here is a piece of information that will make you feel a little less uncomfortable with the idea of tolerating "pests": predators and parasites of some of the insect pests do not show up until the population of their prey, the pest, has increased enough to support them. You must have noticed aphids on so many garden plants in the very early spring—the beginning of the growing season. If you pull out the insecticide, you delay the appearance of natural predators. If you ignore them, or use water washes and other nonharmful methods of suppression, their enemies—ladybugs, lacewings, parasitic wasps—will eventually appear.

In nature, there are cycles of pest—and therefore, predator—abundance that can be related to several factors including severe temperatures in winter or extreme wetness or dryness in spring weather. Even if pests proliferate and seem more numerous in spite of the work of predators for a couple of seasons, a disease outbreak or other means of control should eventually occur to reduce their populations.

There are some ways the gardener can assure a balanced scale:

• Keep your plants healthy. Plants are more susceptible to pests and infections if they are weak or stressed in some way, just as you are more susceptible to a cold when tired or "run down."

• Select plants suitable to your ecological region. Plant them in habitats similar to their natural ones. Give them the advantages of living in a garden: less competition with other plants, room to grow, and water during dry spells.

• Grow a mix of plants that, collectively, will offer continuous bloom for as much of the growing season as possible to feed the many predators and parasitoids of insect "pests" dependent on obtaining nectar and pollen for egg laying.

Since wildlife gardeners are gardeners first, they'll find pest control an appealing result of attracting some fauna usually considered lowlifes. Following are facts about some of the creatures considered beneficial in the model organic garden. If you find one of the listed less than appealing, read the description of its prey—it may look gorgeous in comparison. Pay attention to specific plants and habitats that attract beneficials; duplicate them in your own wildlife garden. But regardless of what plants you grow, you know that what's really attracting this wildlife to your garden is other wildlife. You've set the stage. Buy field guides to insects, butterflies, and moths so you'll know the characters and can tell the good guys from the bad. Then sit back and watch the show!

Beneficial Wildlife[2]

INVERTEBRATES

NON-INSECT ARTHROPODS

Arachnids (Class Arachnida)

Spiders (order Araneae) eat grasshoppers and other insects. The huge number of spiders places them among the dominant predators in any unpoisoned terrestrial community. They, in turn, may be prey for birds, toads, and wasps. Low-growing ground covers or flowers such as ageratum, asters, petunias, knotweed, sweet alyssum, and hypericum will provide safe living, breeding, and hunting grounds for garden spiders.

Predatory mites (order Phytoselidae) eat pest mites such as red or two-spotted spider mites and their eggs, as well as thrips and other organisms. Attractants/habitat: temperatures above forty degrees and high humidity. They are found in the upper layers of soil and in moss, humus and animal manures, and on plants that host pest mites. The tiny free-living mites, predatory and pest, can number millions per acre in soil and organic debris.

Centipedes (Class Chilopoda)

Centipedes have fifteen or more pairs of legs, short of the total referred to in their nickname "hundred-legs." Clawlike front appendages on flat bodies give them a deservedly ominous look. Their bite can be painful to humans and lethal to the flies and other insects and insect relatives on which they prey. They are common in soil and debris, under bark, in rotting wood and other protected places.

INSECTS (CLASS INSECTA)

Dragonflies and Damselflies (Order Odonata)

Larvae and adult dragonflies (suborder Anisoptera) and damselflies (suborder Zygoptera) eat mites, aphids, leafhoppers, mosquitoes, midges, larvae, and other small plant pests. Since their nymph stages are aquatic, more adults will be found in a garden with a pond than without, but they are strong fliers and will fly far to pursue their prey, so any garden with lots of insects will lure these colorful beauties.

Grasshoppers, Katydids, Crickets, Mantids, Walkingsticks, Cockroaches (Order Orthoptera)

The praying mantis (Mantidae family) is an unaggressive predator, which will grab, paralyze, and eat whatever comes its way: aphids, various beetles and bugs, leafhoppers, flies, ants, caterpillars, butterflies, beneficial bees and wasps and even other mantises. Larger mantids, over an inch long, may even eat salamanders or frogs.

Predaceous Bugs (Order Hemiptera)

Strangely shaped ambush bugs (Phymatidae family), whose abdomens flare beyond their wings on either side of their bodies, eat mites, scales, thrips, and occasionally even larger wasps or bees. They attack prey from hiding places in flowers like complicated goldenrod blossoms.

Assassin bugs (Reduviidae family) are either brownish-black and oval shaped or elongated and long-legged like walkingsticks. They stalk plant foliage, preying on caterpillars, aphids, Mexican bean beetles, Colorado potato beetles, Japanese beetles, leafhoppers, hornworms, and honeybees. Sunflowers are said to be especially good attractants.

Damsel bugs or damselflies (Nabidae family) are yellowish-brown or shiny black with well-developed wings. They are common on low vegetation where they seek prey such as mites, aphids, leafhoppers, larvae, and other small plant pests.

Lacewings (Order Neuroptera)

Green lacewings (Chrysopidae family) and brown lacewings (Hemerobiidae family), the names of which describe their exquisite wings, are famous for feeding on aphids, but they also eat pollen, nectar, spider mites, whiteflies, mealybugs, leafhoppers, thrips, corn earworm and other caterpillars and their eggs, and honeydew and the bugs that produce it. Green lacewings are found on grass, weeds, and shrubs in relatively open areas. Brown lacewings are less common than green and are found in wooded areas. Lacewings are drawn to plants of the Umbelliferae family such as angelica, wild Queen Anne's lace, carrot (*Daucus carota*); sunflower family members such as camphorweed (*Heterotheca subaxillaris*), red cosmos, coreopsis, tansy, goldenrod, and wild lettuce (*Lactuca canadensis*); and oleander (*Nerium oleander*).

Beetles (Order Coleoptera)

Pretty little ladybugs need no description. Even severe insectaphobics love them. Really lady beetles (Coccinellidae family), not bugs, they prey on aphids, scale, mealybugs, whiteflies, psyllids (jumping plant lice), other insects and insect eggs, and mites. Most common of the many species in North America is *Hippodamia convergens*, the convergent lady beetle. The plants that attract ladybugs are, of course, the ones that draw aphids and other creatures ladybugs eat. Milkweeds such as *Asclepias tuberosa,* parsley family members such as angelica, and composite family members such as marigold, yarrow, goldenrod, and sunflowers are considered particularly effective attractants. I look for clues that the ladybugs have arrived to lay their eggs on aphid-infested clumps of daylilies in spring and fall, such as the bugs themselves, as well as dried and empty orange-and-black segmented outer skins of ladybug larvae stuck to aphid-infested leaves. They pupate in their larval skin, which splits to release grown-up ladybugs.

Ground beetles (Carabidae family) are usually shiny-backed and can be black or brightly colored. Adults and their larvae are predaceous on mites, earthworms, slugs, snails, and caterpillars of some of our most threatening agricultural and garden pests—such as the introduced gypsy moth, geometer moths (cankerworms), and noctuid moths (cutworms), satin moth, brown-tailed moth, tussock moth—as well as on fly maggots and other insect larvae. Ground beetles themselves may be food for mammals such as hedgehogs, shrews, moles, bats, and mice, and for birds, frogs, toads, spiders, predaceous robber flies, and ants. Evening primrose *(Oenothera)* and amaranth (*Amaranthus)* species are said to attract them. Nocturnal, they hide during the daytime beneath objects such as fallen tree branches and flat rocks on the ground. The gardener who prefers a neat garden can substitute overturned flower pots, flat rocks and pieces of wood for the debris under which they would hide in a natural setting. Some species (*Calosoma* genus, the caterpillar hunters) will climb trees and shrubs in search of caterpillars.

Rove beetles (Staphylinidae family) have a distinctive look imparted by their elongated bodies and short wing covers that leave their abdominal segments exposed. Different species prey on a variety of insects and their larvae—including ants and termites—and mites; some are scavengers of decaying animal or vegetable matter, some are parasitic on fleas, ants, and termites. I am not recommending you leave animal carcasses or dung around to attract the larger rove beetles. There will be enough decaying animal and vegetable matter for them to eat in any garden that is not too well tended. These beetles may be found on the ground or under objects such as stones, under bark, in moss and fungi, on dung, on flowers, in ant and termite nests, in compost piles, and in and under mulches and other decaying vegetable matter.

Carrion beetle (Silphidae family) adults and larvae are scavengers on carrion and decaying vegetation. The flat-bodied adults are black and sometimes have yellow, orange, or red markings.

Tiger beetles (Cicindelidae family) are brown, black, or green, iridescent or very colorful, fast-flying, fast-crawling predators of ants, flies, small beetles, bugs, caterpillars, spiders, aphids, marine fleas and grasshoppers. Their larvae hide in vertical tunnels in the ground, preying on insects that pass too near. They are found in bright sunlight in open sandy areas, on sandy beaches, and on open paths and lanes.

Lightning bugs or fireflies (Lampyridae family) are really luminescent beetles that fly in spring and early summer; their larvae live on the ground, under bark, and in moist swampy places where they feed on invertebrates, including snails.

Soldier beetles (Cantharidae family), shaped like lightning bugs, are soft-bodied and colorful: black, brown, or yellow with red, yellow, or orange markings. Adults of various species feed on pollen and nectar, and on aphids, grasshopper eggs, cucumber beetles and an array of caterpillars such as cabbage loopers, imported cabbage worms, Mexican bean beetles and many other "harmful" pests. Larvae are found under bark or on the ground where they also prey on insects. *Chauliognathus* species adults are found on goldenrod.

Hister beetles (Histeridae family) are hard-bodied, shiny and black; some have red markings. Adults and larvae feed on other insects attracted to decaying organic matter such as carrion, dung, decaying plants, and oozing sap. Some live under loose bark, some in the galleries of wood-boring insects.

Butterflies and Moths (Order Lepidoptera)

There are 765 species of butterflies in North America, but 10,500 known species of moths! Butterflies are ornamental, and though we know their caterpillars are destructive to plants, we feel they're worth it. But we're not so indulgent of moth caterpillars. Some of them are the most notorious pests of cultivated plants. Both butterflies and moths play roles in the pollination of certain plants. But the importance of the Lepidoptera to the wildlife gardener is their natural enemies: all the creatures who consider them food. The garden that hosts Lepidoptera may also host lots of other insects and spiders, many species of birds, reptiles, amphibians, and mammals such as skunks and raccoons. Moth caterpillars are a major source of food for baby birds in spring.

Habitat for butterflies and moths should offer the plants that host their larvae and an assortment of nectar-producing butterfly and moth plants. Most caterpillars eat leaves outright, but there are larvae of moths that are leaf miners, others that are borers into wood, and still others that stimulate a plant to form galls in which they pupate. Some caterpillars even prey on other caterpillars! Garden mulch and undisturbed soil are important habitat elements, too, because most moth larvae burrow into earthen cells in the ground to pupate. Others spend their pupal stage in dead leaves or other debris on the ground or in decaying wood or hollow stems.

Flies (Order Diptera)

Robber flies (Asilidae family) eat flying insects such as beetles, butterflies, leafhoppers, and grasshoppers. Larvae eat eggs and grubs of undersoil pests. Habitat is ground covers and other low plants.

Syrphid or hover flies (Syrphidae family) may be solidly black or brown or brightly striped with yellow. They are important pollinators like the wasps and hairy bees they resemble, and they even buzz as they hover near flowers, but they do not bite or sting. Maggoty larvae of some prey on aphids, mealybugs, thrips, leafhoppers, and other soft-bodied insects; others are scavengers, occupying dung, carrion and decaying vegetation. Their favorite flowers are composite family members such as coreopsis, gloriosa daisies, marigolds, and cosmos; mint family members such as spearmint; baby blue-eyes, *Nemophilia* species, of the waterleaf family; and morning glories.

Many tachinid flies (Tachinidae family) are larger than the houseflies they resemble and are sometimes more colorful, in shades of yellow, red, brown. They eat flower nectar or honeydew secreted by certain insect pests. They are considered *very* important in pest control because of the creatures they parasitize: beetles, bugs, caterpillars, and grasshoppers. Mother flies may deposit live maggots inside the body of the host or lay eggs on plants or on hosts' bodies. They are especially drawn to plants in the buckwheat family, *Rumex* species, *Polygonum* species and *Eriogonum* species.

Chalcids, Ants, Wasps, Bees (Order Hymenoptera)

Bees (superfamily *Apoidea*)—both the more than 3300 North American species, one of which is a honeybee—and the imported, domesticated honeybee are the most important pollinators of significant numbers of our favorite ornamental and necessary agricultural plants. The more pollinators there are, the more plants set seed and fruit. Bees are attracted by the nectar and pollen in flowering plants. To many people, bee = sting, but bees are not aggressive. Most stings occur when a bee is stepped on or brushed away violently, or when the hive is threatened. Bumblebees can sting repeatedly, but the honeybee, which is eviscerated and dies in the process, would probably rather not sting. Some bees may land on your skin, attracted to perspiration; they're called sweat bees and all they want is to drink.

The group called predatory wasps (superfamily Vespoidea) includes aggressive and nonaggressive wasps that feed on pollen and nectar. All prey on soft-bodied insects like tent caterpillars, spiders, or small animals, and some are also scavengers. But the solidly beneficial role of wasps is overshadowed in garden lore by the pain inflicted to humans by some, particularly the aggressive female yellowjackets and hornets (subfamily Vespinae) the stings from which are multiple and painful. The wildlife gardener can limit negative human encounters with wasps without eliminating the creatures from the scene. Remain quiet and move slowly around foraging wasps. Calmly brush them off if they land on your skin. Do not swat yellowjackets; the squished body releases a chemical alarm that signals other wasps to attack! Eliminate constantly available human protein or sugar food sources such as open garbage or dishes of moist pet food. Wear shoes when you stroll through the garden. Survey building eaves, chimneys, lawns, and gardens periodically during warm months to locate wasps' nests so you can remove them or at least avoid disturbing them inadvertently. Wasps will be attracted to their favorite flowers, composite family members such as oxeye daisies, strawflowers, black-eyed Susans, goldenrod, and yarrow. They also like ripe fruits and berries.

Parasitic wasps (division Parasitica) are "mini-wasps," which do not sting. They may be the size of a small ant, or even tinier and patterned or solidly colored, dark or bright, in black, browns, reds, oranges, yellows. They are technically parasitoids because, unlike parasites, they kill their host. They eat pollen and/or nectar and parasitize insect "pests"; their modus operandi is to lay eggs that hatch into larvae that hollow out victims from the inside! Their prey may include adult and larvae of insects such as aphids, scale, mealybugs, beetles, moths, and butterflies and arachnids such as spiders.

Parasitic wasps fall mainly into two superfamilies: Chalcidoidea, which includes chalcid wasps (Chalcidedae family) and tiny, trichogramma wasps (Trichogrammatidae family) and Ichneumonoidea, which includes brachonid wasps (Brachonidae family) and ichneumon wasps (Ichneumonidae family). Many brachonids and ichneumon wasps are host-specific, attacking particular insect pests or their larvae rather than a variety of insects. This makes them more important pest-control agents than, say, the high-profile ladybug, which would rather glut on the heaviest infestations of several species of aphids and other insects than wipe out a whole colony of one species, which the highly species-specific parasatoid wasp will do. To maintain a predator/prey balance in your garden throughout the season, plant a successively blooming assortment of parasitic wasps' favorite flowers—small, single-blossomed wildflowers or flowering herbs including parsley family members like carrots, celeriac, fennel, dill, cumin, anise, coriander and caraway, or composite family members like artichoke, lettuce, endive, daisy, dandelion, edible chrysanthemum, sunflower, yarrow, artemisea, marigold, zinnia, and aster.

Ants (superfamily Formicoidea) are considered pests when they enter houses; when species such as carpenter ants hollow out decayed areas in buildings; when, like imported fire ants, they bite; and when they protect aphids, scales and other insect pests from attack by their natural predators. But even the bothersome species can be beneficial when they prey on termites, caterpillars, boll weevils, and many other insects; when they aerate the soil through construction of tunnels; and when they act as scavengers to clean up dead animals and debris in the garden.

Vertebrates

MAMMALS (CLASS MAMMALIA)

Bats (Order Chiroptera)

Bats eat from 150 to 600 flying insects per hour. They are the greatest living devourers of mosquitoes, moths, grasshoppers, beetles, and lots of other insects, including some of the most notorious agricultural pests. Important citizens of a healthy ecosystem, they are heroes of the night! For that, you would think they would get respect. Education is changing things, but, thanks to misconceptions held by many and perpetuated in a few cases by misinformed public health officials and in many cases by unscrupulous pest control companies who stand to earn a lot more by exploiting the public's fears than by quieting them, bats continue to be much-maligned mammals. Their numbers are dwindling fast due to the careless use of pesticides and to pollution, but even more so because of direct persecution by humans and the loss of roost sites. The big fear—that of rabies—is unfounded. The deadly disease does occur in bats, as it does in dogs, but as George Lowery pointed out in *The Mammals of Louisiana*, "No one would dare recommend that all dogs be eliminated just because a few are found to be rabid."

Bat babies and adults may be prey for owls, opossums, and some species of snakes. Bat parasites and mites are host specific; they are not interested in any other species but the one with which they have evolved. They don't want to live on you or your dog or cat.

Bats are found where there are insects. To attract them, avoid the use of pesticides in your garden. Mount an outside night-light twenty feet high on a pole or tree to bring bugs.

AMPHIBIANS (CLASS AMPHIBIA)

Toads (Order Anura, Family Bufonidae)

Toads do for insect pests on the ground what bats do in the air. These warty little creatures hide under leaf litter and debris, beneath logs, or in burrows by day, to emerge at night, hungry. They will eat anything that moves! Their diet consists of insects and other invertebrates, especially those considered pests by gardeners—cutworms, armyworms, other caterpillars, bugs, beetles, weevils, sowbugs, snails, and slugs. One toad consumes up to ten thousand pests a season, Rhonda Hart estimates. Toads have some predators: skunks, snakes and some large birds. In my neighborhood, automobiles and nighttime joggers are the greatest hazards.

Toads are everywhere. But to increase the numbers of these pest-control machines in your garden, create more of the dark, moist places where they hide. In addition to providing layers of leaf litter and other organic mulch, you can dig shallow holes and partially cover them with stones, bark, boards, or a real log. Upside-down flower pots, the ones with a section broken out, make perfect toad-tels.

One way to find out how many toads you really have, and to

make even more, is to build a pond! Even a small pond will lure loads of toads, all of them amorous, on the first spring night when the temperature and humidity are right. They lay their eggs, which are imbedded in gelatinous strands, in the water. I found fifteen coupled toad couples—that's thirty toads—in my three-foot-by-four-foot pond one morning! Within four weeks, eggs had become tadpoles, and tadpoles became legions of tiny toads hopping out into the garden. Who will eat them?

REPTILES (CLASS REPTILIA)

Turtles (Order Testudines)

Box turtles (family Emydidae, *Terrapene* species) are the turtles most likely to find their way into gardens. Gopher tortoises (order Testudines, family Testudinidae, *Gopherus* species) are possible in some areas of the Southeast. Box turtles eat insects, slugs, snails, fungi, grasses, leaves, wild fruits and berries, even carrion. They are creatures of shady forests, though they may be found in open fields. In your garden, they will appreciate vegetative ground cover and leaf mulch. They may lie in shallow water, like a ground-level birdbath, on hot days. Gopher tortoises live in burrows they excavate in loamy, well-drained soils in open forested places. They eat grasses and herbaceous plants.

Lizards and Skinks (Order Squamata, Suborder Lacertilia)

Lizards and skinks eat earthworms, snails, insects, spiders, and other small arthropods. Some, like horned lizards, eat only ants; eastern fence lizards favor ants. Larger species eat small vertebrates, also. Garden habitat for lizards and skinks includes dense shrubbery, various ground covers, grass clumps, dead leaves, rotting logs and stumps with loose bark, flat boards, brush piles, fences and the sides of buildings, and sawdust piles.

Snakes (Order Squamata, Suborder Serpentes)

Snakes can be valuable predators of garden pests. I'm not suggesting you lure venomous snakes to your garden! Tread lightly around any snake you can't identify. But, luckily, even the dangerous ones are not usually aggressive. The brown, green, and garter snakes, most common in urban gardens, eat insects, slugs, and snails, which they extract from their shells, and earthworms. Garter snakes may eat toads, but if you have a pond in your garden, you'll have plenty to spare. If you're in a suburban or rural area and really lucky, you may find a king snake in your yard. He'll eat mice, rats and other snakes. A hog-nosed snake will eat toads, frogs, and salamanders. A rat snake will eat lizards, mice, rats, rabbits and squirrels!

Unfortunately, some of the larger, tree-climbing snakes will eat birds and bird eggs. That's why predator guards are important on birdhouses. But snakes are natural predators of birds and are considered useful checks in the balance of nature.

In addition to food sources, snakes like watering places, hiding places, and sunning spots.

CHAPTER SIX

Soil and Other Substrates (Mulch, Wood, Snags)

WHEN I FIRST READ ABOUT MYCORRHIZA, the symbiotic relationship between below-ground fungi and the roots of trees, I pictured a cartoon for Gary Larson's *The Far Side*: a cocktail party in the forest to which all the trees in an ecosystem were invited with subterranean view showing them interconnected by fungal extensions on their root

Illustration: Holly, cedar waxwings

tips, looking like long-fingered hands holding other long-fingered hands. "There's a fungus among us!" one tree whispers secretively to another. How strange, to think there's so much going on right under my feet when I walk through the woods.

According to *Forest Primeval, The Natural History of an Ancient Forest*: "Woody plants in particular require mycorrhizal fungi for survival. Many herbaceous plants also depend on the fungus-root association, and most of those that do not depend on this partnership grow far better with the fungi than without them."[1] There must be mycorrhizal fungi in garden soil, too, I thought. How much more to everything there is than meets the eye!

Soil is habitat for an intricate system of organisms, many more living things than you would find above ground in the most elaborate wildlife garden. That explains why soil qualifies for coverage in *National Wildlife* magazine. An article in the February-March, 1985, issue describes the vast populations of bacteria, fungi, viruses and protozoans that inhabit the microscopic worlds formed by each particle of sand or clay in soil and the moisture-film atmosphere that surrounds it—organisms that kill, like those causing tetanus and botulism, and those that cure, producing penicillin and streptomycin. But, according to the article, "the teeming life of the soil has far more powerful significance than disease or medicine. For it is the bacteria and fungi in the soil that break down the complex molecules of dead organic matter, the cellulose and lignin of wood and leaf, into molecules which plants can use for food. Only the microbes can take the salts out of soil minerals and make them available to plants. Only bacteria can oxidize ammonia into nitrite."[2]

Different communities of organisms thrive in different layers of the soil and in varying conditions of moisture, temperature and acidity. Soil flora and fauna go through successional stages, just like above-ground plant and animal life, as this example from the Piedmont of Georgia illustrates: "Plant succession changes soil conditions from inhospitable red-clay subsoil to a true organic-rich top soil with abundant micro-organisms. Kuo documented this change from pine (age 20-30 years), through mixed pine-hardwood (69-90 years) to hardwood climax (120 years) in the Georgia Piedmont. He found little change in pH (from 5.4 to 5.8). He did find definite changes in the floral community of the soil. The pine community favored the fungi, the mixed pine-hardwood favored the actinomycete fungi, and the hardwood forest soils, with their high organic content and low carbon-nitrogen ratio, had the most bacteria. The soil showed steady improvement through these forest stages."[3]

How cultivating must disrupt all the balanced little underground ecosystems. With each thrust of the shovel a world is turned inside out! And there's no end to the disturbance in the disturbance climax of a garden. Is it all necessary? How does nature cultivate her garden without the help of humans?

I wouldn't call my friends to brag about wildlife I had lured to my soil the way I would if a yellow-breasted chat showed up in my garden, but I could. More wildlife below ground means better conditions above. Thousands of species of bacteria, rotifers, protozoa, roundworms, fungi, springtails, beetles, mites, actinomycetes, earthworms, slugs, snails, mites, millipedes, maggots, sowbugs, flatworms, rove beetles, ants, ground beetles, pseudoscorpions and more make up the food web in healthy soil—another way of saying that the ones that don't eat plants or organic debris eat each other. Doesn't that sound just like the way things are above ground?

What results from the repetitive feasting, excreting, and dying of all these creatures is humus, the dark substance that makes up the organic portion of the soil. The top few inches, called topsoil, are the richest and hold the greatest growth potential. The soil is cultivated, with less organic subsoil being brought from deeper layers to the surface so it can be enriched by ants, worms, and larger burrowing beasts like mice, moles and voles, nature's double diggers.

Of these, earthworms play the greatest role. Naturalist Charles Darwin wrote: "It may be doubted whether there are many other animals which have played so important a part in the history of the world. . . ."[4] You might wonder how a creature as small as an earthworm could accomplish so much, but there are lots of them doing nothing but eating and excreting: eating their way down into the earth and then backing out of their burrows to excrete enriched castings on the surface. The accumulated work of all the worms amounts to extensive underground tunnels and a lot of castings—enough, over the ages, speculated Darwin, to bury the massive monuments of ancient cultures and even cause the sinking effect of the monoliths at Stonehenge!

And earthworms are food for lots of wildlife: toads, box turtles and garter snakes; birds such as woodcocks, robins, hermit thrushes and wood thrushes; mammals such as woodchucks, shrews and moles. When they're washed into water, fish, frogs, and turtles chug-a-lug them.

Aren't some of the creatures in the soil damaging to plants growing in the garden? Of course, but remember, each living thing has predators, parasites and pathogens that keep it in check. Conditions that support diversity are most conducive to creating a balance. Again, an organic gardener's approach is most likely to produce outcomes desired by the wildlife gardener.

Have you ever noticed a flurry of white-winged creatures

ahead of your footsteps through mulch, ground-cover habitats or lawns? They're moths! Many moth larvae pupate in the ground or among dead leaves, in grass thatch and other debris. Lichen is host to larvae of some, like the American idia moth; dead leaves host others, including larvae of the common idia moth. Grasses and ground covers, the low-growing flowering plants, host many species, including the notorious armyworm moth, cutworm moth, and sod webworm.

Webworms are known to meticulous gardeners as one of the greatest threats to the perfect lawn. The organic or wildlife gardener might see them as food for other creatures that will abound in healthy habitat: the four species of ants and mites that eat webworm eggs; the robber fly that captures webworm moths; the spiders, vespid wasps, native earwigs, carabid beetles and rove beetles that prey on various stages of webworms; the ground-foraging birds that eat them; parasitoids such as a braconid wasp and two species of flies that parasitize them; a fungus and two species of protozoans that attack them and the beneficial nematodes that are their parasitoids.[5] See how it works?

Is a chinchbug a terrible pest that sucks the last drop of juice from drought-stressed lawn grasses or is it food for beneficial big-eyed bugs, parasitic wasps, and beneficial fungus? Let bad beetles abound! In the wildlife garden, they will be balanced by insect predators, parasitic nematodes, ground-foraging grackles, cardinals, meadowlarks, catbirds and even pesky starlings. Moles may tunnel under the meadow or lawn in pursuit of pestiferous beetle larvae, spiders, centipedes, and earthworms. Mice and voles follow in their footsteps munching subterranean plant parts such as roots, seeds, and bulbs. You can block mouse mischief by leveling the ridges and watering the grass well. In suburban and rural gardens in some parts of the Southeast, armadillos may

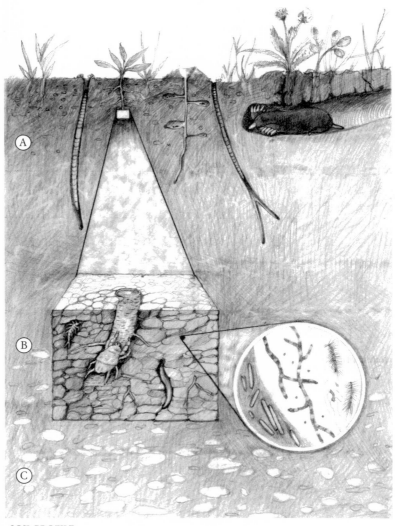

SOIL PROFILE:

The "A" horizon is the top layer, dark, humus-rich, full of roots and other organic matter. Billions of creatures live here and enrich the soil: larger ones such as worms, ants, and moles; smaller ones like the mites, springtails and nematodes shown in the cubical inset; and microscopic organisms like bacteria, fungi, and others shown in the circular inset. The "B" horizon has less air and water and therefore less microscopic life than topsoil; it is stripped of clay and iron as water filters through it. The "C" horizon is just above bedrock. Many of the minerals leached from soil above are deposited here. (Borrowed from Peter Steinhart's article "Soil, the Miracle We Take for Granted" in *National Wildlife*, February-March 1985, 15-22.)

grub for crop pests and other insects by pushing their long snouts into leaf litter and digging when they sense an insect below. A little disturbed earth is a small price to pay for an armadillo in the garden! They may also eat frogs, snakes and birds if they can catch them, and eggs, fruit, and carrion as well.

What goes around comes around, and around, and around, and around!

How to Make the Soil Good Habitat

• In a natural setting each tree and shrub lives within a system that includes a mulch of its own shed leaves and organisms of decay adapted to convert those leaves into a form reusable by the plant. It's a continuous cycle. Perpetuate this system in your garden. Allow leaves and twigs shed by the tree to remain on the ground. Leave clippings from mowed grass or pulled weeds lying where they fall, or secrete them under fallen leaves. You can rearrange things to tidy up a little: rake up leaves and run them through a chopper-shredder, or use a leaf vacuum that chops and bags them, then return them to the garden in a neater form.

• Add organic matter like leafmold or compost to protect the soil from wind and water erosion, severe temperature fluctuations, and rainfall compaction; to conserve moisture and improve nutrient levels and texture; and to create the best possible habitat for plants and function as habitat for animals like ground-dwelling predators of plant pests.

• To make "pest-suppressive soil," apply organic matter such as composted manure, sewage sludge, sifted garden compost, or pulverized bark to the soil in your lawn and garden regularly. They will increase the diversity and activity of microbes and favor the presence of "antagonists" of disease organisms.

Antagonists are organisms such as beneficial fungi that either kill the "bad" organisms or out-compete them for food and habitat.[6]

• Grow clovers (*Melilotus, Trifolium* species) to produce surplus nitrogen and encourage the presence of beneficial soil microorganisms. Nodules on the roots of legumes house bacteria that absorb nitrogen from the air and convert it to an organic form. When clovers die and decay, this nitrogen is added to the soil. Soil fungi, part of the mycorrhizal relationship, also support nitrogen-fixing bacteria, both within and on their surface.

HOW TO ACHIEVE DIVERSITY IN GROUND-LEVEL HABITATS

• Grow a variety of plants: low-growing plants or rambling vines as ground covers in some spots, short grasses in another, wildflowers somewhere else. Aside from the complex of insects associated with each family of plants and edible to an assortment of predators and parasites, plants give all kinds of creatures places to lurk and prowl.

• Use several types of organic mulches to shelter and hide different creatures.

• Create a spot to resemble the areas of bare earth that are natural in a forest, such as strips exposed by fires in pine forests and earth banks at rivers' edges. Birds may take dust baths in little patches of bare earth or sand in the garden. Offer birds a shallow tray or box filled with dry dust, such as road dust. A suggested size is two feet wide, three feet long, two inches deep.

• Put stone borders along planting beds or provide rock piles for creatures that use rocky places in the wild, such as snakes shedding their skins or basking along with skinks and lizards on sunny rock tops. Toads, snails, slugs, and other invertebrates, as well as snakes, will hide underneath.

• Provide overturned flowerpots; they make good hiding crevices.

Wood as a Habitat

Trees remain significant to wildlife even as they die. Natural cavities that form in the trunks of aging sycamores and oaks stricken with heartrot fungus are nesting sites for birds and mammals. Dead trees still standing, called snags, attract beetles and borers that dismantle their limbs and are food for bark gleaners (nuthatches, black-and-white and yellow-throated warblers, brown creepers) and foraging woodpeckers. Wood-peckers may excavate nesting cavities in the rotting bark. Secondary nesters like wrens, chickadees, and titmice might use them in succeeding years if flying squirrels, white-footed mice, tree frogs, arboreal snakes and lizards don't.

Hollowed-out downed logs in wild places may shelter mink, otter, and raccoon. Logs, stumps, and sawdust piles are basking places for all manner of beasts that may also feast on the grubs and beetles that infest them.

Boards or bark laid on the ground may conceal larvae of soldier beetles and glowworms that are predaceous on other insects and invertebrates, including snails.

Log or brush piles can serve as butterfly hotels for overwinter-ing butterflies or as safe places to pupate (i.e., spend the chrysalis or cocoon stage).

Systems of fungi and mold as extensive as the mycorrhiza of the soil invade dying trees through cracks and crevices and through the galleries and tunnels dug by wood-boring beetles, permeating woody tissue and furthering decay. Checkered bee-tles prey on bark-boring beetle grubs; handsome, pleasing, or hairy fungus beetles eat fungus on and in rotting trees. Tooth-necked fungus beetles live in slime molds and under tulip trees and willow bark and false click beetles in rotten beech and maple. Even in death, trees are alive!

Snags

Either you have one or you don't, right? Not necessarily. The importance of dead trees in the forest is common knowledge among the environmentally aware. If a garden tree dies, you know to leave as much standing as you safely can to lure a multitude of creatures. But what if you don't have a snag in your garden and want one? You can do what some wildlife gardeners do. They "plant" dead trees. Following are some guidelines adapted from articles by Scott Shalaway in *Birder's World*, August 1993[7] and *WildBird*, June 1992[8]:

• A snag should extend at least eight feet above the ground and be six inches in diameter at eye level. Locate a snag of suitable size in a woodland or woodlot. Ask permission, then harvest the tree.

• Choose the largest snag you have the facility to transport and "plant." It helps if you have manpower, a pick-up truck, and a winch for hoisting the snag into a hole. A snag hole should be four to six feet deep and eight inches wider than the diameter of the base. Hoist it into place, stabilize it with braces, make sure it is vertical, then pour concrete into the hole.

• If you can, find a snag with horizontal branches, which offer good perching stations and places to hang bird feeders.

• Grow vines up your snag to provide cover for lots of creatures and nectar for hummingbirds and insects.

• Place a birdbath near the snag. You may lure birds that don't usually visit birdbaths!

CHAPTER SEVEN

Trees, Shrubs, and Vines for Backyard Habitats

O F COURSE, THE WILDLIFE YOU CAN ATTRACT is limited to creatures whose overall range coincides with your garden. You know you're not going to draw koala bears to Birmingham, no matter how much eucalyptus you plant! You can't attract what's not there. Residents of suburbs near undeveloped natural areas will have an edge over inner-city residents, except for those who live in inner cities bisected by

Illustration: Gaillardia, Ratibida pinnata, mourning doves

rivers where the willow-thicketed edges shelter wandering raccoons and opossums or built around large parks where forests of
oaks are inhabited by screech owls and lakes are full of bullfrogs
and night herons. Anywhere, though, the right trees not only
can lure more species of resident birds year-round but can also
entice more birds that winter in your area, as well as giving
spring and fall migrants, headed for breeding or wintering
grounds in parts north or south, a reason to drop in. If you're
growing indigenous trees and shrubs, take pleasure in the knowledge that nature has already scheduled bird migration to coin-
cide with times of blooming or fruiting or seed-bearing of trees
and plants. Pull out a field guide to preview the stunning birds
you may glimpse in your red mulberry or black cherry or parsley
hawthorne during spring or fall migration.

Trees are vertical gardens, whole communities of life! A large
specimen produces more of everything you expect from a plant:
flowers to draw nectar and pollen-seeking butterflies and other
insects; leaves and bark to feed and support microbes, fungi,
insects, mites, spiders and their eggs and larvae, all of which are
food for foraging birds and tree frogs; seeds, fruits or nuts, for
even more species of birds, insects, and squirrels and other mammals. With understory shrubs at its feet, mistletoe or Spanish
moss draped from its limbs, and vines scaling its height to the tip
of its crown, flowering and fruiting all the way, a tree is a verita-
ble cafeteria to wildlife!

If mature trees already grow on your property, you're off to a
good start as a wildlife gardener. The information in this chapter
will help you evaluate what grows in your garden now and serve
as a basis for additional selections. Remember, the goal is diversity. In a smaller garden, since you can plant fewer species of
trees and shrubs, you must select well. Choose species that have

the most to offer: more berries, fruit, or seeds over a longer period of time. Be sure to consider evergreen plants, as they will offer cover during the winter when deciduous trees and shrubs have dropped their leaves.

Some Practical Considerations

DEFINING NATIVE

For the gardeners growing native plants to achieve lower maintenance, there is another consideration: they must not only pick species that grow in the immediate region but must also choose individual specimens grown in nurseries nearby, within one hundred miles of where they live. This is more important in selecting trees than other plants, because they require the biggest investment of time and money. Plants are adaptable, but within limits. Sally Wasowski tells about the freeze that killed half the live oaks in Dallas—the half from growers in Houston and south Louisiana. The other half—from Fort Worth nurseries—were totally undamaged. She explains, "For a plant (especially a tree) to withstand all of the vagaries that the weather might produce, it needs to be from the same latitude, from the same altitude, the same distance from the moderation of the ocean, and the same distance from the mountains that affect rainfall patterns. Also, it must have the same kind of soil porosity, with the same range of alkalinity or acidity. Otherwise, some norther or drought will damage it."[1] Ask your nurseryman where a tree came from before you purchase it.

A PERSPECTIVE ON PESTS

In a forest untouched by humans, trees and shrubs are growing where they were meant to grow, or they wouldn't be there at all. That's obvious. They have developed adaptations not only to a site but to fauna with which they have been associated through years of evolution, such as acquiring mechanisms for protection against the damaging activities of insect associates. As trees age, they are subject to decomposition resulting from the work of insects, fungi, microbes and other organisms. Again, many of these are specific to particular plants: the larvae of wrinkled bark beetles bore beneath bark of decaying beech, ash, elm, and pine; the larvae of reticulated beetles seek rotting oak, chestnut, and pine; the larvae of micromalthid beetles bore in oak that has reached the red-rotten stage of decay or in yellowish-brown decayed chestnut.[2] As the life cycle is completed, minerals locked up in tree tissues are returned to the soil for use by other plants.

Trees have adapted to herbivores, vertebrates like browsing hares and deer as well as insects like moth and butterfly caterpillars, by developing defensive chemicals—phenols, tannins, terpenes—which they secrete during different parts of the growing season or in response to insect-caused defoliation. Defensive compounds work in several ways. Some interfere with insect digestion; others inhibit growth and development of the insect and therefore limit reproduction; still others reduce plant digestibility or palatability, making the leaves taste nasty. In certain trees, new growth is higher in the compounds, with better protection against attack, than more mature growth. Fast-growing trees on "good sites" have lower amounts and different types of defensive chemicals and are more subject to injury from insect herbivores than slow-growing species, especially those on poor sites. Some trees respond to herbivore attack by producing compensatory growth.[3]

Obviously, some herbivores break through plant defenses.

That's a good thing, because if some caterpillars didn't eat enough leaves to pupate in cocoons and chrysallises, there would be no moths and butterflies. Without moths and butterflies laying eggs, there would be no caterpillars, which are the main source of food for baby birds each spring. Caterpillars are as important in a wildlife garden as in nature.

Problems result when the system is thrown off balance. Stress or weakness in a tree gives the leaf-eaters an edge. Under stress, a tree may manufacture fewer pest-killing or pest-repellent substances in its leaves; if weak, it may be more easily damaged by wind, which exposes inner bark to assault by fauna and fungal enemies.

How can you maintain the balance in your wildlife garden? Protect your trees, vines, and shrubs from stress. Keep them healthy!

The most destructive species of moths and insects, like the gypsy moth, have generally been introduced. But natives, such as caterpillars of the spring cankerworm moth and maple and elm spanworm larvae, may be "serious defoliating forest pests," too.[4] Just remember that cycles of pest and predator abundance are natural. You must give predator populations a chance to grow large enough to confront the pests effectively; allow time for birds to spread the word. It may be very difficult to develop a completely balanced system in a city wildlife garden. If you must resort to other defenses, don't feel guilty. Try the least toxic solutions for pest control first; use insecticides as a last resort. Remember, a completely pest-free tree isn't much good in a wildlife garden.

Guidelines for Healthy Trees

Select species indigenous to your ecological region.
Choose a variety of species for your garden to complement

species growing in nearby yards and increase the diversity of your neighborhood forest.

Choose trees and shrubs naturally associated in plant communities of your region. (Review "Profiles of Some Common Southeastern Plant Communities/Wildlife Habitats" in chapter 3 to find natural associates.)

Plant trees and shrubs in habitats similar to their natural ones. Water and protect them; give them room to grow.

Keep soil around your tree roots properly aerated by mulching to prevent compaction wherever there is foot traffic. Remember that roots (especially feeder roots) may extend beyond the drip line of the tree.

Do not use herbicides on lawns and ground covers around trees. Vaporized in the air, they can damage leaves; dissolved in water, they can harm roots.

Use a slow-release fertilizer if one is needed at all. Overused nitrogen fertilizers can stimulate the growth of populations of aphids and scale.

Learn proper techniques for pruning your trees to prevent the entrance of decay organisms.[5]

Sex and Flowers

Flowers are perfect, or bisexual, if they have both pollen-bearing or staminate (male) and seed-forming or pistillate (female) parts. If they have only staminate or only pistillate parts, they are called imperfect. If perfect flowers, or imperfect flowers, both staminate and pistillate, are found on the same plant, the plant is called monoecious. When staminate and pistillate flowers grow on different plants, the plants are called dioecious.

Make sure you know whether a tree is dioecious or not before you buy it. If you are growing it for its flowers only, the sex doesn't matter. Butterflies, bees and other insects will visit males or females for nectar and males for pollen. If you are growing it for its fruit or seed, which will be edible by vertebrate wildlife, choose seed- and fruit-bearing females. You'll still need a male in your garden or somewhere nearby, or the pistillate flowers on your tree will not be pollinated and won't set seed or fruit. One staminate plant can pollinate five to ten pistillate. Grow the less ornamental males in out-of-the way parts of the garden.

Selecting Trees for Wildlife[6]

The Overstory: large trees will make up your forest canopy. If they grow in your yard already, you're lucky. Large trees are magnets for birds. If you're starting from scratch and have the money to invest, the bigger the tree the better. Otherwise, you'll have to wait for progression from seedling through sapling to maturity.

Midstory/Understory/Edge: in a forest, the understory makes niches for shrub nesters, singing posts for songbirds, cover for rabbits, and browse for deer. Though some species are found naturally in the shade of taller trees, they will not flower and fruit as heavily in shade as in sun.

Include plants from all these categories in each vegetation layer:

 • conifers and other evergreens for nest sites and cover in winter; for cover, sap, buds, and seed in summer
 • summer-fruiting plants
 • fall-fruiting plants
 • winter-fruiting plants
 • plants that produce nuts and acorns

Conifers

Cupressaceae (Cypress Family)

Overstory The cypress family is represented in the southeast United States not by the bald cypress, which is a redwood, but by junipers and cedars, not to be confused with the real cedars, which are members of the pine family. "Cedars" are evergreen. Eastern red cedar (*Juniperus virginiana*) and southern red cedar (*Juniperus silicicola*) like alkaline soil. Atlantic, or southern white cedar (*Chamaecyparis thyoides*), grows in acid soils. Male pollen cones and female seed cones—bluish, berrylike fruit—form on different plants. Fruit matures in the fall and winter.

Other Cupressaceae for gardens include *Thuja occidentalis*, white cedar or American arborvitae (a northeastern United States native) and *T. orientalis* (oriental arborvitae) and *Juniperus* species (junipers or cedars), both United States natives and exotics, in forms from prostrate ground cover to upright shrub or tree.

These trees provide cover and nesting sites. Female oriental arborvitae bear fruit that may be eaten by birds in fall and early winter. Some junipers form berries. The best wildlife plants in this family are the red cedars—the fruiting female trees attract opossums, armadillos, and fifty species of birds, including tree swallows, cedar waxwings, mockingbirds, robins, yellow-rumped warblers, bluebirds, flickers, yellow-bellied sapsuckers, bob-whites, and mourning doves. Red cedars host the caterpillars of olive hairstreak and pine elfin butterflies and those of juniper geometer, curve-lined angle, and evergreen bagworm moths. Cedars are an alternate host to apple rust; plant them near your rose family trees only if you want to attract this fascinating fungus. Apple rust causes black spots on fruit and leaves of rose family trees in the first half of its life cycle; in the second, it forms ball-shaped brown galls on cedar twigs that ooze brown gelatinous threads after heavy rain.

Pinaceae (Pine Family)

Overstory Pines, *Pinus* species, are evergreen. Their small pollen cones (male) and larger seed cones (female) are borne on the same tree. Seed cones are almost always present, either on the tree or on the ground below.

The seeds are eaten by squirrels, rabbits, hares, raccoons, coyotes, black bears; by nearly all game birds, including wild turkey; and by songbirds, including pine siskins. Trees provide cover and nesting sites for birds. Trunks of mature pines may become habitat for beetles and ants and draw bark-insect feeding birds such as downy woodpeckers and white-breasted and brown-headed nuthatches. From needles in the crowns of pines, pine warblers glean insects such as hairy fungus beetles, which feed on pine pollen. Kinglets, chickadees, and pine warblers may forage for insects in pine saplings or trees. Southern pine beetles and their larvae excavate galleries into the bark of older pines, providing access by fungi that eventually rot the bark, but not before they draw fungus-eating beetles and a multitude of other invertebrates, all food for foraging mammals and birds. Cavities develop and may be used by nesting owls or woodpeckers. A declining pine can be as valuable a wildlife tree as a sapling; just keep all rotting limbs trimmed for safety. The scrub pine (*Pinus virginiana*) is a larval host plant for the eastern pine elfin butterfly (*Incisalia niphon*). Pines may host larvae of the polyphemus, esther, southern chocolate angle and other moths.

Taxodiaceae (Redwood Family)

Overstory Bald cypress (*Taxodium distichum*) and pond cypress (*T. ascendens*) are deciduous. Pollen and seed cones form on the same plant.

The Carolina parakeet, now extinct, used to distribute cypress seeds in its droppings. Bald cypress growing in standing water attracts bird-voiced tree frogs. Cypresses provide shelter and insect habitat for birds, as well as nest sites for yellow-throated and other warblers. Their seed cones are eaten by squirrels, ducks, and some songbirds, and they are larval host of the cypress sphinx and angle-winged emerald moths. Epiphytic Spanish moss, which offers hiding places for bats and hibernation spots for butterflies, may grow on cypress.

BROAD-LEAVED PLANTS

Acanthaceae (Acanthus Family)

Midstory/Understory/Edge Flamingo plant (*Justicia carnea*) is a tender South American evergreen shrub with fluffy clusters of pink flowers that bloom during summer and attract hummingbirds. It is the larval host of the Texan crescentspot butterfly.

Firespike (*Odontonema strictum*) is a Central American perennial shrub with scarlet spikes of flowers, present spring into winter, which are loved by hummingbirds.

Shrimp plant (*Justicia brandegeana, Beloperone gutatta*) is a tender Mexican weak-stemmed shrub with maroon-and-white blooms appearing summer into winter. It is an important Gulf Coast winter hummingbird plant and is larval host to the Cuban crescentspot butterfly. It is also a butterfly and bee nectar plant, and birds such as orange-crowned warblers, mockingbirds, house finches, and white-crowned sparrows eat the nectar-filled bases of the flowers.

Aceraceae (Maple Family)

Overstory Red maple (*Acer rubrum*), swamp red maple or Drummond's maple (*Acer rubrum* var. *drummondii*), Florida sugar maple (*Acer barbatum*), silver maple (*A. saccharinum*) and chalk maple (*A. leucoderme*) are southeastern species. The maples are deciduous and dioecious. Showiest is the red; its late-winter red flowers are followed by seeds encased in red double-winged papery samaras that persist three to four weeks on female plants only.

Maples provide nesting sites for birds. Seeds are eaten by some birds, including bobwhite, chickadee, purple finch, American goldfinch, and yellow-bellied sapsucker, and by mammals, such as squirrels. Inner bark of maples is eaten by porcupines; twigs are eaten by cottontail rabbit, hare, and white-tailed deer. Sap that flows in early spring from holes drilled by woodpeckers or from broken twigs is food for hummers and other nectarivorous birds, as well as for insects, which, in turn, become food for insect-eating birds. Maple flowers provide pollen and nectar for honeybees, which are hungry after winter. The trees are larval hosts for moths, including unicorn caterpillar, morning-glory prominent, maple prominent, white-dotted prominent, wavy-lined heterocampa, Baltimore bomolocha, maple zale, saddleback caterpillar (stinging), promethea, cecropia, white spring, and red humped caterpillar.

Midstory/Understory/Edge Box elder or ashleaf maple (*Acer negundo*) is a medium-sized deciduous and dioecious tree. Flowers appear in spring; fruits, on female trees only, are seeds paired in papery, V-shaped cases that hang in clusters, maturing in autumn and persisting into winter. These are nesting trees for birds and provide nectar for bees. Sap that flows in early spring is used by hummingbirds and insects. Squirrels and songbirds eat the seeds. Trees are larval hosts for tortricid family moths such as the tufted applebud.

Anacardiaceae (Cashew Family)

Midstory/Understory/Edge The famous members of this family are poison ivy, poison oak and poison sumac, well used by wildlife but not recommended for the garden! Sumacs are decid-uous, dioecious, thicket-forming shrubs and small trees known for their brilliant red fall color: shining, winged, or dwarf sumac (*Rhus copallina*), common or smooth sumac (*R. glabra*), and staghorn sumac (*R. typhina*). Spikes of yellow-green flowers appear midsummer on female plants; dense clusters of red berries follow and persist into winter, unless, as is usual with winged sumac, they have been consumed by then. They provide nest sites and berries that are eaten by rabbits and deer and by bob-white, turkey, and many other birds, although only, one source hints, during late winter when nothing else is available. Another source suggests grubs of insects that lay eggs on the berries are the lure. *R. copallina* hosts larvae of red-banded hairstreak butter-flies. All sumacs may host larvae of the spring azure butterfly and of the following moths: bordered sallow, variable antepione, spotted datana and showy emerald. Staghorn sumac also hosts the dark marathyssa moth.

Annonaceae (Annona [Custard-apple] Family)

Midstory/Understory/Edge Pawpaw or false-banana (*Asimina triloba*) is a small, deciduous tree. The dwarf form is *A. parviflora*. Dark maroon blooms appear before the leaves in spring; small, velvety, green banana-like fruits mature in fall. It is monoecious, but two cultivars are necessary for fruiting.

The flowers are pollinated by flies. Twigs are wildlife browse. The fruit is eaten by opossums, squirrels, raccoons, foxes, and birds. It is the larval host for the zebra swallowtail butterfly and for the pawpaw sphinx, pink-spotted hawk and tulip-tree beauty moths. *Omphalocera munroei* moth larvae bore into pawpaw fruit.

Apocynaceae (Dogbane Family)

Midstory/Understory/Edge The exotic oleander (*Nerium oleander*) attracts beneficial insects such as minute pirate bugs, big-eyed bugs, assassin bugs, lady beetles, soft-winged flower beetles, lacewings, syrphid flies, and parasitic wasps. It is the larval host of the colorful day-flying polka-dot wasp moth larvae (oleander caterpillar), a neotropical species found only in Florida and spots along the Gulf Coast. I saw them on lantana in Dauphin Island, Alabama.

Aquifoliaceae (Holly Family)

Midstory/Understory/Edge Small to medium-sized shrubs to trees. Though they are adapted to understory, they bear more fruit in sunnier spots. All like acid-to-slightly-acid soil; yaupon will thrive in alkaline, also. Some are deciduous; most, ever-green. They are dioecious. Tiny, white flowers bloom in early spring; colorful berries, on females only, mature in autumn and persist into winter. Choose plants during fruiting season to be sure of what you're getting. You'll need at least one pollen-bearing male nearby, or females will not produce berries.

Possum haw or deciduous holly (*Ilex decidua*), Sarvis holly (*I. amelanchier*), and winterberry or black alder (*I. verticillata*) are deciduous and red-berried. American holly (*I. opaca*) is the largest holly, evergreen tree or shrub and has red berries. Other evergreen hollies, either small tree or shrub in form, include red- or yellow-berried yaupon (*I. vomitoria*), black-berried inkberry or gallberry (*I. glabra*), myrtle holly (*I. myrtifolia*), and dahoon holly (*I. cassine*), with bright red berries and heavy-fruiting habit. Hybrids of native hollies are available, such as Savannah, Fosteri, and East Palatka, crosses of *I. opaca* and *I. cassine*. Dwarf forms of yaupon (*I. vomitoria*) are males and do not produce berries at all.

Hollies are important as wildlife cover and nesting sites. Flowers are early spring sources of nectar for bees. Many song-birds, game birds, and mammals, including opossums and raccoons, eat holly berries. Berries of some species, like American holly (*I. opaca*) are eaten early in the season; others, like possum haw (*I. decidua*), are eaten later or not at all. One source suggests that it's a matter of taste—that birds turn to the least-favored hollies after they have run out of foods they like better. But Sally Wasowski suggests that the birds are saving the best for last. They know, she hypothesizes, that the product of several winter freeze-and-thaw cycles is fermented berries, just the thing for a spring fling![7] Plant several species of hollies for bird food throughout the winter. They are the larval host for striped hair-streak butterflies.

Females of the nonindigenous Chinese holly (*I. cornuta*) will produce berries without males.

Araliaceae (Ginseng Family)

Midstory/Understory/Edge Hercules'-club or devil's walkingstick (*Aralia spinosa*) is a small deciduous thicket-forming understory tree with prickly stems and leaves. Blooms are upright clusters of tiny white flowers that appear in late summer; shiny black fruits mature in autumn. Flowers are visited by bees and wasps. Mammals and many birds love the fruit.

Japanese angelica tree (*A. elata*) is a nonindigenous aralia. It also produces fruits eaten by birds.

Betulaceae (Birch Family)

Overstory *Betula nigra*, river birch, is a deciduous tree. Flowers are long catkins that appear in spring; the fruit, winged nutlets, matures in summer.

The trees provide nesting sites. Many songbirds, such as chickadees and small finches, as well as game birds, eat the seeds and buds; several mammals eat the twigs and bark. Trees may host larvae of the following moths: polyphemus, curve-toothed geometer, promethea, variable oakleaf caterpillar, four-barred and bent-line gray, porcelain gray, small engrailed, chocolate prominent, and black waved flannel. Sap that flows in early spring from holes drilled by woodpeckers or from broken twigs is used by hummers and insects, which become food for insect-eating birds. In bad nut years, even squirrels consume tree sap.

Midstory/Understory/Edge These smaller birch family members are deciduous. They bloom in spring; the flowers are small catkins. The fruit, in various forms—nuts, winged or wingless nutlets—matures in late summer/autumn.

Ironwood or American hornbeam (*Carpinus caroliniana*) and eastern hop hornbeam (*Ostrya virginiana*) are small trees. Deer and rabbits browse on twigs and buds. Grouse, pheasants, wild turkey, quail, cardinals, grosbeaks, purple finch, goldfinch, and gray squirrels eat the nutlets. *Carpinus* is larval host to red-spotted purple, hop merchant, and tiger swallowtail butterflies and to mustard sallow, sleeping baileya, eyed baileya, and white spring moths.

Hazel alder or tag alder (*Alnus serrulata*), green or mountain alder (*A. crispa*), and hazelnut (*Corylus americana*) and beaked hazelnut (*C. cornuta*) are shrubs. The bark of alders is food for deer and mourning doves and is used by beavers for food and lodge construction. Hazelnuts (called filberts) and twigs are used as food and browse by mammals such as squirrels, chipmunks, and deer and by many birds, including jays, grouse, quail, and pheasant. Alders host larvae of the four-barred and bent-line gray, Doubleday's baileya, and bordered sallow moths.

Bignoniaceae (Bignonia Family)

Overstory Southern catalpa (*Catalpa bignonioides*) is a deciduous tree with dramatic large leaves and abundant, showy, fragrant, white blossoms that appear in late spring and are followed by long seed pods maturing in autumn.

This tree is known for its pests: catalpa mealybugs, catalpa midges, and the catalpa worm, larva of the catalpa sphinx moth, which is choice fishing bait, and, one source says: "one of the most spectacular insect pests."[8] The worms can completely defoliate catalpas but are so subject to parasitism by chalcid wasps that few pupate and become adults. How many birds and lizards enjoy the worms as much as fish do?

Midstory/Understory/Edge Cape honeysuckle (*Tecomaria capensis*) is a South African, tender, vinelike shrub used as ground cover or hedge. Its blooms, yellow to red-orange tubular clusters, appear summer into winter and attract hummingbirds.

Caprifoliaceae (Honeysuckle Family)

Midstory/Understory/Edge Elderberry (*Sambucus canadensis*) is a clump-forming, deciduous shrub. Flat-topped clusters of white flowers bloom in early summer and sporadically until frost; dark purplish berries follow, with flowers and berries appearing on the shrub at the same time. Bees and butterflies visit the flowers for nectar. Many species of birds eat the fruit. The plant hosts larvae of the elder shoot borer moth.

Coralberry or Indian currant (*Symphoricarpos orbiculatus*) is a small deciduous shrub that spreads by suckers, forming thickets of erect and arching branches. Clusters of small white flowers appear in early summer; coral-red berries follow in fall and persist for months. The plant provides nectar for bees and butterflies and nest sites and cover for birds. Leaves are larval food for hummingbird moths and faint-spotted palthis moths. Flowers attract beneficial flower and tachinid flies. Birds eat the berries in winter.

Arrowwood (*Viburnum dentatum*), swamp blackhaw or swamp viburnum (*V. nudum*), and rusty blackhaw (*V. rufidulum*) are some of the many native viburnums for garden use. These shrubs or small trees are deciduous, although they may be evergreen in regions with warmer winters. Blooms are flat or round-topped clusters of white flowers appearing in spring or summer; dark, berry-like fruit matures in summer or fall and persists into winter on some. Berry crops vary depending on weather conditions when the pollen is produced and the resulting success or failure of cross-pollination. Beware the large-flowered introduced "snowball" viburnums! All show, they are sterile and do not produce berries. Viburnum blossoms are nectar sources for bees and butterflies. Berries of native viburnums are eaten by songbirds and game birds and by mammals such as foxes. Foliage is browsed by deer and rabbits. Maple-leaf viburnum (*V. acerifolia*) hosts larvae of the spring azure butterfly. Viburnums attract the harvester butterfly, the larvae of which eat infestations of woolly aphids, and the saddleback caterpillar (stinging), pink prominent, and chestnut schizura moths.

Glossy abelia (*Abelia x grandiflora*), is a semievergreen shrub, a hybrid of oriental species, with small, tubular, pink-to-white flowers that bloom spring to frost. It is well used by nectar-feeding butterflies and hummingbirds. Old-fashioned weigela, *Weigela florida*, is a deciduous shrub of Asian origin. Rose-pink clusters of funnel-shaped flowers appear before the new leaves in spring and are used by hummingbirds and other nectar drinkers.

Celastraceae (Bittersweet Family)

Midstory/Understory/Edge Strawberry bush or wahoo (*Euonymous americana*) is a thicket-forming deciduous shrub that requires acid soil. Small dark red or purple flowers bloom in late spring and early summer; the fruits are warty, rose-colored capsules with husks that mature in fall and split open to expose reddish-orange seeds. Deer and rabbits browse on the leaves and stems. Wild turkeys and songbirds use the seeds.

The *Euonymous* species offered by many nurseries are Asian introductions. In fall, some produce berries eaten by birds.

Cletheraceae (White-alder Family)

Midstory/Understory/Edge Summersweet or hairy pepperbush (*Clethra alnifolia*) is a small, thicket-forming, deciduous shrub. Its fragrant white spikes of flowers appear over a four-to-six-week period in summer; its brown seed capsules mature in fall and persist on spikes. Bees, butterflies, and hummingbirds visit the flowers for nectar; seeds are eaten by many birds and small mammals.

Compositae or Asteraceae (Sunflower or Composite Family)

Midstory/Understory/Edge Groundsel bush or silverling (*Baccharis halmifolia*) is a semievergreen, dioecious shrub. Clusters of tiny white-to-yellowish flowers bloom in fall and are followed by silvery-bristle fruits on the female plants only. Butterflies use its nectar.

Cornaceae (Dogwood Family)

Midstory/Understory/Edge Flowering dogwood (*Cornus florida*) is a small deciduous tree famous for its early spring flowers, which are clusters surrounded by white bracts. Red berries mature in fall. Other native dogwoods less showy but just as useful to wildlife include roughleaf dogwood (*C. drummondii*), with round-topped clusters of white flowers in spring and white berries in fall, and red-osier dogwood (*C. stolonifera*), with flat-topped clusters of white flowers in spring and summer and white fruits maturing summer to fall. Choose a dogwood from your ecological region. Flowers are visited by bees; berries are eaten by seventy-five species of songbirds and game birds. Berries and twigs are eaten by skunks, deer, rabbits, and squirrels. *Cornus* species are larval host for spring azure butterfly and for dogwood borer, saddleback caterpillar, and dogwood probole moths.

Cyrillaceae (Titi Family)

Midstory/Understory/Edge Swamp cyrilla or titi (*Cyrilla racemilflora*) is a large shrub or small tree, semievergreen. Its blooms, appearing in early summer, are tiny, white, fragrant and profuse on four-to-six-inch-long racemes clustered near twig ends; tiny brown beadlike fruits mature in late summer to autumn and persist into winter.

Buckwheat bush or black titi (*Cliftonia monophylla*) is a shrub or small tree that is evergreen, sometimes thicket-forming, and grows in acid soils. Its blooms, slender erect spikes of fragrant pink or white flowers with orange anthers, appear in spring; its fruit, showy and lime-green to yellow, turns brown as it matures in autumn. It persists through winter.

Both plants offer cover to birds and may be browsed by mam-

mals and visited by honeybees and butterflies for their nectar
when in bloom.

Elaeagnaceae (Elaeagnus Family)

Midstory/Understory/Edge There are American eleagnus species,
like American silverberry (*E. commutata*), from more northern
latitudes, but the ones likely to be found in southern nurseries
are European and western Asian imports.

Russian olive (*Elaeagnus angustifolia*) is a small, deciduous tree
that has escaped cultivation and become a pest in some parts of
the country. It flowers in late spring; its berry-like yellow-to-
brown fruit matures late summer to fall. Thorny elaeagnus or
Russian olive (*E. pungens*) is an evergreen shrub. It has fragrant
white flowers in fall and berries maturing in spring. Gumi or
many-flowered silverberry (*E. multiflora*) is an evergreen shrub
with fragrant spring flowers and red berries in fall.

All elaeagnus species offer nesting sites and cover for birds,
nectar for bees and berries eaten by birds.

Ericaceae (Heath Family)

Midstory/Understory/Edge Huckleberries (*Gaylussacia* species)
are small to medium-sized semievergreen shrubs growing singly
or in colonies in acid soil. White-to-pink clusters of flowers
bloom in spring; fruit is small blue-to-black berries following in
late spring to fall. Berries are eaten by mourning doves, grouse,
bobwhite, and wild turkey. The plant is larval host for Henry's
elfin butterfly.

Sourwood (*Oxydendron arboreum*) is a medium-sized, deciduous
tree that requires acid soil. White lily-of-the-valley type flowers
on spikes bloom midsummer; fruit matures in the fall, with seeds
remaining attached into winter. Deer browse the foliage. Bees
that visit the blooms make esteemed honey. Seeds are eaten by

small mammals, such as turkey and grouse, and by songbirds. It hosts larvae of the friendly probole moth.

There are many rhododendrons and azaleas (all are *Rhododendron* species) native to the Southeast. All require well-drained, acid soil. Some are evergreen and others deciduous. All are known for their beautiful flowers, which appear in early or late spring (honeysuckle, piedmont, or wild azalea, *R. canescens*; Florida flame azalea, *R. austrinum*; great laurel, *R. maximum*; Catawba rhododendron, mountain rose-bay, *R. catawbiense*) and summer (swamp azalea, *R. viscosum*). Dry fruits mature in fall and may persist on the plant into winter. The ornate azaleas considered traditional in much of the South are oriental imports.

The nectar of azaleas is used by bees, hummingbirds, and butterflies and is favored by pipevine swallowtail butterflies. Azaleas host larvae of the azalea sphinx moth and rhododendrons host larvae of the copper underwing moth.

Blueberries or deerberries (*Vaccinium* species) are deciduous or evergreen shrubs requiring acid soil; winter huckleberry or sparkleberry (*V. arboreum*) can become a small tree and is more adaptable. These are self-pollinating, though berry production may be greater if additional specimens are nearby for cross-pollination. Blooms appear in spring; blue-to-black berries follow and mature in fall. Berries are sought by many songbirds, game birds, and mammals. *Vaccinium* species host larvae of the striped hairstreak, Henry's elfin and spring azure butterflies and of the half-wing, Andromeda underwing, and plain schizura moths. Butterflies use the nectar.

Euphorbiaceae (Spurge Family)

Overstory Chinese tallow or popcorn tree (*Sapium sebiferum*) is a deciduous tree introduced from the Orient. Its flowers appear in spring; its fruit, a hard-shelled nut maturing in autumn, splits open to expose three shiny white seeds that persist through winter. It has become a serious threat to native plant communities in parts of the Southeast where it reseeds rampantly, crowding out indigenous species and their animal associates and reducing diversity. It is a beautiful tree, very attractive to birds, who have helped spread its seeds, but do not plant it. Help eradicate it by pulling seedlings wherever appropriate.

Ebenaceae (Ebony Family)

Midstory/Understory/Edge Persimmon (*Diospyros virginiana*) is a deciduous tree, sometimes thicket forming and shrublike, of medium size. Its inconspicuous blooms appear in spring; the fruit, appearing in autumn on female trees, falls to the ground when fully ripe, usually not until a hard freeze. Bees visit the flowers for nectar. Fruit is important for mammals such as foxes, opossums, and skunks and for many birds, including wild turkey, robin, yellow-rumped warbler, and cedar waxwing. It hosts the persimmon borer, larva of a clearwing moth and also larvae of the large necklace, small necklace, variable antepione, pecan carpenterworm, the penitent, southern flannel, small purplish gray, red humped caterpillar, fine-lined gray and Echo moths.

Fagaceae (Oaks, Beeches, and Allies)

Overstory This family includes many species of oaks (*Quercus*), the American beech (*Fagus grandifolia*), and chinkapins (*Castanea* species), small trees or shrubs of the same genus as the blighted American chestnut.

American beech is deciduous. Oaks can be evergreen or deciduous. Flowers appear in early spring; nuts or acorns mature in fall.

Oaks are divided into red oaks, with bitter acorns that take two years to mature, and white oaks, with more palatable (to people) acorns that mature in one season. Some white oaks are white oak (*Quercus alba*), live oak (*Q. virginiana*), chinquapin oak (*Q. muehlenbergii*), bur oak (*Q. macrocarpa*), and overcup oak (*Q. lyrata*). Red oaks include southern red oak (*Quercus falcata*), water oak (*Q. nigra*), willow oak (*Q. phellos*), shumard oak (*Q. shumardii*), laurel oak (*Q. laurifolia*), and Nuttall oak (*Q. nuttallii*). Animals use acorns of both.

Dense branches and hollows in older specimens of beech offer shelter and nesting sites for birds and other animals. Beechnuts are eaten by game birds such as ruffed grouse, wild turkey, bobwhite, and pheasant; by other birds including woodpeckers, blue jays, titmice, nuthatches, grackles, cardinals, and towhees; and by mammals such as black bear, raccoon, red and gray foxes, white-tailed deer, cottontail rabbit, gray, red, and flying squirrels, porcupine, and opossum. It is larval host for the following moths: red-lined panopoda, colorful zale, variable oakleaf caterpillar, saddleback caterpillar (stinging), and eyed baileya.

Large oaks offer shelter and nesting sites for birds and mammals, both within their branches and foliage and in the natural cavities that develop in older oaks stricken by heartrot. Acorns are eaten by nearly all herbivorous birds, including many songbirds (especially blue jays), woodpeckers (especially red-headed), and game birds such as quail, grouse, bobwhite, wild turkey, pheasant, mourning dove, and wood duck; and by mammals such as white-tailed deer, black bear, red and gray fox, raccoon, opossum, gray, fox, red, and flying squirrels, chipmunks and ground squirrels. Deer and cottontail bunnies eat their twigs, and porcupines eat the growing layer beneath the bark. Oaks are habitat for a multitude of insects that become food for insectivorous creatures like warblers. Oaks support Spanish moss, an epiphyte that is used as nesting material by birds, as a nest site for seminole and red bats, and as a habitat for overwintering butterflies and other insects. Oaks may host larvae of butterflies such as the white M hairstreak, Edward's hairstreak, banded hairstreak, striped hairstreak, southern hairstreak, gray hairstreak, and sleepy dusky wing, and the larvae of moths such as buckmoth, io, polyphemus, dot-lined white, lappet, scalloped sack-bearer, confused meganola, variable oakleaf caterpillar, palmerworm, pecan carpenterworm and others. Filbertworms (larvae of the filbertworm moth) feed on "oak apples," galls formed on oak leaves by cynipid wasps. Another cynipid (gall moth) forms woolly galls on oak leaves. The caterpillars of a blastophid moth feed inside acorns hollowed out by acorn weevils. Heliodinid moth larvae are internal parasites of oak scales. Chestnut, chinkapin, and oak may attract the dyseriocrania moth (larvae is a leaf miner).

Midstory/Understory/Edge Allegheny chinkapin (*Castanea pumila*), running or Florida chinkapin (*C. alnifolia*) and others are small deciduous trees or thicket-forming shrubs that grow in oak and hickory forests. Early spring flowers are visited by bees and butterflies for their nectar. The fruit, a nut encased in a spiny bur, matures in autumn and is eaten by many forms of wildlife.

Hamamelidaceae (Witch Hazel Family)

Overstory Sweet gum (*Liquidambar styraciflua*) is known for its star-shaped leaves and its prickly, ball-shaped clusters of seeds. Deciduous, it flowers in late winter, and its fruits mature in late summer.

The tree provides nest sites and food for birds, including mallard, bobwhite, chickadee, purple finch, American goldfinch, pine siskin, pine warbler, dark-eyed junco, yellow-bellied sapsucker, white-throated sparrow, rufous-sided towhee, Carolina wren, titmouse, cardinal, and quail and for mammals such as

foxes, raccoon, squirrels, and deer. It is larval host for the following moths: luna, mustard sallow, promethea, pygmy paectes,
large paectes, royal walnut, and imperial.

Midstory/Understory/Edge Witch hazel (*Hamamelis virginiana*) is
a deciduous shrub to small tree that grows in slightly acid soil.
Fragrant yellow flowers resembling clusters of shredded paper
form on the branches as the leaves fall in autumn and winter;
woody brown seed pods mature a year after flowering and eject
two shiny black seeds as far as thirty feet.

Witch hazels are pollinated by and are larval host plants for
winter moths of the subfamily Cuculliinae (mustard sallow,
Bethune's pinion); for the three-spotted Nola, contracted datana
Tortricidia testacea, Argyrotaenia quercifoliana moths. They host
species of aphids that are eaten by the carnivorous caterpillars of
the harvester butterfly. Seeds, buds, or twigs are food for squirrels, white-tailed deer, cottontail rabbit, beaver, pheasant, bobwhite, and grouse.

Hippocastanaceae (Buckeye {Horse-chestnut} Family)

Midstory/Understory/Edge Red buckeye (*Aesculus pavia*) is a
deciduous shrub that usually stays small in cultivation but can
become a thirty-foot tree in some settings. Spikes to ten inches
above the foliage bear clusters of bright red to yellow-red tubular
flowers, which bloom with new foliage in spring; the fruit, a
capsule holding brown poisonous seeds, matures in autumn.
Nectar is used by butterflies (favored by spring azure) and hummingbirds.

Hypericaceae (St.-John's-wort {Hypericum} Family)

Midstory/Understory/Edge There are several species of St.-
John's-wort suitable for garden use: St.-John's-wort or St.-
Andrew's-cross (*Hypericum hypericoides*), golden St.-John's-wort

(*H. frondosum*), and St.-John's-wort (*H. densiflorum*). These small evergreen shrubs are short-lived, but reseed themselves. Yellow flowers bloom in early summer, some continuously into fall; capsules of black seeds follow.

St.-John's-worts provide cover for lots of creatures, including spiders. Seeds are eaten by juncos and several other finches. The plant is larval host of the gray hairstreak butterfly and the gray half-spot moth.

Hypericum, St.-John's-wort, or Aaron's beard (*H. calycinum*) is Eurasian.

Juglandaceae (Walnut and Hickory Family)

Overstory Southeastern species are sweet pecan (*Carya illinoensis*), black walnut (*Juglans nigra*), mockernut hickory (*Carya tomentosa*), shagbark hickory (*Carya ovata*), coastal pignut hickory (*Carya glabra*), nutmeg or swamp hickory (*Carya myristiciformis*), and bitternut (*Carya cordiformis*). All are deciduous. They flower in spring; fruit is a nut that matures in autumn.

Nuts/drupes of various species are sought by wildlife including squirrels, mice, wood ducks, blue jays, woodpeckers, and crows. Bitternut (*Carya cordiformis*) seeds, which may be unpalatable to most wildlife, are eaten by rabbits. Pignut hickories acquired their name in colonial times after hogs were observed eating their nuts. Forest hickories sprout from their stumps in the summer, providing succulent leaves within reach of deer and other browsing animals. Large trees offer shelter and nest sites for birds and mammals and provide habitat for insect life consumed by warblers and other insectivorous birds that visit. Webworms and tent caterpillars may infest walnut and pecan trees and will attract predators like predaceous wasps, ground beetles, and—though it is not very likely in urban areas—yellow-billed cuckoos. Hickory and/or walnut trees are larval host for the banded hairstreak butterfly, and for the following moths: polyphemus, red humped caterpillar, luna, walnut sphinx, walnut caterpillar, royal walnut, sad underwing, variable oakleaf caterpillar and others. Pecans host larvae of the hieroglyphic, the penitent, and southern flannel moths; pecans and hickories host larvae of the pecan carpenter worm and small purplish gray moths. Pecans, walnuts, and hickories host larvae of several species of underwing moths.

Lauraceae (Laurel Family)

Midstory/Understory/Edge The best-known southern representative of this family, which includes the French bay tree, the leaves of which are used for seasoning, is sassafras (*Sassafras albidum*), a deciduous, aromatic tree or thicket-forming shrub. Usually dioecious, it blooms in early spring; its fruit, bluish-black berries on red stalks on the female trees only, matures in autumn. Sassafras hosts larvae of the spicebush swallowtail butterfly and of the following moths: black-waved flannel, small necklace, *Archips purpurana* moths, tortricid family moths, common metarranthis, imperial, tulip-tree beauty.

Red bay, swamp bay (*Persea borbonia*) and swamp red bay (*P. palustris*) are evergreen trees with leaves that are used as a substitute for French bay leaf. Spring flowers are followed by dark blue, fleshy berries in late summer/fall.

Spicebush (*Lindera benzoin*) is a dense, aromatic, deciduous shrub that grows in acid soil and is dioecious. Fragrant, yellow-green flowers appear before foliage in spring; red berries follow in fall on female plants only. Male and female forms are necessary for fruit. This is a good bee plant.

Bays and spicebush are valuable for wildlife. Fruits (on female trees) are eaten by many birds, including bobwhite, wild turkey, catbird, great-crested flycatcher, eastern kingbird, mockingbird, eastern phoebe, brown thrasher, thrushes, red-eyed vireo, and white-eyed vireo, and pileated woodpecker and by mammals such as black bear. Twigs are browsed by rabbits, deer, and opossum. The plant hosts larvae of palamedes swallowtail and spicebush swallowtail butterflies and of promethea moths.

Leguminosae (Legume Family)

Overstory Honey or sweet locust (*Gleditsia triacanthos*), water locust, (*Gleditsia aquatica*) and black locust (*Robinia pseudoacacia*) are spiny-branched deciduous trees. They bloom in spring; seed pods persist into winter. Honey locust's seeds are surrounded by a sweet pulp; water locust's pods are short, while other locust pods are long. Black locust's flowers are showy and very fragrant. Thornless and almost seedless locusts have been developed; consult with your nurseryman before buying to make sure your tree has thorns and seeds. Flowers of all are nectar sources for bees.

Thorny branches afford safe nesting sites for birds. Seeds are eaten by birds such as mourning dove, bobwhite, and pheasant and by mammals including deer, rabbits, and squirrels. Bark of black locust sprouts and seedlings are winter food for rabbits. Locust leaves are larval food for dreamy dusky wing and Zarucco dusky wing butterflies. Honey and water locust host larvae of the little underwing and three-staff underwing moths. Honey locust hosts larvae of the following moths: the betrothed, the magdalen underwing, married underwing, honey locust, and moon-lined. Black locust hosts larvae of silver-spotted skipper butterflies and pesty velvet caterpillar moths.

Midstory/Understory/Edge Sweet acacia or Huisache (*Acacia farnesiana*) is a thorny-branched, thicket-forming, evergreen shrub that grows in coastal and warmer areas of the South. Its fragrant, yellow ball-shaped blooms in spring are followed by long seed pods. It provides cover and nest sites for birds and is a honey plant for bees. Tender foliage and pods are browsed by deer. It hosts larvae of the silver-spotted skipper butterfly and bagworm moth. Other *Acacia* species grow in the Southeast, too.

Red bud or Judas tree (*Cercis canadensis*) is a small deciduous tree known for its profuse, showy bloom in early spring before leaves appear. Long, flat seed pods form and split open to reveal beanlike seeds, then fall to the ground in late autumn or winter. Early blooms are visited by bees for pollen and by bees, butterflies, and hummers for nectar. Bobwhite and a few songbirds eat the seeds. It is larval host to Henry's elfin butterfly and to red bud leaffolder, grapeleaf skeletonizer, and white flannel moths.

Indigo bush, false indigo, or leadplant (*Amorpha fruticosa*) is a deciduous shrub or small tree. Flowers are lavender spikes with yellow-orange stamens in spring; small kidney-shaped seed pods follow in late summer. It is larval host for the dogface (a sulphur), silver-spotted skipper, and mottled dusky wing butterflies. Butterflies use the nectar. *A. canescens* is also called leadplant.

Eastern coralbean, cardinal spear, or mamou (*Erythrina herbacea*) is a spiny shrub that becomes a small tree in southern Florida but may die back to the ground each winter and behave more like a perennial herb the further north it grows. Dramatic, spurlike red flowers cluster along the leafless stalks in late spring to early summer, followed by pods of shiny red poisonous beanlike seeds that mature in late summer. Hummingbirds and butterflies visit the flowers for nectar.

Mimosa or silk tree (*Albizia julibrissin*) is a deciduous tree imported from the Orient. Spring/summer flowers are pink puffs of extruded stamens; long seed pods follow. Attractive to hummingbirds and occasional butterflies. Invasive by seed in native plant communities.

Golden-yellow flowered cassias, both the wildflower forms indigenous to the Southeast and the tender tropical imports, are larval hosts for cloudless sulphur, orange-barred sulphur, Mexican sulphur, and little sulphur butterflies. Recommended tropical ornamental semievergreen shrubs include candlestick (*Cassia alata*), which blooms in late summer and fall; senna or golden shower (*C. corymbosa*), which blooms summer to frost; and golden wonder (*C. splendida*), which produces a spectacular display of flowers in autumn.

Many legume family members are host for larvae of the gray hairstreak butterfly.

Lythraceae (Loosestrife Family)

The oriental crape myrtle (*Lagerstroemia indica*) is a deciduous ornamental tree, shrub or groundcover. It blooms through summer, with clusters of crinkly white, pink, red or lavender flowers. Hummingbirds may visit for nectar. Birds may eat the seeds.

Mexican cigarflower or cigarette plant (*Cuphea micropetala*) is a tender shrub with small, orange, tubular, yellow-tipped flowers that bloom summer to fall. Hummingbirds and butterflies use the nectar. Other orange and red C. species are useful, too.

Magnoliaceae (Magnolia Family)

Some magnolias are evergreen and others deciduous. Their seeds are berries that form in conelike clusters and mature in autumn. Southern magnolia (*Magnolia grandiflora*), an evergreen, is known for its fragrant white flowers followed by cones with crayon-red seeds. Its dense shade and competitive root system make the ground at its base a poor spot for underplanting, but a good spot for foraging birds if leaf and flower debris dropped from the tree are left as habitat for invertebrates. Cowcumber or big-leaf magnolia (*M. macrophylla*) is deciduous; sweet bay magnolia (*M. virginiana*) is semievergreen. There are other native species for garden use and some showy oriental magnolias, including the pink-flowered ones. The imports are less valuable for native wildlife.

Tulip tree, tulip poplar, or yellow poplar (*Liriodendron tulipifera*) is deciduous. Its spring flowers are followed by cone-shaped clusters of winged seeds that mature in autumn and persist on the tree in winter. It can be long-lived and grow very tall.

All magnolia family members are good cover and nesting sites for songbirds. Fruit of various magnolias may be eaten by yellow-bellied sapsuckers and other woodpeckers, rufous-sided towhees, and red-eyed vireo. Mammals such as squirrels, white-tailed deer and others may either eat the fruit or browse on leaves and twigs. *M. virginia* is larval host for the palamedes swallowtail butterfly and the sweetbay silkmoth. The tulip tree's seeds, eaten by birds and squirrels, remain on the tree through winter. It is a larval host plant of the tiger swallowtail butterfly and the tulip-tree silkmoth, promethea moth, and tulip-tree beauty moth. Hummingbirds and bees visit the flowers for nectar.

Malvaceae (Mallow Family)

Midstory/Understory/Edge Flowering maple (*Abutilon pictum*) is a tender Brazilian shrub whose bell-like blooms lure hummingbirds.

Althaea or rose-of-Sharon (*Hibiscus syriacus*) is an oriental, deciduous shrub with showy single blooms, summer to fall, which appeal to hummingbirds. Semi-doubles are less useful to hummers.

Tropical American turk's cap or sultan's turban (*Malvaviscus arboreus* var. *drummondii*) is a tender, vine-like evergreen shrub. It has bright red blooms summer to frost and red berry-like fruit eaten by birds such as cardinals. Its nectar attracts hummingbirds, bees and butterflies. Turk's cap (*M. arboreus* var. *mexicanus* or *M. arboreus grandiflorus*) is a tender evergreen shrub with pendulous, scarlet flowers appearing from summer into fall. Both are important Gulf Coast winter hummer plants.

Moraceae (Mulberry Family)

Overstory Red mulberry, our native American mulberry (*Morus rubra*), is too messy for the taste of many gardeners, but, as Bill Fontenot says, "Don't mention this to a rose-breasted grosbeak, or a northern oriole, or a scarlet tanager, for mulberries stand at the very top of their menu as preferred food sources."[9] The popularity of the fruiting red mulberry is no secret to birdwatchers, nor is the litter that falls underneath, some dropped by feasting birds. Most bird lovers will consider the trade even. Plant your mulberry away from sidewalks, patios, and house, and you'll be safe. Some clever nursery developed a fruitless variety for people who want the fast-growing, broad-canopied mulberry without the mess. Make sure your nurseryman understands that you want a fruiting cultivar, or dig a seedling from beneath a tree in your region, but realize that mulberries may not fruit until they are six to eight years old. They provide nesting sites for birds. Fruit produced in spring is eaten by squirrels, opossums, raccoons, chipmunks, coyotes, and other mammals and by many birds, including cardinals, catbirds, crows, great-crested flycatchers, grackles, rose-breasted grosbeaks, blue jays, eastern king-birds, mockingbirds, orioles, tanagers, thrushes, woodpeckers (including pileated), tufted titmice, brown thrashers, summer tanagers, and cedar waxwings. Associated insects are the mulberry white fly (pest).

There are other garden mulberries. White mulberry (*Morus alba*) is a widely naturalized introduction to the United States from the Orient. Birds eat its fruit, which is produced for a shorter period than that of the long-fruiting native red mulberry. Black mulberry (*Morus nigra*), another Asian introduction, has large, juicy fruits. The Mediterranean fig tree (*Ficus carica*) produces the brown, pear-shaped fruit considered delicious by people and wildlife. Certain species of figs are pollinated by the fig wasp.

Midstory/Understory/Edge Osage orange or bois d'arc (*Maclura pomifera*) is a spiny, thicket-forming shrub that matures into a small tree. Deciduous and dioecious, it grows in alkaline soils. It blooms in spring, and its fruit, large, warty globes on the female trees only, is green in summer, turning yellow-orange when mature in autumn. Seeds are eaten by birds such as grosbeaks, goldfinches and purple finches after squirrels drop the fruits to the ground to split open the tough outer covering. The cedar-like aroma of the fruit is reputed to repel insects, including roaches. It is larval host for the Hagen's sphinx moth.

Myricaceae (Bayberry [Wax Myrtle] Family)

Midstory/Understory/Edge Several species of these evergreen shrubs or small trees are found in the Southeast: bayberry or wax myrtle (*Myrica cerifera*), odorless wax myrtle (*M. inodora*), dwarf wax myrtle (*M pumila*), bayberry or bigleaf wax myrtle (*M. heterophylla*). They are dioecious. Tiny, waxy, gray berries that form along stems of the female plants only mature in fall and persist into winter.

Small spring flowers are high in nectar for bees. Berries are eaten by many species of birds, including yellow-rumped warblers, white-eyed vireos, ruby-crowned kinglets, dowitchers, catbird, eastern bluebird, meadowlark, and quail. Flocks of tree swallows swarm to feed on the berries. The plants are possible larval host to the red-banded hairstreak butterfly and to the following moths: *Condylolomia participialis*, the little wife, skiff, black-waved flannel, and plain schizura.

Myrtaceae (Myrtle Family)

Midstory/Understory/Edge Crimson or lemon bottlebrush (*Callistemon citrinus*) is an evergreen shrub from Australia with bristly bright red flowers, blooming spring to summer, that are attractive to hummingbirds.

Nyssaceae (Gum Family)

Overstory Black gum (*Nyssa sylvatica*) and tupelo gum (*N. aquatica*) are deciduous and dioecious trees. Late spring blooms are followed in autumn by berry-like fruit, a half inch long and blue-black on black gum, purplish and one inch long on tupelo gum, and found on female trees only.

Flowers, very high in nectar, are important for bees. Autumn fruit is eaten by many species of birds, including woodpeckers, blue jays, bluebirds, cardinals, catbirds, eastern kingbird, mockingbird, brown thrasher, summer tanager, cedar waxwing, rose-breasted grosbeak, grouse, pheasant, wild turkey, and wood ducks and by mammals such as opossum, gray squirrel, white-tailed deer, and black bear. Hollows in old trees are used for cover and nests by birds and mammals. It is larval host for the Hebrew moth.

Oleaceae (Olive or Ash Family)

Overstory Green or red ash (*Fraxinus pennsylvanica*) and white ash (*Fraxinus americanus*) are popular shade trees. Pumpkin ash (*F. tomentosa*) is another southeastern native. Arizona ash (*F. velutina*) is widely used, too. The trees are deciduous and dioecious. Flowers appear in early spring. Seeds are winged, shaped like canoe paddle blades, clustered, present on female trees through summer; they ripen in fall.

The trees provide nest sites for birds. Twigs are browse for deer. Flowers on male trees produce pollen important to bees. Seeds may be eaten by birds like wood duck, bobwhite, wild turkey, cardinal, and purple finch and by mammals such as deer. White ash seeds persist on the trees (female only) through winter. Ashes may be larval host plant for tiger swallowtail butterfly and the following moths: Franck's sphinx, Johnson's euchlaena (white ash), laurel sphinx, waved sphinx, greater red dart, cecropia, and the penitent.

Midstory/Understory/Edge Fringe tree or grancy graybeard (*Chionanthus virginicus*) is a small, deciduous and dioecious tree. Flowers in spring are white, drooping clusters, with those on males longer-fringed and showier; grape-like bunches of dark blue berries mature in fall on females only. Fruits are eaten by many birds and mammals. Larval host of the rustic sphinx, waved sphinx, and laurel sphinx moths.

Swamp privet (*Forestiera acuminata*) is a deciduous, thicket-forming, dioecious shrub. It blooms in spring, with male flowers in yellow clusters and female flowers inconspicuous; dark purple fruit forms on females only and matures in summer. Florida privet (*F. segregata*) is evergreen, thicket-forming, and dioecious. Small, yellowish-green blooms appear in spring; purplish-black fruit matures during summer on the female plants. Nectar attracts bees, butterflies and other insects, which become food for migratory warblers; fruit is eaten by songbirds, waterfowl, and quail.

Devilwood or American olive (*Osmanthus americanus*) is a large shrub or small evergreen tree, usually dioecious. Clusters of small, fragrant yellow or white flowers appear in early spring; dark blue, three-quarter-inch-large pitted fruit matures in fall and persists through winter on female plants. Fruit is eaten by birds and mammals, including deer.

Most of the evergreen trees and shrubs called privets (*Ligustrum* species) so common in American gardens are Asian, even though one (*L. ovalfolium*) is called California privet. Chinese privet (*L. sinense*) self-seeds rampantly and currently threatens native plant communities in southern natural areas.

In ligustrums not severely clipped into hedges, clusters of white flowers bloom spring to summer; the fruit, dark berries maturing summer to fall, persists on the plants in winter. Ligustrums offer nectar to bees and butterflies. Honey from privets has an unpleasant taste. Berries are eaten by songbirds and game birds in winter.

Platanaceae (Sycamore Family)

Overstory Sycamore (*Platanus occidentalis*) is a deciduous tree that flowers in the spring; seeds clustered in little stemmed balls mature in autumn and persist in winter. Sycamores offer nesting sites for birds. The hollow trunks of old trees were once used as homes by chimney swifts; cavities in older trees can be nest and shelter sites for wood ducks, opossum, and raccoon. Twigs are eaten by deer and muskrats. Insect associates include sycamore lace bug, terrapin scale, and drab prominent moth.

Rhamnaceae (Buckthorn Family)

Midstory/Understory/Edge Carolina buckthorn or Indian cherry (*Rhamnus caroliniana*) is a deciduous large shrub or small tree that self-sows and can be weedy. It grows in acid soil. Greenish-yellow bell-shaped clusters of flowers bloom in late spring and early summer; red berries become black with maturity in late summer and autumn and may persist on branches. Berries are eaten by many birds and mammals.

New Jersey tea (*Ceanothus americanus*) is a small, deciduous shrub. It bears clusters of tiny white flowers in spring; seeds mature in fall. The plant provides nectar for bees, butterflies, and hummingbirds; it is a favorite of hairstreak butterflies. Some birds, including bobwhite and wild turkey, eat the seeds. It is larval host to Pacuvius dusky wing, spring azure, and brown elfin butterflies.

Rosaceae (Rose Family)

Overstory Wild cherry (*Prunus serotina*) is a deciduous tree with clusters of white flowers in early spring that are followed by pendulous clusters of small black cherries in summer.

Wild cherry is an important wildlife tree, with bees visiting the flowers and birds nesting there. Cherries are eaten by birds such as thrushes and mockingbirds, catbirds, thrashers, grouse, pheasant, and bobwhite and by mammals such as raccoon, black bear, red fox, white-tailed deer, cottontail rabbit, and gray squirrel. It is larval host for the tiger swallowtail, coral hairstreak, and red-spotted purple butterflies and for the following moths: dowdy pinion, straight-toothed sallow, Morrison's sallow, red-winged sallow, forked euchlaena, saddleback caterpillar moth (stinging), American swordgrass, dubious tiger, cecropia, tufted bird-dropping, white furcula, black-waved flannel, and many species of underwing moths. Eastern tent caterpillars may infest and defoliate cherry and other *Prunus* species in spring if predators such as predaceous wasps, ground beetles, and carnivorous caterpillars don't get them.

Midstory/Understory/Edge Southern crab apple (*Malus angustifolia*) and wild crab apple (*M. coronaria*) are native deciduous, thicket-forming shrubs to small trees. Fragrant pink flowers appear on long stalks in spring; small apple-like fruit matures in late summer. Buds and blossoms of the early blooms are eaten by house finches and other birds. Flowers offer nectar to bees. Sap, which flows in early spring from holes drilled by woodpeckers or from broken twigs, is food for hummers and other nectarivorous birds and for insects, which, in turn, become food for insect-eating birds. Apples are eaten by birds such as thrushes, mockingbirds, catbirds, thrashers, bobwhites, grouse, and pheasants and by mammals including rabbits, squirrels, opossums, raccoons, skunks, and foxes. Crab apples and others that hold fruit all winter offer additional food in the form of bugs overwintering in the fruit. Apples host larvae of the following moths: tufted apple-bud, southern flannel, black-waved flannel, saddleback caterpillar (stinging), and several species of underwing moths.

The many hawthorns are thorny-branched, deciduous shrubs or small trees, sometimes thicket forming. Grow species indigenous to your region. Parsley hawthorn (*Crataegus marshallii*) has the easiest foliage to identify; mayhaw (*C. opaca*) is famous for its jelly. Small, fragrant white-to-pink blossoms appear with new foliage in early spring. Most hawthorns produce yellow-to-red berry-like fruit that matures by fall and may persist into winter; mayhaw's fruit matures in late spring.

Hawthorns are important honey plants. Their dense, thorny branches make them popular with birds seeking cover and safe nest sites. Berries are fall and winter food for birds such as bob-white, partridge, pheasant, grouse, thrushes, mockingbirds, catbirds, thrashers, wood duck, American robin, fox sparrow, and cedar waxwing and for mammals such as squirrels, foxes, cotton-tail rabbit, white-tailed deer, otters, and raccoons. Hawthorns are larval host for striped hairstreak, northern hairstreak, and red-spotted purple butterflies and for tufted bird dropping, white spring, and several species of underwing moths.

Small trees of the genus *Prunus* indigenous to the Southeast include the evergreen cherry laurel (*Prunus caroliniana*) and decid-uous cherries and plums such as wild plum (*P. americana*), Chickasaw plum (*P. angustifolia*), and Mexican plum (*P. mexicana*). Profuse early spring bloom is followed by fruit that matures late summer to fall and, in the case of cherry laurel's dark berries, persists on the tree through winter. All are visited by bees during early spring bloom. The petals and nectar of the flowers may be consumed by cedar waxwings and orioles. Butterflies may come for nectar.

Cherry laurel's dense foliage makes it a good nest site for birds. Its berries are available in winter, when food sources are limited. Foliage is toxic to livestock.

Plum fruits are summer-fall food for songbirds and game birds and for mammals such as foxes. Wild plum is the larval host for Henry's elfin butterfly. All *Prunus* species host larvae of the coral hairstreak and striped hairstreak butterflies and of the following moths: cecropia, eastern tent caterpillar, gray spring, white spring, black-waved flannel, and several species of underwing. Plums host tufted bird dropping moths.

The nonindigenous *Prunus* species (cherry, plum, peach, flow-ering almond, apricot) are nectar sources for bees and other insects and provide bird and mammal food.

Indian pear or downy serviceberry (*Amelanchier arborea*), a small, deciduous tree, is one member of a genus with species also called juneberry and shadbush. Fragrant clusters of white flowers bloom in spring before leaves; long, drooping clusters of purple berries appear in early summer. It is a nectar plant for bees and butterflies. Berries are sought by many songbirds, wild turkey, grouse, bobwhite, and mourning doves and by skunk, red fox, raccoon, black bear, red and gray squirrels, and chipmunks. Twigs are browsed by rabbits, beavers, white-tailed deer, and moose.

Red chokeberry (*Aronia arbutifolia*) is a deciduous shrub. White blooms appear in early spring; clusters of brilliant red berries mature in autumn and persist into winter if not consumed by birds. Fruit is eaten by birds such as cedar waxwing, eastern bluebird, thrasher, and robin. It is larval host to several species of underwing moths.

Roses (*Rosa* species) are thorny deciduous shrubs or climbing shrubs. Showy blooms appear spring to fall, depending on the species, and are followed by fruits called hips that persist on the plant if not pruned off. Carolina rose (*R. Carolina*), prairie rose (*R. setigera*), and others are indigenous to the United States. Cherokee rose (*R. laevigata*), Chickasaw or Macartney rose (*R. bracteata*) and multiflora rose (*R. multiflora*) are Chinese species that have escaped cultivation to become naturalized in the United States. The oriental roses, especially multiflora rose, are invasive pests that threaten native plant communities.

Species and hybrids of roses are useful in the wildlife garden to the extent that they produce hips and can thrive without being doused with chemicals. The showy blooms are poor sources of nectar but do offer pollen for honey and bumblebees. Hips persist on the shrubs all winter and are eaten by wild animals, although, as one source says, "mostly incidentally or where preferred foods are lacking."[10] If you must have roses—and some of us must—stick with native species or cultivars chosen from among those called "old roses." Roses may host tufted bird dropping moths, southern flannel moths, and others.

There are other rose family imports. Japanese plum, loquat, or mespilus (*Eriobotrya japonica*) is a tender, small, evergreen tree. White, fragrant flowers appear in fall; yellow-orange pear-shaped fruit appears in spring. Wintering hummingbirds and orioles may visit the flowers. The fruits are eaten by birds, squirrels, and insects, which draw more birds. Butterflies visit the flowers for nectar. *Cotoneaster* species shrubs are evergreen and sprawling-to-prostrate in form. Clusters of small pink or white blossoms in spring are followed by berries. Bees visit the flowers, and birds eat the berries. Chinese photinia (*Photinia serrulata*) is an evergreen shrub that produces clusters of white flowers in spring. Red berries should follow in fall and winter, but may not always in warmer climates. Berries are eaten by some birds. Pyracantha (*Pyracantha coccinea*) is a thorny-branched, evergreen shrub. Small white flowers bloom in spring; red-orange or yellow berries appear in profuse clusters, fall through early spring. Bees visit the flowers; birds eat the berries. It provides a safe nesting site for birds. Bradford flowering pear (*Pyrus calleryana* Bradford) is a deciduous tree. It produces a profusion of white flowers in spring; small fruit follows in fall. Flowers are a source of nectar. Birds eat the fruit.

Rubiaceae (Madder Family)

Midstory/Understory/Edge Buttonbush (*Cephalanthus occidentalis*) is a deciduous shrub that grows in or near water and adapts to dryer garden settings. Flowers, in summer, are fragrant, white globes; fruit matures into hard, round clusters of reddish-brown nutlets and persists on the plant into winter. It is a cover and nesting plant. Hummingbirds, bees, and butterflies such as painted lady and sachem, as well as moths including the hummingbird clearwing love its nectar. Seeds are eaten by waterfowl. Deer browse its foliage. It is the larval host plant for the hydrangea sphinx and beautiful wood-nymph moths.

Firebush (*Hamelia patens*), a small evergreen shrub indigenous to Florida and the West Indies, will die to the ground with cold weather in other areas, but frequently returns from the roots. Clusters of orange-red tubular flowers appear throughout the year where the plant is native; in other areas, bloom begins and is heaviest in hot weather, then decreases as weather cools. Small, blue-black berries appear during season of bloom. It is an excellent nectar plant for bees, hummingbirds and butterflies, and the berries are eaten by mockingbirds, cardinals, and others.

Rutaceae (Rue {Citrus} Family)

Midstory/Understory/Edge Common hoptree (*Ptelea trifoliata*) is a large shrub or small tree, deciduous. Clusters of small, greenish flowers bloom in spring; drooping clusters of waferlike, disk-shaped seeds mature in summer, remaining closed and persisting on the tree in winter.

Prickly ash or toothache-tree (*Zanthoxylum clava-herculis*) is a small deciduous and dioecious tree that derives its name from the fact that people chewed the aromatic leaves, fruits, or bark covered with prickle-tipped corky knobs as a cure for toothache. Clusters of tiny, yellow-green flowers bloom in spring on female trees. Dense clusters of fruit mature and crack open in late summer, falling to reveal shiny black seeds.

Seeds of both are eaten by birds. All citrus family members may host caterpillars of the giant swallowtail and eastern black swallowtail butterflies.

Imported citrus (*Citrus* species), the oranges, lemons, limes and grapefruit, have been grown in parts of the United States through the years. The fragrant blooms of citrus offer nectar to bees, hummers, and butterflies, and the fruit is edible. Orange trees host larvae of the southern flannel moth. Citrus species host larvae of the bagworm moth.

Salicaceae (Willow Family)

Overstory Cottonwood or poplar (*Populus deltoides*), swamp cottonwood (*P. heterophylla*) and black willow (*Salix nigra*) are fast-growing, short-lived, soft-wooded, deciduous and dioecious trees. Seeds are windspread, tiny with cottony hairs, and are released in late spring. Other poplar/willow species are cultivated, too, including the Chinese import, *Salix babylonica*, the weeping willow.

In the garden, poplars and willows should be placed at a distance from drainage and sewer pipes to prevent clogging by their fibrous roots. The silky "cotton" of female cottonwoods is considered messy by some, so many of the cultivars sold in nurseries are male. Since you may prefer the seed-bearing female trees for wildlife, question your nurseryman before you buy.

Leaves, seeds, buds, and twigs of poplars/willows are food for birds such as grouse and ptarmigan and for mammals such as elk, white-tailed deer, moose, beaver, muskrat, porcupine, cottontail rabbit, and black bear. The "cotton" is used as nest lining by some birds. Willows are favored nest sites for songbirds, and cottonwoods are important, too. Older trees may develop cavities used by hollow-tree nesters such as raccoons, opossums, flying squirrels, wood ducks, owls, and woodpeckers. Willows and cottonwoods may host larvae of the tiger swallowtail, red-spotted purple, viceroy, and mourning cloak butterflies and of the following moths: giant leopard, one-eyed sphinx, the once-married, plain schizura, frigid owlet, small engrailed, red humped caterpillars, porcelain gray, and others. Willows may also host larvae of the striped hairstreak, faunus anglewing (green comma), and spring azure butterflies and of the following moths: luna, huckleberry sphinx, twin-spotted sphinx, merry melipotis, darling underwing, rustic quaker, and others. Caterpillars are important food for baby birds. Pollen and nectar of early spring willow flowers are an important source of food for bees.

Saxifragaceae (Saxifrage Family)

Midstory/Understory/Edge Oak-leaf hydrangea (*Hydrangea quercifolia*), wild or mountain hydrangea (*H. arborescens*) and sweetspire or Virginia willow (*Itea virginica*) are deciduous understory shrubs. All bloom in early spring, producing flowers that brown and persist on the plant into fall. The hydrangeas are available through nurseries in "improved" forms some feel are not as attractive as the species. Oak-leaf hydrangea likes acid soil, while wild hydrangea is more adaptable. Hydrangeas like shade; Virginia willow will grow in sun or shade.

Oak-leaf hydrangea (*H. quercifolia*) seeds are eaten by songbirds, game birds, and mammals. It hosts larvae of species of tortricid moths. Wild hydrangea (*H. arborescens*) flowers are visited by bees; the flowers and seeds are eaten by wild turkey and white-tailed deer. The twigs are eaten by deer. It is the larval host plant for hydrangea sphinx moth. Virginia willow (*Itea virginica*) flowers are visited by butterflies and bees; the seed is eaten by birds.

Styracaceae (Styrax Family)

Midstory/Understory/Edge Silverbells (*Halesia diptera, H. carolina*) are small deciduous trees requiring slightly acid soil.

White, bell-shaped blooms appear in spring; dry pods of sour citrusy-tasting fruit follow late summer to autumn and persist during winter. Hummingbirds visit the blossoms for nectar.

Symplocaceae (Sweetleaf Family)

Midstory/Understory/Edge Sweetleaf or horse sugar (*Symplocos tinctoria*) is a deciduous shrub. Fragrant, small yellowish-white blooms appear in early spring before new foliage; orange-brown fruit matures in early fall. Foliage is wildlife browse. The plant is larval host of the king's hairstreak butterfly.

Tiliaceae (Basswood {Linden} Family)

Overstory American basswood (*Tilia americana*), white basswood (*T. heterophylla*), and Carolina basswood (*T. caroliniana*) are all called "bee tree." They are deciduous and have clusters of fragrant pale yellow/lime flowers on long, drooping stems in late spring, followed by nutlike seeds.

Basswood is an important honey plant and is absolutely enveloped in bees while in bloom. It is a butterfly nectar plant, also. Buds, leaves, twigs, and inner bark are favored by porcupines and also eaten by deer and cottontails. Buds and fruit are eaten by ruffed grouse, quails, squirrels and chipmunks. It is larval host plant for the tiger swallowtail and question mark butterflies and for the following moths: curve-lined acontia, Linden prominent, nondescript dagger, ochre dagger, confused woodgrain, Angus' datana, definite tussock, the half wing, saddleback caterpillar (stinging), and the promethea.

Ulmaceae (Elm Family)

Overstory In the Southeast the elm family is represented by the hackberries (*Celtis*) and several species of elms (*Ulmus*). All are deciduous.

Elms flower in spring and release their small seeds, encased in papery "samaras," shortly afterward. The September elm (*Ulmus serotina*) produces flowers and seeds in autumn. American elm (*U. americana*) is threatened in much of its range by the Dutch elm disease, a fungal disease accidentally introduced to the United States in 1930 and spread by elm bark beetles. Other elms—winged or small-leaved elm (*U. alata*), September elm (*U. serotina*), slippery elm (*U. rubra*), and cedar elm (*U. crassifolia*)—may be less susceptible.

The small, greenish flowers of hackberries bloom in spring and are followed by small berries, colored brown or orange-red to yellow, which mature late summer through autumn and persist during winter. Hackberry's nutlike fruits are eaten by many species of birds, including the bluebird, cardinal, flicker, sapsucker, grackle and other blackbirds, blue jay, crow, mockingbird, catbird, eastern phoebe, American robin, brown thrasher, tufted titmouse, rufous-sided towhee, and cedar waxwing and by mammals such as gray fox, raccoon, squirrels, and deer. Hackberries host larvae of the hackberry, Empress Flora, tawny emperor, snout, and question mark butterflies and the thin-lined owlet, palmerworm, and southern flannel moths. Galls on the underside of hackberry leaves are formed by insects called psyllids, which are related to aphids and whiteflies. Psyllids are parasitized by chalcid wasps.

Elms are early, though brief, sources of seeds for many songbirds, including finches, sparrows, and grosbeaks and for mammals such as fox and gray squirrels and rabbits. Elms and hackberries are important as nesting sites for birds. Elms are larval food for a butterfly called the comma and for moths such as the double-toothed prominent, morning-glory prominent, red humped caterpillar, and variable oakleaf caterpillar. Slippery elm hosts the white-lined bomolocha moth. Elms and hackberries host larvae of the question mark and mourning cloak butterflies.

Verbenaceae (Vervain Family)

Midstory/Understory/Edge American beautyberry or French mulberry (*Callicarpa americana*) is a deciduous shrub. Pinkish flowers bloom in summer; clusters of juicy, rosy purple berries encircle the stems in fall, persisting after the leaves drop. Bees visit the flowers. Berries are eaten by many species of birds and by mammals such as raccoon and deer.

Some nonindigenous (to the southeast United States) vervains have become important in providing extended profuse bloom and lots of nectar for hummingbird and butterfly gardens. These include several lantanas. Ham and eggs (*Lantana camara*) is a tropical American perennial shrub, naturalized in many southern areas, not completely hardy. It flowers in combinations of white, vivid pinks, yellows, orange-reds, and solids, summer to frost. Dark berries appear in fall. Texas lantana (*L. horrida*), a south Texas native, has orange and yellow flowers that turn red as they age. Weeping or trailing lantana (*L. montevidensis*) has a sprawling, mounded form and rosy-lilac flowers. Flowers of all species are attractive to bees, butterflies, and hummingbirds. Berries are eaten by some birds.

Palmae (Palm Family)

Overstory Cabbage palm (*Sabal palmetto*) grows in southern coastal areas, both Atlantic and gulf. An evergreen, it has white blooms in summer and black fruit in fall. Flowers are visited by bees and other insects; the black fruit that follows is eaten by birds including robins, grackles, mockingbirds, thrashers, red-bellied woodpeckers, catbirds, and fish crows and by mammals such as raccoons. Birds use palm thatch for building nests. The crown of the plant collects moisture and serves as a habitat for frogs, lizards, and insects. It is a larval host plant for the monk butterfly.

Midstory/Understory/Edge Dwarf palmetto (*Sabal minor*), saw palmetto (*Serenoa repens*), and needle palm (*Rhapidophyllum hystrix*) are evergreen shrubs, though dwarf palmetto (*Sabal minor*) can become a small, palmlike tree under certain conditions. Flowers appear in spring and berrylike fruit in autumn. The plant offers excellent cover, the flowers provide nectar for honeybees, and the fruit is eaten by several bird species and by raccoons. Saw palmetto is larval host plant for the palmetto arpo skipper and palmetto-borer moths.

Ginkgoaceae (Ginkgo Family)

Overstory Ginkgo or maidenhair tree (*Ginkgo biloba*), which is native to China, is the only member of this once-widespread, ancient family; it is a living fossil, extinct everywhere except in gardens. The tree is deciduous and dioecious.

The tree provides nest sites for birds. Female trees develop a fruit reputedly eaten by raccoons, but which has such an unpleasant smell (foul! rancid! objectionable!) that only male trees are recommended.

Vines and Brambles for Wildlife Habitats

The wildlife gardener with space limitations can provide cover and food for lots of wildlife in a vertical garden by planting a varied selection of vines and brambles on a trellis.

Anacardiaceae (Cashew Family) Poison ivy (*Rhus radicans*) is not recommended for planting but does make berries eaten by many species of birds and does host larvae of light marathyssa and eyed paectes moths.

Apocynaceae (Blue Star or Dogbane Family) Climbing dogbane (*Trachelospermum difforme*) blooms fragrant, funnel-shaped, yellowish-green flowers spring to fall. It is deciduous.

Araliaceae (Ginseng Family) The ivies (*Hedera* species) are introduced from Africa, Asia, and Europe. They make good ground cover habitat for lots of wildlife. English ivy (*H. helix*) blooms in late fall and is visited by honeybees, bumblebees, wasps, butterflies, and small flies; fruit is eaten by birds in winter and spring. Algerian ivy (*Hedera canariensis*) is favored habitat of Norway and roof rats![11]

Aristolochiaceae (Ginger Family) Dutchman's pipe (*Aristolochia* species) blooms are unique brownish-purple, curved flowers in spring. It is larval host plant for pipevine swallowtail and polydamas swallowtail butterflies.

Bignoniaceae (Bignonia Family) Trumpet creeper (*Campsis radicans*) is larval host for plebeian sphinx moths; *Clydonopteron tecomae* moth pupates in its seed pods. Its orange-to-red trumpet-shaped flowers appear from June to October and attract hummingbirds.

Cross vine (*Bignonia capreolata*) blooms orange and yellow trumpet-shaped flowers April to August and attracts hummingbirds. Bill Fontenot saw raccoons eating the bouillon-cube-scented flowers.[12]

Caprifoliaceae (Honeysuckle Family) Coral honeysuckle (*Lonicera sempervirens*, other *L.* species) nectar is favored by pipevine swallowtail butterflies and silver-spotted skippers; it is host to the alternate woodling moth larvae. The blooms, appearing spring to fall, attract hummingbirds. Yellow-flowered Japanese or Hall's honeysuckle (*L. japonica*), a threat to native

plant communities in many natural sites, is visited by hummingbirds and insects; the fruit is eaten by birds and mammals.

Celastraceae (Bittersweet Family) American bittersweet
(*Celastrus scandens*) blooms small, green, clustered flowers in
spring. Ornamental orange pods that open to expose scarlet
seeds are present fall into winter. Fruit is eaten by songbirds,
ruffed grouse, pheasant, bobwhite, and fox squirrel. Cottontail
eats bark and twigs.

Compositae or Asteraceae (Sunflower or Composite Family)
Pale lavender flowers of *Mikania scandens*, climbing hempweed,
resemble those of *Eupatoriums*. This twining perennial vine climbs
over low vegetation in moist edges, blooming summer to fall. It
hosts larvae of the scarlet bodied wasp moth.

Convolvulaceae (Morning Glory Family) Twining, vining
morning glory family members are popular with bees and may
host larvae of the straight-lined seed moth. *Convolvulus sepium*,
bindweed or woodbine, hosts larvae of the common spragueia
moth. *Ipomoea* species, nonindigenous garden morning glories,
are butterfly nectar plants and are favored by cloudless sulfurs;
they host black-bordered lemon moth larvae. Red morning glory,
I. coccinea, is an annual that sometimes runs wild, but so do hummingbirds and butterflies when they find its blooms. I grow it
intertwined with passionflower, and lure flocks of fritillaries! *I.
quamoclit*, cypress vine or cardinal climber, is a feathery-foliaged
tropical American twining vine with small, crimson blooms; it is
also a hit with hummingbirds and butterflies. Dwarf morning
glories attract syrphid or hover flies, the larvae of which eat
aphids and other insect pests. Sap beetles (*Conotelus* species) are
found in morning glory flowers. Birds eat morning glory seeds.

Leguminosae or Fabaceae (Pea or Legume Family) American
wisteria (*Wisteria frutescens*), a native that Sally Wasowski feels

"has the potential to be far superior to the commonly used Asian species,"[13] hosts larvae of the Zarucco dusky wing, long-tailed skipper, and silver-spotted skipper butterflies. Nonnative *Phaseolus coccineus*, scarlet runner bean, attracts hummingbirds and hosts larvae of eastern-tailed blue and long-tailed skipper butterflies.

Liliaceae (Lily Family) Greenbrier (*Smilax* species) tangles provide good cover and nest sites. It is basically spring flowering and fall fruiting, but fruit can persist year-round if not eaten by a number of songbirds, game birds and small mammals like rabbits. It is larval host to the curve-lined owlet moth.

Loganiaceae (Logania Family) Carolina jessamine (*Gelsemium sempervirens*) blooms yellow, tubular flowers in late winter and early spring. Hummingbirds visit.

Menispermaceae (Moonseed Family) Carolina moonseed (*Cocculus carolinus*) is dioecious; red berries form on the female plants in fall and are eaten by birds. It hosts larvae of the moonseed moth.

Passifloraceae (Passionflower Family) Passionflower vine (*Passiflora incarnata*) is the native, purple-flowered maypop. It flowers and forms edible fruit May to September. It is larval host of the gulf fritillary, variegated fritillary, and zebra butterflies and of the plebeian sphinx moth.

Rhamnaceae (Buckthorn Family) Rattan vine or supplejack (*Berchemia scandens*) blooms greenish-white flowers in spring. Blue fruits, appearing summer through fall, are eaten by many birds such as wood duck, mallard, bobwhite, and wild turkey.

Rosaceae (Rose Family) The thorny canes of blackberry, dewberry, and brambles (*Rubus* species) are excellent cover for nesting birds, wintering birds, and other wildlife. Flowers are visited by butterflies for nectar. Berries are important food for many bird species including thrushes, grosbeaks, buntings, sparrows, orioles, vireos, quail, and woodpeckers and for raccoons, squirrels, and box turtles during spring and summer. Seed left from fruit fallen on the ground may be eaten by birds in winter. Dewberries host larvae of the small purplish gray moth.

Schisandraceae (Schisandra Family) Smooth woodbine or star vine (*Schisandra coccinea*, formerly *S. glabra*) is an aromatic, climbing woody vine with glossy leaves and drooping blooms that appear spring to fall, followed by red berry-like fruit in clusters. It is useful as a ground cover.

Vitaceae (Grape Family) Peppervine (*Ampelopsis arborea*) is a deciduous, woody vine. Its clusters of flowers are followed by blue-black fruits June to October. It can be invasive. It provides food for wildlife and is larval host to the pandorus sphinx, achemon sphinx, gaudy sphinx, Abbot's sphinx, lettered sphinx, nessus sphinx, and grapeleaf skeletonizer moths.

Virginia creeper (*Parthenocissus quinquefolia*) is a ground cover or climbing vine with tendrils. Its flowers, blooming May to August, are visited by bees. Small dark berries are eaten by mockingbirds, robins, bluebirds, thrashers and others. It is larval host to the lettered sphinx, grapeleaf skeletonizer, eight-spotted forester, beautiful wood nymph, and smoky moths.

Wild grapes (*Vitis* species) are deciduous woody vines. Some are dioecious. Make sure you're buying a self-pollinating variety, or purchase a staminate plant to pollinate your pistillate plants, or grapes will not develop. Tangles provide good cover; bark is used by some species for nesting; fruit is eaten by a variety of insects and birds, as well as by skunks, foxes, raccoons, rabbits, opossums, and squirrels. It is larval host for the grapevine epimenis, beautiful woodnymph, eight-spotted forester, grape root borer, grapeleaf skeletonizer, grape plume, and smoky moths, which attract parasitic wasps.

CHAPTER EIGHT

The Herbaceous Layers

Flowers for Wildlife

WHAT KIND OF WILDLIFE CAN YOU ATTRACT with flowers? Nectarivores, the nectar-sippers like butterflies, hummingbirds, and orioles? Granivores, like pine siskins, American goldfinches and white-throated sparrows, which dine on flowers gone to seed? Of course! But if you look carefully in a flower garden dedicated to wildlife, you'll find lots more beasts among the blooms, like yellow-faced bees, shining flower beetles, banded thrips, soldier flies, pirate and ambush

---

Illustration: Sycamore log, wood fern, box turtle, toad, skink

bugs. There will be pollinating insects, insect pests, spiders and insects that parasitize the pests or eat them—all the creatures in addition to butterflies and birds that associate with flowers. You may not think some of them appealing, but you'll certainly appreciate the creatures that consider them gourmet fare—migratory warblers and flycatchers, slug-eating toads and other amphibians, green anole lizards and other reptiles.

Native flowering plants live their life cycles intertwined with specific insects and arachnids. Consider, for example, the intimate involvement of milkweed and dogbane family members with milkweed butterflies, like the monarch, which lays its eggs on no other plants. Milkweed flowers are very high in nectar, and the plants themselves host the larvae. Gold-and-black adults sip nectar from the blooms, then lay their eggs on the stems and leaves; caterpillars hatch, grow fat munching on the succulent foliage, form jade-green chrysalises studded with gold spots, and hatch into winged beauties like their parents. Milkweeds' other intimates include coppery-tinged, iridescent blue-green dogbane beetle adults, which patrol the leaves, and their larvae, which feed on the foliage and roots; plant-eating aphids, which lure predaceous ladybug beetles and lacewings; and more.

And milkweed is nothing compared to goldenrod, a flowering plant that is a wildlife garden all by itself! More than a thousand different beetles, bees, flies, butterflies and moths (such as the goldenrod stowaway, goldenrod flower moth, green leuconycta, and lichen) feed on goldenrod or use its abundant nectar. Soldier beetles and locust borers eat its pollen; tiny red aphids adhere to its stems. Goldenrod gallflies and goldenrod gall moths lay their eggs inside the plant itself; the larvae that hatch are sought by chickadees and downy woodpeckers. The bee-like syrphid fly visits the golden flowers; its larvae eat aphids. Wasps, ambush bugs, crab spiders and other garden spiders come to prey on various creatures. At summer's end, the goldenrod's flowers become fluffy seeds that persist long into winter when they may be eaten by birds like goldfinches and dark-eyed juncos. The plants themselves, if left, become goldfinch winter cover. More than a hundred species of goldenrod grow in the United States. "Goldenrod's too invasive for a garden," say people who think the beautiful but tall and unruly field goldenrod (which is invasive) is typical of the *Solidago* genus. But they don't know about elm-leaved goldenrod, seaside goldenrod, and other restrained species. A goldenrod belongs in every wildlife garden!

GUIDELINES FOR WILDLIFE FLOWER GARDENING

Plants indigenous to a region attract more wildlife within that region than plants introduced from faraway places. When I say "more wildlife" I am including insects and other invertebrates, which are less charismatic than birds but are an important element of natural systems of your ecological region and serve as basic wildlife food. The patch of my garden that, to me, epitomizes the concept of the wildlife garden, is the one planted with indigenous members of the composite, mint, lobelia, and dayflower families. On sunny days from spring to late fall it is absolutely teeming with life. If I stand quietly by blooming goldenrod and wild ageratum, I see nature's miniature version of "The Young and the Restless," with dramas more intense and infinitely more complex and interesting!

On the other hand, it would be hard to create the unnatural abundance of flowers for a continuous supply of nectar over an extended period of time that makes the most enchanting butterfly garden without including exotic complements to the natives. And most of the flowers gardeners use to attract wintering hummingbirds to Gulf Coast gardens are alien to those ecological regions. Choose plants—indigenous, foreign natives, and introductions from far away—that suit your own designs for your wildlife garden. Emphasize natives.

Curtail the use of pesticides. Remember, if you kill pests, you also kill their predators. Grow a diversity of species of flowering plants, including members of the parsley, composite, mint, and mustard families, to attract parasitic wasps, syrphid flies, and other beneficial insects, which, along with insectivorous birds, reptiles, and amphibians, will maintain order in the garden. If conditions are such that you must intervene, use the least toxic approaches to pest control. *Common-Sense Pest Control* is a good resource.[1]

Stressed plants are more susceptible to attack by pests. Space and occasionally divide plants to prevent overcrowding and allow air circulation between them; reduce competition by controlling weeds; water plants deeply and early in the day to prevent overnight wetness and fungal infections.

Pruning or deadheading some species of flowers will prolong the period during which they bloom and produce nectar and pollen for beneficial insects. But when flowering diminishes, leave seedheads in place as food for seed-eating wildlife.

Though mulching is important, there are guidelines for mulching flowerbeds:

Do not mulch the immediate area around wildflowers requiring well-drained soils with limited organic matter (such as butterfly weed, some penstemons, mulleins).

Do not cover basal rosettes of plants such as the lobelias—cardinal flower and blue lobelia, rudbeckia, and others—that actively grow in winter.

Volunteers of self-seeding perennials will be suppressed if mulch is applied around the plants in fall to last through winter. Unless you want to block new seedlings, wait until they appear in spring, then apply mulch.

CONSERVATION GUIDELINES FOR USING NATIVE PLANTS

If it isn't enough that native plants are endangered by invasive exotic species and by human expansion into natural habitats, as they become more popular with gardeners, some species are put at risk by commercial—and individual—plant collectors, too. Conservation guidelines for native plant enthusiasts (adapted from Brooklyn Botanical Garden Handbook *The Environmental Gardener*[2]) follow:

Do not take plants from the wild except in areas of impending development and after getting permission from property owners! Instead, collect small quantities of seed you can germinate yourself.

Learn about propagation and cultivation requirements of native plants from sources such as *Growing and Propagating Wild Flowers* (Phillips) and *Gardening With Native Wild Flowers* (Jones and Foote) before you select plants from commercial sources. Your knowledge will enable you to avoid buying the ones less easily propagated or slow to flower, which may have been collected from natural habitats. Buy commercially grown plants of easily propagated species. Nursery stock labeled "field grown" or "nursery grown" may have been dug up in the wild and grown in a container for a short period of time. Look for "nursery propagated" plants. Ask the origin of plants before you purchase them.

Try to use plants grown from seed collected within a fifty-mile radius of your garden; they have had eons to adapt to your precise conditions. Besides, botanists fear nonlocal plants may jeopardize the genetic integrity of the same species in local plant communities.

Don't be so fast to weed seedlings that appear from nowhere in your garden. Some may be wildflowers whose seeds, spread by birds or wind, have sprouted because they're in the perfect habitat. The fact that a plant is dispersed by birds proves that it's valuable to wildlife. Two times, I collected seeds of plants I admired in wild settings; then, once I had identified their foliage, I recognized them growing in my garden. What besides seaside goldenrod and bird peppers have I pulled and replaced with species I had to beg to thrive? When a dark-green-leaved plant appeared in moist areas shaded by a tall, board fence in my yard, I watched. In fall, its tight buds burst into fuzzy, white flowers— it was snakeroot, *Eupatorium rugosum*, a white version of the blue wild ageratum, *E. coelestinum*, with which it intermingled. The butterflies love it!

WEEDS FOR WILDLIFE

For the most part, weeds—those early successional plants with habits of seed production and growth that make them objectionable in the garden—should be controlled. They compete for nutrients, moisture and sunlight with plants we've chosen for our gardens. But the adventurous gardener may be open to reasons for allowing some to grow, such as those that provide habitat and are nectar sources for beneficial insects or that indirectly attract beneficial insects by serving as "trap crops" for pest insects. An appalling thought? Here are suggestions for making it more palatable:

Most insects feed on plants in a certain family and reject those not related. If there is a less invasive plant in the same family as a weedy one known to attract beneficials, you can grow it instead of the weed and hope the insects will accept it.

Hide your weeds in an herb garden; many so-called weeds are herbs escaped from cultivation, anyway.

Any handbook of weeds will include native wildflowers with rowdy behavior. Don't reject all of them; find the more restrained species or varieties within each genus. Try pruning the tall or rangy ones to create more compact growth.

Should you grow weeds or rambunctious wildflowers in your wildlife garden? Not unless you want to. But if you're courageous enough to brave the criticism, your reward may be wildlife beyond your wildest dreams.

Weeds useful for wildlife include *Rumex* species, *Polygonum* species, and *Eriogonum* species (of the buckwheat family), especially attractive to tachinid flies (Tachinidae family), which eat flower nectar or honeydew secreted by certain insect pests. Tachinids are very important in pest control because they parasitize beetles, bugs, caterpillars, and grasshoppers. Composite, parsley, mint, and mustard family plants have small, single-blossomed, shallow-throated flowers that put pollen and nectar within easy reach of parasitic wasps and other tiny beneficial insects.

Selecting Flowering Plants for Wildlife[3]

Regardless of the value of a plant to available fauna, we, as gardeners, want it to be beautiful, too. But luckily, beauty is in the eyes of the beholder. The plants described below are just some of the possibilities for a wildlife garden. You may want to try others, either ornamentals developed for garden use or wildflowers you've discovered growing in nearby wild places. Plants with the following characteristics are useful to wildlife:

- Small, juicy leaves or blossoms at ground level for birds and other wildlife that forage on the ground, or higher for browsing animals.
  - Large quantities of edible seeds or fruit.
  - Flowers with high nectar content. Observe which ones the butterflies and bees are visiting.
  - Associations with insects eaten by wildlife. Again, observe or identify the plants and research their natural histories.

Use the list in the appendix, "Flowers by season of bloom," as a guide for selecting plants that bloom each season so your garden will offer continuous flowering as much of the year as possible.

Acanthaceae (Acanthus Family) Both natives and tropical American *Ruellia* species—the wild petunias—flowered blue and pink, are available in nurseries. They are butterfly nectar plants and host larvae of the buckeye, Cuban crescentspot, and Texan crescentspot butterflies.

Agavaceae (Agave Family) Yuccas and agaves host larvae of the giant skipper butterfly. *Manfreda virginica (Agave virginica)*, rattlesnake master or aloe, is a succulent perennial found in dry, sandy open areas and thin woods. Non-showy but fragrant flowers bloom early summer on a scape to four feet tall. There are forty species of yucca (*Yucca* species) indigenous to the warmer parts of North America, including several to coastal areas of the Southeast. They grow in sunny spots in sandy loam. Their beautiful white flowers occur spring to fall depending on the species; some bloom twice a year. Unless the appropriate species of moth in the subfamily Prodoxinae (yucca moths) is present to carry pollen to the ovary, the plant will not set seed. If you grow yucca, try to host yucca moths; find a yucca of the species indigenous to your ecological region.

Amaranthaceae (Amaranth Family) Amaranths produce seeds or small fruits that are eaten by certain birds; some seeds may be retained on the plants until winter. Amaranths host the spotted beet webworm moth. *Amaranthus* species attract ground beetles and host common sooty wing butterfly larvae.

Some species that are useful but classified as "weeds" are *Amaranthus albus,* tumbleweed; *A. hybridus,* green amaranth; and *A. retroflexus,* pigweed. Pigweeds host larvae of the mottled dusky wing and southern sooty wing butterflies.

Introduced ornamentals that produce seeds eaten by birds are *Amaranthus caudatus*, love-lies-bleeding or tassel-flower; *A. tricolor,* Joseph's coat and fountain plant; and *Celosia cristata,* cockscomb. *Gomphrena globosa,* globe amaranth, is a butterfly nectar plant. *A. hypochodriacus* and *A. gangeticus* are ornamental and food crop amaranths—for humans and birds.

Amaryllidaceae (Amaryllis Family) *Hymenocallis caroliniana* and other *H.* species, spider lilies, are indigenous to swampy areas of the Southeast but will grow in moist garden soil, also. They form dark green clumps of strap-like leaves with beautiful white flowers during summer in sun or shade. They host larvae of the Spanish moth; flowers may be visited by hummingbirds.

Agapanthus species are South African perennials with clusters of white or blue flowers visited by hummingbirds and butterflies.

Apocynaceae (Blue star or Dogbane Family) Nectar of native dogbanes is very attractive to butterflies and other insects. John Dennis[4] reports that he observed thirty-eight butterfly species visit the small greenish-white-to-pinkish flowers of a dogbane. Dogbane family members may host larvae of the snowberry clearwing and dogbane tiger moths and the dogbane beetle. Species for the garden: *Apocynum androsaemifolium,* spreading dogbane, and *A. cannabinum,* Indian hemp, the nectar of which is the favorite of dun skipper butterflies. *Apocynums* may host larvae of monarch butterflies and delicate cycnia moth. Of several useful species of the blue-flowering perennial *Amsonias*, the most common in nurseries is *A. tabernaemontana*, woodland blue star.

Everybody knows and grows introduced ornamental dogbane, *Catharanthus roseus,* or Madagascar periwinkle, which is useful as a butterfly nectar plant.

Aristolochiaceae (Ginger Family) Shuttleworth's ginger, *Asarum shuttleworthii* (= *Hexastylis shuttleworthii*), and other wild gingers, such as *A. arifolium and A. virginicum*, are good shade-tolerant ground covers, indigenous to various parts of the Southeast. Their maroon flowers occur at ground level, are fertilized by beetles, fungus gnats, scavenger flesh flies, and other ground-feeding insects. They host larvae of the pipevine swallowtail butterfly.

Asclepiadaceae (Milkweed Family) *Asclepias* species, the milkweeds, are perennials with flowers that are very rich in nectar. They are popular with many insects, including butterflies like the hairstreaks. Milkweed is larval host for monarch and queen butterflies and for the milkweed tussock, delicate cycnia, and unexpected cycnia moths. Milkweed attracts aphids and their predators, ladybugs and lacewings; and dogbane beetles.

Asclepias tuberosa, butterfly weed, is the milkweed most frequently found in nurseries; its nectar is favored by silver-spotted skipper and sachem butterflies. It will not tolerate wet soil. *A. variegata* and *A. syriaca* like dry situations, too, as do *A. viridis*, spider milkweed, and *A. humistrata*, sandhill milkweed. For wet areas, grow *A. incarnata*, swamp milkweed, a favored nectar source of the pipevine swallowtail, and *A. lanceolata* and *A. rubra*. *A. quadrifolia* is attractive and long-blooming in moist spots.

The introduced *A. currassavica*, Mexican milkweed, is fast growing, long blooming, and well used by butterflies and lots of other insects.

Balsaminaceae (Balsam or Touch-Me-Not Family) Jewelweed or spotted touch-me-not, *Impatiens capensis*, is our native impatiens. It is hummingbird adapted and a butterfly nectar plant. The popular introduced impatiens (*I. wallerana*), an African native, and oriental garden balsam or lady's slippers (*I. balsamina*) are also attractive to hummingbirds and butterflies.

Boraginaceae (Borage Family) Native perennials, puccoon, *Lithospermum carolinense*, and hoary puccoon or Indian paint, *L. canescens*, grow in sandy dry soils and are bee and butterfly nectar plants.

Introduced ornamentals and herbs in the same family that are also good nectar sources for bees and butterflies include the beautiful blue-flowered borage (*Borago officinalis*), Chinese forget-me-not (*Cynoglossum amabile*), heliotrope (*Heliotrope arborescens*), garden forget-me-not, (*Myosotis sylvatica*), and comfrey, healing herb, or boneset (*Symphytum officinale*), which has escaped cultivation and grows as a weed in parts of the United States.

Borago and *Myosotis* species host larvae of the American painted lady and painted lady butterflies and *Cynoglossums* host larvae of the gray hairstreak.

Bromeliaceae (Bromeliad or Pineapple Family) Flowers of some *Tilliandsia* species, found in southern Florida, are hummingbird adapted. Spanish moss, *Tilliandsia usneoides*, an epiphyte found in the Southeast on trees such as oaks and bald cypress, is used as nesting material by birds, as a nesting site for seminole and red bats, which roost within the clumps, and as a habitat for overwintering butterflies and other insects. It hosts larvae of the black-winged dahana moth in Florida. Collect it from the ground where it will perish if someone doesn't save it. It may "take" on the right garden tree.

Cactaceae (Cactus Family) Species of *Opuntia*, the prickly pear cactus, are indigenous to many sandy, sunny habitats in the Southeast. The fruit is persistent, and fruit and/or seeds may be eaten by raccoons, gopher tortoises, box turtles, and eastern woodrats, as well as by several species of birds, including woodpeckers and cardinals; the fleshy pads and fruit may be eaten by deer. Cacti provide nesting sites for several species of birds and for the wood rat. It hosts insects such as cactus flies and larvae that live in or near decaying cactus. Cactus-associated insects are eaten by birds such as flycatchers, gnatcatchers, and warblers. In bloom, prickly pear is a butterfly nectar plant.

Cannaceae (Canna Family) *Canna flaccida* is native to the Southeast; *C. indica* is tropical American, naturalized in the South. They host larvae of the Brazilian skipper and long-tailed skipper (bean-leaf roller) butterflies. Hummingbirds visit the red *C. indica* and the brightly colored, nectar-filled garden hybrids.

Capparaceae (Caper Family) Spider flower, *Cleome hasslerana*, is a South American native naturalized in parts of the Southeast. A bee and butterfly nectar plant, it is larval host plant for the checkered white and great southern white butterflies. The John James Audubon print of rufous hummingbirds shows them visiting a spider flower. Mourning doves will eat the seeds.

Caryophyllaceae (Pinks Family) Fire pink, *Silene virginica*, is a hummingbird-adapted native, available in nurseries. Other species suitable for the garden are *S. caroliniana* and the southernmost occurring *S. subcilliata*, scarlet catchfly. Other pinks are soapwort, *Saponaria officinalis*, a Eurasian species naturalized in the United States, and the native, giant chickweed *Stellaria pubera*, larval host of the dwarf yellow sulphur butterfly. Seed capsules of pinks are food for larvae of the capsule moth.

Chickweed, *Stellaria media*, the European winter annual, is an invasive weed in all cultivated areas of North America. If you can't beat it, accept its value to some wildlife: it hosts larvae of the dainty sulphur butterfly, and quail, finches and other ground feeders may eat its leaves and seeds.

Ornamental pinks of exotic origin include pink, dianthus, or sweet williams, *Dianthus* species, butterfly nectar plants and rock soapwort, *Saponaria ocymoides*.

Chenopodiaceae (Goosefoot Family) The *Chenopodiums* are classified as weeds. Pollen of the Eurasian *C. album*, lamb's-quarters, and *C. paganum,* pigweed, is windborne, meaning that it triggers fall allergies. On the other hand, *Chenopodiums* are aphid traps and also—*C. album* especially—host larvae of the common sooty wing butterfly and of the eight-spot and *Blepharomastix ranalis* moths. Pigweed hosts the agreeable tiger moth. *Chenopodiums* retain many of their seeds, offering winter food for seed-eating birds. Mexican tea, *C. ambrosioides,* cultivated for its essential oils, attracts beneficial assassin bugs, big-eyed bugs, and lady beetles.

Introduced ornamental summer cypress, *Kochia scoparia* and its various cultivars attract grasshoppers.

Commelinaceae (Dayflower Family) Spiderwort, *Tradescantia* species, are native perennials and provide good ground cover in wet and shady areas. Bees and butterflies visit the three-petaled purple, blue, pink, or white triangular half-a-day blooms. The pretty blue flowers of dayflower, *Commelina erecta*, make seed eaten by mourning doves, quail, and some songbirds. *C. communis*, also called dayflower, is a weedy annual from Eurasia naturalized in the United States. It's probably the species in my garden. While they last, the ephemeral dayflowers get a lot of attention from insects.

Compositae or Asteraceae (Sunflower or Composite Family)
There are species of composites blooming almost year-round, and
nearly all are important nectar sources for bees, butterflies, and
other insects. The small, single-blossomed, shallow-throated
composite flowers put pollen and nectar within easy reach of
parasitic wasps and other tiny beneficial insects. Pollen in daisies,
goldenrod, and yarrow attracts predatory wasps. The succulent
spring growth of some composites may be eaten by birds. If
allowed to remain uncut after they go to seed, the larger composites create cover and food for birds and other wildlife long
into winter.

Many of the composites are quite tall and would just as soon
sprawl as stand upright. You may want to stake them or place
them in the wilder reaches of your estate.

Antennaria plantaginifolia, field pussytoes, has rosettes of leaves
that make silvery patches of ground-cover hiding places. Their
fuzzy white-to-purplish blooms appear in spring.

Asters, *Aster* species, such as New England aster, *A. novae-
angliae* are favored by buckeye, checkered skipper, fiery skipper
and sachem butterflies for their nectar. Asters host larvae of the
pearl crescent and American painted lady butterflies and of the
following moths: spotted straw, sharp-stigma looper, dimorphic
gray, Arcigera flower, goldenrod flower, small brown quaker, the
asteroid, white-dotted groundling, brown-hooded owlet.

Bidens species, the Spanish needles, host larvae of the goldenrod stowaway, the confederate, and Mobile groundling moths.
Their nectar is favored by the hairstreaks and Zarucco duskywing
butterflies. *Bidens aristosa*, beggar ticks or sticktight, is recommended for late-summer-to-fall yellow in wild gardens. *Bidens
pilosa*, shepherd's-needle, is quite invasive, but if you can tolerate

little patches of it—if it can be contained in little patches—it blooms spring to frost with its yellow-centered white daisy-flowers producing nectar favored by sleepy orange butterflies, gulf fritillaries, and checkered skippers. It hosts larvae of the dwarf yellow sulphur butterfly.

Chrysanthemum species, especially daisy forms such as shasta and oxeye daisies, lure many insects. Some birds may eat their seeds. The more highly cultivated many-petaled doubles are less valuable to wildlife than the basic ones.

Nectar of the tickseeds, *Coreopsis* species, is favored by buckeye butterflies. Easy to grow, long-blooming garden plants, coreopsis attract beneficial green lacewings and syrphid or hover flies, the larvae of which eat aphids and other insect pests, and dimorphic gray moths. Goldfinches and others may eat the seeds.

Echinacea species, perennial purple coneflowers, are essential, both for their beauty and for their value to nectar- and pollen-loving insects and to birds that eat their seeds.

Erigeron species, fleabane, hosts larvae of checkered white butterflies. Its nectar is favored by checkered skippers and lynx flower moths. *Erigeron pulchellus*, Robin's-plantain, and other fleabanes bloom in early spring when nectar is scarce.

Eupatoriums are significant nectar sources for butterflies and other insects. They host larvae of the burdock borer and clymene moths. There are white-flowered species, the bonesets, and *E. rugosum*, white snakeroot, that bloom in shade. It's poisonous to livestock. Beautiful blue wild ageratum, hardy ageratum or mistflower, *E. coelestinum*, blooms in shade or sun. It is called invasive, but has not become a problem in my garden. It hosts larvae of the yellow-winged pareuchaetes moth.

There are several species of joe-pye weed, all similar to *E. fistulosum*. They grow in sunny moist places. Their heights vary, but the appeal of the pollen and nectar of their purple-to-pink flowers to insects does not. They are considered the quintessential butterfly flower and are the favorite of silver-spotted skippers. Eupatorium borer moth larvae eat their roots, and three-lined flower moth larvae eat their leaves.

Red and yellow *Gaillardia* species, firewheels or blanketflowers, come in perennial and reseeding annual forms. Blossoms are always buzzing with bees and other insects. They bloom absolutely forever, shedding seeds that mourning doves and cardinals eat.

Helianthus species, the sunflowers, host larvae of the painted lady butterfly and of the yellow bear, frothy, Isabella tiger, giant leopard, and common pinkaband moths. They attract beneficial assassin bugs, as well as aphids and predaceous ladybugs and lacewings. Swamp sunflower, *H. angustifolius*, is everybody's favorite garden wildflower; prune it back in summer so you won't have to stake it in fall. *H. annuus* is the source of sunflower seeds; there are many garden cultivars.

Helenium autumnale, Helen's flower or sneezeweed, hosts larvae of dwarf yellow sulphur butterflies. It blooms in late summer in moist places. Garden cultivars of Helen's flower and other *Helenium* species are available in yellows, oranges, and bronze-reds. Summer-blooming *Heliopsis helianthoides*, oxeye, is available as beautiful garden cultivars Summer Sun, Gold Greenheart and others. The singles are better than doubles for nectar-seeking insects.

Yellow-flowered *Hieracium venosum*, rattlesnake weed or poor-Robin's-plantain, flowers in spring and summer in light shade. Camphorweed, *Heterotheca subaxillaris*, attracts lacewings, tachinid and syrphid flies, lady beetles, and sand, ichneumonid and braconid wasps. Other *Heterotheca* species are useful in the garden, also.

Wild lettuces, *Lactuca canadensis* and *L. floridana,* attract soldier beetles, lacewings, earwigs and syrphid flies. *Liatris spicata* blooms with purple spikes in late summer and early fall; it hosts larvae of the glorious flower moth.

Though Bill Fontenot praises *Polymnia uvedalia,* bear's foot or bear-paw,[5] few others acknowledge admiration for the tall perennial of woods and edges named for its large leaves; it's called "rank" and worse in other sources. Its small yellow blooms occur summer into fall. I'm trying it from seed.

Rudbeckia hirta is the gloriosa daisy. Its nectar is favored by pearl crescent butterflies and its seeds by birds. It attracts syrphid or hover flies, the larvae of which eat aphids and other insect pests. Other black-eyed Susans include the long-lived garden perennial Goldsturm, cultivar of *R. fulgida,* and cutleaf coneflower, *R. laciniata.*

Ratibida columnifera and *R. pinnata,* Mexican hat, are incredibly attractive and easy-to-grow perennials that bloom from spring into winter. Their central cones project over drooping petals, purple or yellow. Butterflies and other insects love them. Dragonflies use their cones as perching posts.

Senecio species host larvae of the painted lady butterfly. Some for the garden are perennial, spring bloomers: golden ragwort (*S. aureus*), obovate ragwort (*S. obovatus*) and annual self-seeder butterweed or yellow-top (*S. glabellus*), which will grow in shade. I transplanted butterweeds from near the railroad tracks to my garden on a partly sunny December day. I stopped to admire them an hour later and counted eight species of insects colored red, orange, yellow, black, and green already combing the blooms and foliage!

Spilanthes americana, creeping spot flower, is a perennial ground cover that might be growing in your southern lawn right now. You may have dismissed it as a weed, but you'll reconsider once you see its beautiful display of little yellow sunflowers and all the tiny insects and butterflies that visit from late spring to frost. I've given it a place of honor in the moist area around my birdbath. South American *Spilanthes* species are called "low growing semi-tropical creepers" in *Seeds of Change* catalog.

The seventy North American species of goldenrod (*Solidago* species), the pollen of which is transported from flower to flower by insects, do not cause fall allergies! Airborne pollen of ragweed, which blooms at the same time, does. Goldenrods recommended for garden use are elm-leaf goldenrod (*S. ulmifolia*), which will bloom in dry shade; seaside goldenrod (*S. sempervirens*), a clumper with growing tips that can be pinched in spring to keep the plant compact; sweet goldenrod (*S. odora*), a noninvasive "sprawler" with anise-scented foliage; and Golden Fleece *(S. sphacelata)*, which, at two feet high, is a dwarf. Craig Tufts, who wrote *The Backyard Naturalist*,[6] grows hard-leaf goldenrod *(S. rigida)*. Rough-leaf goldenrod (*S. rugosa*) "produces a few stolons, but for the most part it stays in a clump" says Allen Lacy, who agrees that my favorite, the sprawling, six-foot field goldenrod (*S. altissima*), which spreads rapidly by underground roots, "lacks real viciousness."[7] More and more species and cultivars developed for garden use are showing up in nurseries. There is absolutely no need for the wildlife gardener—and the creatures of his or her backyard world—to live a life without goldenrod!

Spring growth of goldenrods may be tender food for grouse. A thicket of goldenrod offers a fall and winter seed feast to birds including goldfinches, juncos, and tree sparrows and good cover for finches and other wintering birds. Goldenrods host the insects that make goldenrod galls; larvae inside the galls may be eaten by chickadees and downy woodpeckers. Goldenrod flowers produce large quantities of nectar, which is loved by many butterflies; it is the absolute favorite of American painted lady butter-flies and monarchs. Goldenrods attract beneficial green lacewings, predaceous beetles, big-eyed bugs, lady beetles, spiders, parasitic wasps, long-legged flies, and assassin bugs and moths such as goldenrod flower, brown-hooded owlets, green leuconyctas, pink-barred lithacodias, white-dotted groundling, spotted fireworm, sharp-stigma looper, the asteroid, and fine-lined sallow.

Stokesia laevis, Stoke's aster, is a lovely pale-blue flowered perennial and butterfly nectar plant that likes good drainage and will bloom in partial shade, spring and summer.

Yellow-rayed *Verbesina helianthoides* and *V. alternifolia*, crown-beards, are sun- to partial-shade loving perennials that host larvae of spring azure butterflies and the gold moth.

Vernonia species, the ironweeds, grow very tall. The fuzzy fall flowers are a unique reddish-purple color you'll see nowhere else. Their nectar is favored by fiery skippers and golden banded skippers; larvae of *Polygrammodes flavidalis* and eupatorium borer moths eat their roots, and ironweed borer moth larvae live off their seeds. Ironweeds also host larvae of red groundling moths, *Polygrammodes langdonalis* and parthenice tiger moths.

Some of the most popular garden ornamentals and herbs are composites. *Achillea* species, the yarrows, are European with some naturalized in the United States. They may attract aphids and ladybug beetles, parasitic wasps of aphids, scales and white-flies and are butterfly nectar plants. Blue-flowered *Ageratum houstonianum*, ageratum or flossflower, is Central American and is a butterfly nectar plant. There are native North American *Artemisia* species, but the best known is the European wormwood or sage, *Artemesia absinthium*, naturalized in parts of the United States. A good nectar plant, it hosts larvae of the painted lady butterfly.

Is the European cornflower (*Centaurea Cyanus*) a garden plant or a cosmopolitan weed? No matter what you call it, bees, butterflies and other nectar-seeking insects love it. Goldfinches, house finches and others may eat its seeds. Along with other centaureas or knapweeds, it can serve as a substitute for thistle—now that's a cosmopolitan weed!

Garden favorites are crimson, pink, and white *Cosmos bipinnatus* and the yellow, orange, and red *C. sulphureus*—Mexican natives valuable as butterfly nectar plants and favored by the painted lady and monarch. They attract praying mantis and syrphid or hover flies, the larvae of which eat aphids and other insect pests. Their ripe seeds may be eaten by goldfinches, white-throated sparrows, house finches, and juncos. Cosmos hosts gray looper moths. Lacewings love red cosmos.

Marigolds are the basic garden flower. Those grown as ornamentals are of middle-American origin. The simpler they are, the more useful for wildlife. Try singles or just barely doubles from among the almost two hundred varieties of French marigold *(Tagetes patula)*. They offer nectar for butterflies and food for birds when gone to seed. The small flowers of signet marigold *(T. tenuifolia)* draw butterflies and beneficial insects. American painted lady, fiery skipper, and sachem butterflies favor marigold nectar. Marigolds attract ladybugs and syrphid or hover flies, the larvae of which eat aphids and other insect pests; they may host larvae of the dwarf yellow sulphur butterfly.

Tansy (*Tanacetum vulgare*), a European herb, attracts beneficial green lacewings and hosts larvae of the cobbler moth. Bees and butterflies love nectar from the yellow-centered orange flowers of Mexican sunflower (*Tithonia rotundifolia*). .

The many forms of garden zinnias, developed from middle and South American *Zinnia* species, are nectar sources favored by monarchs, gulf fritillaries, red-spotted purples and silver-spotted skippers. Gone to seed, they are food for goldfinches and other seed-eating birds.

You may know some composites as weeds. The infamous *Ambrosia* species, ragweeds, are native plants and excellent bird food. Though not intrinsically beautiful, they can look quite ornamental—for instance, when they are crowded with brunching indigo buntings like the one I saw at Dauphin Island, Alabama. Ragweed produces windborne pollen that's one of the principal causes of fall allergies, so I'm not recommending you plant it. But you should know that *Ambrosia* species host larvae of the common sooty wing butterfly and of the ragweed flower and olive shaded bird dropping moths. *A. artemisiifolia* attracts lady beetles, assassin bugs, and spiders. Giant ragweed, *A. trifida*, hosts larvae of Thoreau's flower moths and black-barred brown moths. Sally Wasowski reports that ragweed grows where the climax vegetation has been disturbed and the soil abused—for example, "along creeks in the backyards of fancy suburban homes or in parks."[8]

Thistles (*Cirsium* species), whether native or alien, are prickly, invasive weeds. Their flowers make nectar sought by hummingbirds and by butterflies such as gulf fritillaries, pearl crescents, and pipevine swallowtails; they produce abundant seeds for goldfinches, clay-colored sparrows and other seedeaters. Goldfinches use thistle down as nest lining. Thistles may host larvae of painted lady butterflies and of parthenice tiger moths.

I'm not recommending you plant the Eurasian weed dandelion (*Taraxacum officinale*), but if you must live with it anyway, realize that when it blooms at ground level after having been mowed in your lawn, foraging birds such as goldfinches, pine siskins, indigo and painted buntings, chipping sparrows and other finches may

eat its seed. Butterflies, especially the spring azure, will appreciate its nectar. It may host larvae of small brown quaker, ruddy
quaker, parthenice, banded tiger and harnessed moths.

Crassulaceae (Orpine Family) The oriental *Sedum spectabile*,
showy stonecrop, and other sedums are good butterfly nectar
plants and host larvae of the variegated fritillary.

Cruciferae (Mustard Family) Yellow or white mustard flowers
provide nectar for beneficial insects, butterflies and bees and host
larvae of *Pieridae* family butterflies, the whites and sulphurs.

Cardamine bulbosa, spring cress, is "fun, easy, and beautiful,"
but is "rarely, if ever offered in the native nursery trade," says Bill
Fontenot.[9] Maybe that will change! Though its normal bloom
period is February to May, during one warm winter a specimen in
Fontenot's garden produced the first of its white delicate flowers
on January 1, and continued "blooming its little heart out"
through a spell of below-freezing temperatures!

My weed book lists several *Brassica* species, the wild mustards
introduced from Europe and Asia. They are widespread. One
came up on its own in my experimental weed patch. *Brassicas*
host larvae of checkered white, great southern white, and
European cabbage (introduced) butterflies and of the sharp-
angled carpet moth. *Barbarea vulgaris*, winter cress or yellow
rocket, is a favored nectar source for gray hairstreak and spring
azure butterflies.

Some introduced mustard family ornamentals are wallflowers
(*Cheiranthus* species and *Erysimum* species), butterfly and bee
nectar plants, and stocks (*Matthiola incana*), pollinated by sphinx
moths. Candytufts are bee and butterfly nectar sources and offer
edible seeds for birds. Rocket candytuft (*Iberis amara*) and globe
candytuft (*I. umbellata*) attract syrphid flies and the diamondback
moth (introduced). Nectar of *Lobularia maritima*, sweet alyssum,

lures bees and (purple alyssum especially) butterflies. Alyssums host European cabbage butterfly larvae (introduced), and larvae of the diamondback moth (introduced). Nasturtium (*Tropaeolum majus*) hosts larvae of the European cabbage butterfly. Other *Brassica* species are ornamental cabbages and flowering kale.

Dipsacaceae (Teasel or Pincushion Family) Common teasel (*Dipsacus fullonum* [*D. sylvestris*]) is a biennial European weed naturalized in the northeastern United States. It is a bee nectar plant.

Ornamentals of the teasel family are *Scabiosa caucasica, S.* species, the pincushions and scabiosas; colorful annuals, they are good nectar plants for butterflies and other insects.

Euphorbiaceae (Spurge Family) Euphorbias are very good sources of nectar for butterflies and other insects. Native wild-flowers include *E. corollata,* flowering spurge, and *E. heterophylla,* wild poinsettia or milkweed. The most famous spurge is the Mexican ornamental *E. pulcherrima*, poinsettia, which may host larvae of the ello sphinx moth.

Geraniaceae (Geranium Family) Cranesbills, wild gerani-ums, *Geranium maculatum* and other *G.* species, are native peren-nials with clusters of pink-to-purple flowers that bloom in part sun during spring. They are good sources of nectar for butterflies and other insects.

Labiatae or Lamiaceae (Mint Family) This family contains some of the most important nectar plants for bees, butterflies, and other insects, as well as for hummingbirds. They are some of the longest blooming and most ornamental garden plants avail-able. You can spot a mint family member by its square stems. Mints host larvae of gray looper moths.

Conradina species, wild rosemary, is aromatic and looks just like Mediterranean rosemary but isn't! Its four species are native to the Southeast. The spring blooms are delicate lavender trumpets attractive to insects.

Monarda didyma, bergamot or bee balm, especially the red cultivars, and *M. fistulosa*, wild bergamot, attract hummingbirds. *M. citriodora*, lemon bee balm, blooms spring to summer and is similar to *M. punctata*, dotted mint or horsemint, which blooms July to October and hosts larvae of the common sooty wing butterfly. Horsemint, my favorite, is very easy to grow from seed, has unusual flowers, and is alive with minute creatures that seek its nectar! Butterflies like the gray marvel love *Monarda* nectar.

Physostegia virginiana, false dragonhead or obedient plant, is a spring-through-fall bloomer, with uncommonly attractive pinkish-purple spikes of flowers used by hummingbirds and bees. It sprawls and spreads with abandon, but is easily controlled.

Pycnanthemum incanum and other species of mountain mints lure insects such as the tiny parasitic wasps and bees. A mountain mint planted near tomato plants will attract braconid wasps to help control pests such as hornworms on tomatoes.

Salvias are the most famous garden mint. Southeastern natives for garden use are the blue-flowered *Salvia azurea* var. *azurea, S. farinacea* and *S. lyrata*, cancerweed or lyreleaf sage, with rosettes that make a nice ground cover. Cancerweed and *S. coccinea*, tropical, scarlet sage or Texas sage, lure hummingbirds, bees and butterflies. Sulphurs love nectar of scarlet sage. There are spring-to-early fall bloomers of *Scutellaria* species, skullcaps. In wild places, animals may browse their foliage. Grow them to see what insects visit. *Teucrium canadense*, wood sage or germander, grows in moist places and blooms July into fall, with long clusters of pink-to-purple to white flowers with extended lower petals that invite insects to perch.

Mint family introductions for southeastern gardens include:

Agastache species, hyssops, natives of Texas and the southwest United States, are showy nectar plants for bees and butterflies. Some attract hummingbirds.

Lavandula angustifolia, English lavender, and other lavenders are butterfly and bee attracters. *Leonotis leonurus*, lion's ear, is a shrubby South African mint with tiers of velvety orange flowers in summer/fall that are attractive to hummingbirds.

Mentha species, spearmint, peppermint, etc., originated in the Old World. They are nectar plants important to bees, butterflies, and other insects. Spearmint attracts syrphid or hover flies, the larvae of which eat aphids and other insect pests. Mint nectar is a favorite of dun skippers and gray marvel butterflies. *Nepeta cataria*, catmint, is a butterfly and bee nectar plant, but it attracts cats. Don't plant it if you want lizards, frogs, birds, beneficial ground beetles and other small creatures house cats like to hunt and kill.

Purple-foliaged perilla, *Perilla frutescens*, is cultivated in Asia for its seeds, which birds will eat, too. Insects visit the spikes of tiny blue flowers. Perilla self-seeds, but is not difficult to control. The foliage contrasts nicely with usual garden greens. *Prunella vulgaris*, heal-all, is widely naturalized in the United States. Though called a weed, it is very attractive to many species of butterflies. Try other *Prunellas*, too, such as *P. grandiflora*. There are many cultivars of the Mediterranean herb rosemary, *Rosemarinum officinalis*. Their flowers, usually blue-violet, entice butterflies and bees.

A seemingly infinite number of *Salvias* are available for use in the garden, including species collected from far and near and hybrids developed by enthusiasts such as Richard Dufresne of North Carolina. Some are ever-blooming; some are seasonal.

The fall/winter bloomers are part of the secret of luring wintering hummingbirds to Gulf Coast areas.

S. splendens is the scarlet salvia from Brazil, traditional in gas station flower beds. It comes in white and purple, too, and blooms in shade. Hummingbirds, bees, and butterflies love its nectar. Other salvias important for hummingbird gardens are rocky mountain or autumn sage (shades of red and peach), *S. greggii*; Mexican bush sage (blue), *S. leucantha*; mountain sage (red) from Texas and Mexico, *S. regla;* pineapple sage (red with pineapple-scented leaves) from Mexico, *S. elegans*; Belize sage (red), *S. miniata*; forsythia sage (yellow) from Mexico, *S. madrensis*; and Mexican fuchsia sage (red-purple), *S. iodantha*. There are many more.

Costa Rican red skullcap, *Scutellaria moiciniana*, is very ornamental and is a good hummingbird plant.

Teucrium marum, cat thyme, is a Mediterranean ornamental that contains dolichodial, a very potent cat stimulant and insect repellant. Do not use it in a wildlife garden. The thymes, *Thymus* species, are bee and butterfly nectar plants.

Leguminosae or Fabaceae (Pea-Legume Family) Peas are best known as soil improvers. Nodules on legume roots house bacteria that absorb nitrogen from the air and convert it to an organic form usable by plants. When legumes die and decay, this nitrogen becomes a part of the soil. Some legumes produce seeds edible by birds. They are important nectar plants for insects. Legumes host the Zarucco dusky wing butterfly and black-spotted and gray-patched prominent moths.

Baptisia species, false indigos, are bee plants and host larvae of butterflies such as the mottled dusky wing, frosted elfin, and eastern tailed blue. *B. tinctoria*, wild indigo, hosts the wild indigo dusky wing butterfly. *Lupinus perennis*, wild lupine, of acid pinelands, hosts larvae of the frosted elfin butterfly and bella moth.

Petalostemum candidum and *P. purpureum* are prairie clovers. There are indigenous and introduced species of *Lespedeza*, the bush clovers. Some are ornamental; others are used for soil improvement and animal forage. Their flowers produce nectar for bees; seeds are good bird food. They are larval host for the common ptichodis and bella moths and for the eastern tailed blue, silver spotted skipper, and northern cloudy wing butterflies.

Thermopsis villosa, Carolina bush pea, is an early bloomer found along woodland edges in the upper South.

You may consider yellow-flowered *Cassia fasciculata*, partridge pea, and other cassias to be weeds or wildflowers. They grow in disturbed places, including perhaps in your yard. They may host larvae of cloudless sulphur, little sulphur, sleepy orange, and alfalfa butterflies. *Lathyrus latifolius*, everlasting or perennial pea, hosts larvae of eastern tailed blue butterflies.

The legumes introduced to the Southeast include the following agriculturally important species:

Medicago sativa, alfalfa, is very high in nectar. It attracts beneficial insects such as minute pirate bugs, big-eyed bugs, damsel bugs, assassin bugs, lady beetles, and parasitic wasps. It hosts larvae of funereal dusky wing butterflies and of small purplish gray moths.

Phaseolus species, including the very ornamental scarlet runner bean (*P. coccineus*), host eastern tailed blue butterflies and long-tailed skippers. Scarlet runner beans attract hummingbirds, too.

Clovers, *Trifolium* species and *Melilotus* species, are European and Asian introductions and are butterfly nectar plants. Clovers, *Trifolium* species, may host clouded sulphur, eastern tailed blue, northern cloudy wing, and dogface butterflies and the following moths: grateful midget, forage looper, clover looper, small purplish gray, tufted apple-bud, and Gelechiid family moth species. Crimson clover (*T. incarnatum*) is larval host to cloudless sulphur, little sulphur, sleepy orange, and alfalfa butterflies. White clover (*T. repens*) is exceptionally high in nectar; it attracts tiny beneficial wasps that are parasites of aphids, scales, and whiteflies.

The vetches (*Vicia* species), some native and some not, are good sources of nectar for butterflies.

Liliaceae (Lily Family) North American native lilies include wild onion (*Allium cernuum*) and wild hyacinth or eastern camas (*Camassia scilloides*). The best-known lily family garden plants which are of European and Asian origin are the daylilies, *Hemerocallis* species, popular perennials that come in yellows, oranges, and reds. They are good sources of nectar for butterflies, and hummingbirds and orioles may visit the flowers, also.

Lobeliaceae (Lobelia Family) This family contains the most stunning of all the native flowers for garden use—cardinal flower (*Lobelia cardinalis*). Its vivid blooms, which appear over three months, summer to fall, are irresistible to hummingbirds, the plant's major pollinator, and are also attractive to butterflies. Growing in moist soil, it is a short-lived perennial, more likely to return in successive years if not mulched in winter (mulch will smother its rosettes and interfere with self-seeding). Blue lobelia (*L. syphilitica*) lures hummingbirds, too.

Loganiaceae (Logania Family) *Spigelia marilandica,* Indian pink, is an easy-to-grow, very ornamental hummingbird-adapted perennial. Its red and yellow trumpet-shaped flowers begin blooming in spring and may continue until fall.

The most commonly grown butterfly bushes, *Buddleia* species, are oriental in origin. They produce beautiful spikes of flowers in white and shades of yellow and purple that are very attractive to butterflies.

Malvaceae (Mallow Family) The mallow family is known for its very ornamental flowers that lure nectar-seeking humming-birds and insects. *Callirhoe* species, the poppy mallows, are sprawling perennials that produce incredible wine-red blooms in spring to summer. *Hibiscus coccineus,* Texas star hibiscus, with brilliant red flowers, and other native *H.* species, the rose mal-lows, are shrub-like perennials that thrive in wetlands. *Kosteletskya virginica*, salt-marsh mallow, is a pale-pink-flowered perennial that grows to six feet, blooming through summer into fall. *Hibiscus* and *Malva* species host larvae of the gray hairstreak butterfly; *Malva* species host checkered skipper butterfly larvae.

The Asian biennial hollyhock (*Alcea rosea*) hosts larvae of the checkered skipper butterfly and of the exposed bird-dropping moth. The European biennial *Malva sylvestris* may host larvae of the checkered skipper butterfly.

Onagraceae (Evening Primrose Family) Evening primroses are perennials with many insect associations: some attract bene-ficial predatory ground beetles; some host larvae of moths such as the proud sphinx, *conchylis oenotherana*, and grape leaf-folder; evening- and night-flowering *O. biennis* is pollinated by sphinx moths; *Oenothera fruticosa* attracts plant-eating flea beetles. *Oenothera fruticosa* and *O. perennis*, both called sundrops, are yel-low-flowering species. Pink- and white-flowered *O. speciosa*, evening primrose or Mexican primrose, hosts pearly wood-nymph moth caterpillars and may attract hummingbirds.

Gaura lindheimeri is a drought-resistant rangy perennial from Louisiana and Texas with stems of willow-like foliage that elon-gate to six feet. It produces small airy pink-tinged white-aging-to-rose blossoms from late spring to November. Allen Lacy praises *Gaura* extravagantly in *The Garden in Autumn*.[10] I'm growing it from seed collected in south Louisiana. *G. biennis* hosts caterpillars of primrose and clouded crimson moths. Texas wildflower *G. suffulta*'s common names, bee blossom and wild honeysuckle, give an idea of the appearance of *Guara* flowers and their attractiveness to insects.

Phytolaccaceae (Pokeweed Family) *Phytolacca rigida, P. americana*, pokeweeds, are perennial herbs that require space, for they grow to twelve feet. The six-inch racemes of white-to-purplish flowers are followed in fall by dark purple fruit eaten by many birds including bluebirds, cardinals, thrashers, thrushes, waxwings, and doves and mammals such as raccoons, opossums and foxes. They reseed rampantly. Every part of the plant is poisonous to humans.

Polemoniaceae (Phlox Family) The colorful native phloxes are butterfly nectar plants and may host larvae of moths such as the spotted straw moth. Some tall native phloxes that bloom in spring and then intermittently to frost are the lavender, pink, and sometimes white-flowered thick-leaved phlox, *Phlox carolina,* smooth phlox, *P. glaberrima,* and *P. maculata*. Woodland or Louisiana phlox, *P. divaricata*, is a low-growing ground cover that blooms carpets of blue flowers in spring. *P. drummondii*, annual or Drummond's phlox, is a Texas native, a colorful late-spring-to-summer bloomer, in white and shades of red to purple.

Standing cypress, scarlet gilia, *Ipomopsis rubra*, is a scarlet-flowered, hummingbird-adapted upright perennial or biennial that grows in well-drained soils in the southeastern United States. It lures butterflies, too.

Polygonaceae (Buckwheat Family) Buckwheats produce flowers very high in nectar, and therefore very attractive to bees and other insects, and seeds relished by birds. Though useful to wildlife, most of the following plants are not very ornamental. Some are considered weeds.

Rumex hastatulus is native wild sorrel. The Eurasian curly dock *(R. crispus)* blooms spring to fall. *R. acetosella* is also Eurasian. Docks host larvae of American copper butterflies and of pink-barred lithacodia moths. The seeds are eaten by birds.

Wild buckwheats, *Eriogonum* species, such as *E. tomentosum*, are butterfly nectar plants and attract sand wasps, tachinid, chloropid and syrphid flies, and minute pirate bugs. Seeds and other parts serve as food for various kinds of wildlife.

Polygonum species, the knotweeds and smartweeds, such as dock-leaved smartweed *(Polygonum lapathifolium)*, produce lots of seeds. Some are retained on the plant, providing winter food for wildlife such as ground-feeding songbirds and game birds and seed-eating small mammals. *Polygonums* may host larvae of bent-line carpet, red twin spot, purple-lined sallow, bidens borer, and the gem moths. Knotweeds are larval host plant for pipevine swallowtail butterflies. Garden knotweed is *P. capitatum*, a Himalayan introduction. Very ornamental as a ground cover, it provides good cover for skinks and spiders and bees love its little pink blooms.

Ranunculaceae (Ranunculus Family) *Aquilegia canadensis*, columbine, is a spring-blooming perennial with spurred red and yellow flowers that are hummingbird adapted. It grows in dry, rocky woods and hosts larvae of the columbine dusky wing butterflies.

Western native larkspurs, *Delphinium* species, are humming-bird adapted. Southeastern larkspurs, *D. carolinianum, D. tricorne, D. exaltatum,* and *D. virescens,* should attract hummers and insects. Mediterranean and oriental *Delphinium* and *Consolida* species, garden ornamentals, lure hummers and bumblebees.

Rosaceae (Rose Family) *Fragaria virginiana*, common or wild strawberry, is a low-growing plant that spreads on runners in fields and sunny woodlands of the eastern United States. The spring flowers, white with yellow centers, are followed by small, sweet, red strawberries. Flowers are nectar sources for butterflies and other insects. Strawberries and other rose family members may host larvae of spotted straw and dolichos armyworm moths, as well as the flannel moth, with larva—the puss caterpillar— that stings! The yellow-flowered strawberry, mock strawberry, *Duchesnea indica*, is an introduced weed in some southeastern cities. Its strawberry-like fruit is flat and tasteless.

The introduced ornamentals meadowsweets or queen-of-the-pasture (*Filipendula* species) are butterfly nectar plants.

Rubiaceae (Madder and Bedstraw Family) Partridgeberry, *Mitchella repens*, is an evergreen ground cover found in rich, acid woodland soils. Its white flowers, blooming May to July, are followed by red berries eaten by game birds, skunks and white-footed mice. Buttonweed (*Diodia virginiana*) is a perennial ground cover that forms thick mats of deep green studded with tiny, snowy white flowers. I removed a nice patch of it growing over part of a bark path because I had read that it was a weed. Now, I have nut sedge to pull. Bill Fontenot remarks that buttonweed "which superficially resembles *M. repens* in form, foliage, color, bloom, and texture . . . is considered no more than a weed. Possessing all of the same qualities (except for the showy red fruits), this widespread, super adaptable species is ignored."[11] I wish I had mine back. It should make a nice ground cover habitat for insects and other invertebrates.

Introduced ornamental *Pentas lanceolata,* Egyptian star-clusters, especially the red variety, is very attractive to hummingbirds. Butterflies like its nectar, also; for them grow the lavenders, pinks, and blues.

Rutaceae (Rue [Citrus] Family) The southern European perennial herb rue (*Ruta graveolens*) hosts larvae of giant swallowtail and eastern black swallowtail butterflies and attracts beneficial ichneumonid wasps.

Scrophulariaceae (Figwort Family) Figwort family members may host larvae of the buckeye butterfly and the chalcedony midget moth. Some native figworts are recommended for garden use.

Culver's root (*Veronicastrum virginicum*) is found in meadows, prairies, and woodland edges. Monkeyflowers (*Mimulus alatus, M. ringens*) grow in moist or wet soil. Penstemons are found in the Southeast, though more of the 250 North American species are western natives. They need very well-drained soil. Species available in nurseries include *Penstemon smallii*, *P. digitalis*, *P. laevigatus*, *P. multiflorus,* and *P. tenuiflorus.* Because penstemons can be finicky, it's best to grow them from seed collected in your own region. They are important nectar sources for bees. Some are visited by hummingbirds.

Variously called weeds or wildflowers, mulleins (*Verbascum* species) are Eurasians widely naturalized in the United States. *V. thapsus*'s three-foot-tall candle-like flower stalk grows from a flat rosette. Fuzz from the soft leaves that line the stalk is used by hummingbirds to line their nests. Downy and hairy woodpeckers will work over the dried flower stalks in midwinter and early spring.

Butter-and-eggs, yellow toadflax or wild snapdragon (*Linaria vulgaris*) is a naturalized Eurasian; toadflax (*L. canadensis* and *L. canadensis* var. *texana)* are United States natives. *Linarias* host larvae of the buckeye butterfly.

Introduced ornamental figworts can also host larvae of the buckeye butterfly. Some suggested for garden use are snapdragons (*Antirrhinum* species); spurred snapdragon or toadflax, from

Morocco *(Linaria maroccana)*, and wishbone flower or bluewings *(Torenia fournieri)* from Vietnam, which bloom in moist shady places. Coral plant or fountain plant *(Russelia equisetiformis)* is best planted in a container. Its tubular, red flowers blooming from late spring through cool weather attract hummingbirds.

Solanaceae (Nightshade Family) Bird peppers, a variety of *Capsicum annuum* that grows wild in parts of the southern United States, are tiny, bright red peppers highly favored by catbirds and mockingbirds. The one that grows in my garden volunteered, probably from seeds left in mockingbird droppings. Any number of the small cultivated peppers would probably be as popular.

A few garden-grown nightshades from faraway places are *Petunia* hybrids, moth and butterfly nectar plants that produce tiny seeds edible by birds. *Nicotiana* species, the flowering tobaccos, include *N. sylvestris*, which lures moths to its blossoms, and *N. alata*, touted as a butterfly and hummingbird nectar plant. Tobaccos may host the tobacco hornworm, gargantuan larvae of the Carolina sphinx moth and larvae of the yellow bear and tobacco budworm moths.

Umbelliferae or Apiaceae (Parsley or Carrot Family) Many species from this family host larvae of black swallowtail butterflies. Umbelliferous flowers, those with many tiny flowers arranged in tight umbels, are good sources of nectar and pollen for many beneficial insects such as the parasitic wasps (trichogramma, braconid, chalcid, and ichneumon wasps), lady beetles, lacewings, sand wasps, syrphid and tachinid flies, green lacewings, minute pirate bugs, big-eyed bugs, assassin bugs and predaceous wasps.

There are a number of native wildflower Umbelliferae. Hairy Angelica *(Angelica venenosa)* is an attractive, white-flowered, long-blooming, widespread perennial not cultivated because it's reputed to be poisonous, though wrongly, speculate Duncan and Foote.[12] Rattlesnake weed (*Daucus pusillus*) is an annual, similar to the introduced Queen Anne's lace, but smaller. Pennyworts or dollar grass (*Hydrocotyle* species) are perennials frequently considered weeds. *H. bonariensis* is found in sandy soils and near saline and brackish marshes. *H. umbellata* and *H. verticillata* are found in wet places, including lawns. You've probably seen them, though you may not have noticed their parsley-family umbels. They will do as moist area ground covers. Golden parsnip, heart-leaved Alexander (*Zizia aptera*), golden Alexander (*Z. aurea*), and *Z. trifoliata* are yellow, spring-flowering perennials.

The following introduced herbs, ornamentals, or weeds, all European or Eurasian, may attract beneficials and host black swallowtail butterflies: Bishop's flower (*Ammi majus*), dill (*Anethum graveolens*), angelica, archangel or wild parsnip (*Angelica Archangelica*, *A.* species), caraway (*Carum carvi*), fennel (*Foeniculum vulgare*), Queen Anne's lace (*Daucus carotus*), parsley (*Petroselinum crispum*).

Urticaceae (Nettle Family) There are native nettles and naturalized species from other parts of the world. In spite of their weediness and their armor of stinging hairs, some—such as Eurasian stinging nettle (*Urtica dioica*)—are cultivated as ornamentals and for medicinal and other uses. Insects will appreciate their flowers; nettles host larvae of comma, American painted lady, and red admiral butterflies.

Valerianaceae (Valerian Family) The Mediterranean native red valerian or Jupiter's-beard (*Centranthus ruber*), is a garden perennial whose round-clustered flowers are good butterfly nectar sources.

Verbenaceae (Vervain Family) There are several species of low-growing, colorful, long-blooming *Verbena* species native to the United States. But those most visible along roadsides in the Southeast are naturalized South American species. These and the garden hybrids, readily available in nurseries and through seed catalogues, are nectar sources for bees. They may host larvae of the buckeye butterfly and the rustic sphinx and verbena moths. Most wild native verbenas, usually called vervain, are erect, rangy plants with spikes of dense, tiny, not very showy flowers. Hoary vervain (*V. stricta*) hosts larvae of the fine-lined sallow moth.

Violaceae (Violet Family) Violets (*Viola* species), both indigenous and introduced, abound in wild and garden settings of the Southeast. They are valuable ground-cover perennials for shady and partly shady settings. They are prolific self-seeders. Their seed and sometimes flowers and leaves are eaten by dark-eyed junco and other finches, ruffed grouse, common ground doves, and cardinals. Certain types of violets host larvae of the variegated fritillary. They are larval host for the dolichos armyworm, grateful midget, and nais tiger moths.

Ferns for Wildlife Habitats

Can you picture a forest without ferns? A shady backyard forest shouldn't be without them, either. Ferns provide cover for wild things that live on and lurk near the ground, for predators and prey. Ferns supply nesting material for birds such as ruby-throated hummingbirds that line their nests with cinnamon fern down. Like the flowering plants, they are habitat for a host of insect associates such as the fern scale and its predator, the beneficial brown lacewings that frequent forests. The following moths are just a few of the species with larvae that feed within ferns, pupate, and emerge as adult members of the food chain:

American angle shades, Virginia chain fern borer, bracken borer, osmunda borer and the sensitive fern borer.

Following are species recommended for garden use.[13] Review the ones listed in "Profiles of Some Common Southeastern Plant Communities/Wildlife Habitats" in chapter 3 to find their plant associates.

WET SOIL

Lorinseria areolata, netted or small chain fern, net-veined chain fern
Matteuccia struthiopteris, ostrich fern
Osmunda cinnamomea, cinnamon fern
O. regalis, royal fern
Woodwardia virginica, Virginia chain fern

MOIST SOIL

Adiantum pedatum, northern maidenhair fern
Athyrium filix-femina, southern lady fern
A. pycnocarpon, glade fern
A. thelypterioides, silver glade fern
Cystopteris protrusa, brittle or fragile bladder fern
Onoclea sensibilis, sensitive or bead fern
Thelypteris hexagonoptera, broad beech fern, southern beech fern
T. kunthii, widespread maiden fern
T. palustris, southern marsh fern

WELL-DRAINED UPLAND SOILS

Asplenium platyneuron, ebony spleenwort
Dryopteris marginalis, marginal wood fern, marginal shield fern
Polystichum acrostichoides, Christmas fern
Pteridium aquilinum, bracken fern

FOR LEDGES AND CREVICES OF ROCK WALLS OR IN COBBLE

Asplenium platyneuron, ebony spleenwort
Asplenium trichomanes, maidenhair spleenwort
Cheilanthes lanosa, hairy lip fern
Polypodium virginianum, rockcap fern, common polypody
Pteris multifida, spider brake

LIME-LOVING FERNS FOR CREVICES IN LIMESTONE OR MASONRY

Adiantum capillus-veneris, southern maidenhair or venus hair
Camptosorous rhizophyllus (=*Asplenium rhizophyllus*), walking fern
Pellaea atropurpurea, purple cliff brake
Pteris multifida, spider brake

GROUND COVER FERNS

Athyrium filix-femina, southern lady fern
Dennstaedtia punctilobula, hay scented fern
Dryopteris marginalis, marginal wood fern, marginal shield fern
Polystichum acrostichoides, Christmas fern
Pteridium aquilinum, bracken fern
Thelypteris noveboracensis, New York fern
Equisetum hyemale, scouring rush, horsetail
Lycopodium digitatum, running ground pine or ground cedar
L. species, club mosses
Selaginella apoda, meadow spikemoss

Grasses for the Wildlife Habitat

Where will you plant your flowers? Probably where you always have, in collections of your favorite specimens in conventional beds and borders. You may integrate native species with exotics, or grow only indigenous flowering plants. If you're really open to experimentation, you may try native grasses, rushes, and sedges along with perennial flowers—there are specimens every bit as beautiful as the Argentine pampas grass and imported bamboos we have cultivated in our gardens for years. If you're seeking the ultimate adventure in habitat re-creation, you will design a small savannah, a mini-meadow or pocket-prairie, using plants typical of savannah, meadow or prairie communities that exist in your region.

Meadows are grasslands in areas of high rainfall. They persist as subclimax stage grasses and perennial wildflowers because they are mowed or grazed, in which case they are pastures. Natural meadows are found in places where insufficient rainfall, fire, bedrock, soil characteristics or other conditions prevent succession to climax forest. Prairies are grasslands in areas where rainfall is inadequate for trees to grow. Savannahs occur where grasslands meet adjacent forests; they consist of grasses and widely scattered trees.

Savannah/meadow/prairie flowers do not occur in the dense zones of color seen when bedding plants are used in formal gardens. Because of the grasses, the effect is more subtle. Tall grasses provide support for herbaceous perennial wildflowers; when the same plants are grown as isolated specimens in gardens, they must be staked, pruned, or allowed to sprawl.

Members of the prairie restoration movement that began in the midwest in the 1930s have developed practical procedures for establishing meadows and prairies on properties large and small. Such landscaping provides sources of food, cover, and habitat for several orders of wildlife and can be a lot less expensive to maintain, once established, than a turf-grass lawn. But there's more to it than opening a meadow-in-a-can and broadcasting seeds—lots more. Vigilant action to eradicate invasive alien plant species is part of the preparation, and weeding is also very important for the several years it can take to establish a meadow. Periodic mowing, a substitute for natural fires, is important for long-term maintenance.

The mixtures of seeds sold for growing "wildflower meadows" will not produce meadows—they contain no grasses. They include flowers such as Queen Anne's lace and cornflower, introduced by European settlers to this country and now naturalized, and flowers such as California poppies that are native to North America but only to western regions. Use them, if you wish. But do not mistake the results for a true meadow.

For more information on planting prairies and making meadows, see *Gardening With Native Wild Flowers* (Jones and Foote), *Nature's Design: A Practical Guide to Natural Landscaping* (Smyser, Rodale Press), *Native Gardening in the South* (Fontenot), *Landscaping with Wildflowers & Native Plants* (Wilson, Ortho Books) and *Requiem for a Lawnmower and Other Essays on Easy Gardening with Native Plants* (Wasowski). To see pine savannah and other plant communities of the Pearl River drainage basin, visit the Crosby Arboretum in Picayune, Mississippi.

Patches of native grasses and sedges in a garden can offer the same benefits to wildlife that they would in a wild setting: a green feast to grazing creatures like white-tailed deer, a banquet of pollinating insects for songbirds, and seeds for voles, mice and other ground-level foragers. A sedge meadow provides safety and food to ground- or shrub-foraging birds, rails, grouse, and sparrows, which eat their triangular seeds. Tall stalks are perching places for singing yellowthroats and swamp sparrows. Insects attracted to the rank growth are food for wrens, swallows, and snipes. Many species of the Satyridae Family of butterflies, satyrs and wood nymphs feed on grasses and pupate on the earth or in mulch or other surface debris.

Bermuda grass (*Cynodon* species) sometimes used as a lawn grass and many times considered a weed, and crabgrasses (*Digitaria* species) some indigenous, some introduced, are larval host plants for fiery skipper butterflies and sachem butterflies. *Andropogon* species, beard grasses, may host larvae of the cobweb skipper butterfly. Various species of grasses host larvae of the broken dash, Carolina satyr, fiery skipper, ocola skipper, least skipper, little glassy wing, southern skipperling, tawny edged skipper, Peck's skipper, and Eufala skipper butterflies and of the feeble grass, small brown quaker, ruddy quaker, striped garden caterpillar, vagabond crambus, microcrambus elegans, and *Urola nivalis* moths. Elachistid moth larvae are leaf miners in grasses and sedges. Grasses such as *Paspalum* species host larvae of the whirlabout butterfly. *Erianthus* species host larvae of the Delaware skipper and clouded skipper butterflies.

Where can you buy grasses?

• More and more nurseries are carrying species of grass. Take a book that lists natives with you, for nursery labels frequently do not differentiate natives from exotics.

• Identify the grasses growing in your region. Collect seeds that you yourself can germinate. *Andropogon glomeratus*, for example, is a formidable lable. It is the botanical name for bushy beard grass or bluestem, "an exceptionally handsome and well behaved ornamental grass"[14] with stems that take on a bluish cast during part of the growing season. But who would think I'd find it along the railroad tracks by the levee just up Magazine Street from my home? Why, I've driven by there daily for years, dreaming of exotic plants in faraway places and failing to see beauty growing at my feet! No more!

• Examine carefully what grows in your own backyard. I assumed that an attractive, low-growing grass that clung to shady spots in my backyard was a useless weed. Had to be if it just came up there, right? It sent up regiments of wispy stalks that leaned in precise angles toward the light, but stopped growing just short of the shade's edge. So pretty! How pleased I was to find it looking like the drawing of basketgrass (*Oplismenus setarius*) in *Grasses of Louisiana*. Author Charles Allen offered vindication: "Basketgrass is very shade tolerant and should be considered as potential groundcover plant to replace the introduced plants such as monkey grass."[15] The American tropical basketgrass (*Oplismenus hirtellus*) is frequent in southeastern edges and forests, too.

Names of some native grasses recommended for garden use follow.[16] Grow the ones natural to your ecological region in conditions that duplicate the ones where they are found. Check "Profiles of Some Common Southeastern Plant Communities/ Wildlife Habitats" in chapter 3 to find natural associates of some of these grasses.

Grass Family (Gramineae or Poaceae)

Aira caryophyllea, hairgrass (dry habitat)
A. elegans, hairgrass (dry habitat)
Andropogon gerardii, big bluestem, turkeyfoot
A. glomeratus, bushy beard grass, bushy broom sedge
A. ternarius, splitbeard bluestem
A. virginicus, broom sedge
Anthaenantia rufa, purple silkyscale (wet habitat)
A. villosa, green silkyscale (wet habitat)
Aristida stricta, wiregrass, three-awn grass
Arundinaria gigantea, native bamboo, canebrake

Bothriochloa species, silver bluestem
Bouteloua curtipendula, side-oats grama
Chasmanthium latifolium, upland sea oats (low light)
Coelorachis cylindrica, Carolina jointgrass
C. rugosa, wrinkled jointgrass (wet habitat)
Ctenium aromaticum, toothache grass (wet habitat)
Eragrostis secundiflora, lovegrass (dry habitat)
E. spectabilis, purple lovegrass (dry habitat)
Erianthus contortus, plume grass, beard grass
E. giganteus, sugarcane plume grass
Glyceria arkansana, Arkansas managrass (wet habitat)
Gymnopogon species, skeletongrass
Leersia virginica whitegrass (low light)
L. species, cutgrasses (wet habitat)
Leptoloma cognatum, fall witchgrass (dry habitat)
Limnodea arkansana, Ozarkgrass (dry habitat)
Melica mutica, melic grass (low light)
Muhlenbergia capillaris, pink muhly, hairgrass (dry habitat)
Oplismenus setarius, basketgrass
Panicum subgenus *Dechanthelium*, panic grasses (low light)
Panicum amarum, beach panic grass
P. brachyanthum, pimple panicum (dry habitat)
P. gymnocarpon Savannah panicum (wet habitat)
P. scabriusculum, panic grass (wet habitat)
P. virgatum, switch grass (wet habitat)
Paspalum repens, water paspalum (wet habitat)
P. species, paspy grasses
Poa autumnalis, autumn bluegrass (low light)
Polypogon monspeliensis, rabbitfootgrass
Schizachyrium scoparium, little bluestem
Sorghastrum nutans, Indian grass, Indian reeds

S. elliottii, slender Indian grass
Spartina pectinata, slough grass, prairie cordgrass
Sphenopholis species, wedgescales
Sporobolus species, dropseeds (dry habitat)
Stipa avenacea, S. leucotricha, needlegrasses (low light)
Uniola paniculata, sea oats

Sedge Family (Cyperaceae)

Carex grayi, Gray's sedge
C. laxiflora, C. pennsylvanica, C. plantaginea, C. platyphylla, other
   sedges
Cymophyllus fraseri, Fraser's sedge
Dichromena colorata, whitetop sedge, starrush
Eleocharis montevidensis, spikerush, spikesedge

Rush Family (Juncaceae)

Juncus coriaceus, J. canadensis, J. dichotomus, J. scirpoides, rushes
Luzula echinata, L. bulbosa, L. acuminata, L. multiflora, wood
   rushes

CHAPTER NINE

Water in the Wildlife Garden

Aquatic Environments: The Pond

I HEAR OF LUCKY PEOPLE in uptown New Orleans who look out their back windows and see a great egret or green heron perched on the edge of their garden pools stalking goldfish. And they don't even think they're lucky! They get mad because those magnificent birds are eating their goldfish. Great egrets and black-crowned night herons fly right over my garden and don't look twice at my little pond. I would sacrifice

Illustration: Pickerel weed, water clover, water lily, bullfrog, dragonfly

any number of fish and maybe even a few frogs for a heron in my garden!

It's not that I'm dissatisfied with the creatures that do live in my wildland. Even a small pond, three feet by four feet and two feet at its deepest with a birdbath dish fountain at one end, like mine, will be a watering hole for birds and mammals and a habitat for the frogs and toads and insects that spend all or part of their life cycles in water. I introduced goldfish, minnows caught in local lagoons, and bullfrog (*Rana catesbeiana*) and leopard frog (*Rana sphenocephala*) tadpoles from a biological supply house because I doubted my urban garden would lure those species, but other creatures have come on their own.

Gulf Coast toads (*Bufo valliceps*) arrived first, announcing the coming of spring with their mating "song," an impressive low trill, guttural and nonmelodic. Within days of their mating, tadpoles hatched—so many that the water was cloudy. Goldfish began to die. In succeeding years, I would fling out excess toad eggs the morning after an orgy, but I finally replaced the goldfish with native minnows. They breed and their population seems stable even with tons of tadpoles.

My first real frog was the green tree frog (*Hyla cinerea*), an emerald creature that makes a "quonk, quonk, quonk!" sound as loud as the call of the toad. We spot them with flashlights and watch their throats balloon in song. Once my ears were tuned, I would note each anuran addition to my yard by the new song in the garden chorus. With a tape of frog and toad calls and Dundee and Rossman's *Amphibians and Reptiles of Louisiana* as a guide, I've identified the new arrivals to the garden: the tiny, introduced greenhouse frogs (*Eleutherodactylus planirostris*) with their cricket-like chirps, and southern cricket frogs (*Acris gryllus*), which make a nasal "gick-gick-gick" sound.

Leslee Reed, with the help of a tape, identified a bronze frog (*Rana clamitans*) who found his way to the pond in her urban garden just a few blocks from mine. His song is a series of banjo-like plunks. She's also hosted a pointy-nosed pig frog (*Rana grylio*) and a bullfrog, Jeremiah, whose spring and summer serenade was a resonant "brrrwoooom!" He left suddenly during torrential rains after several years as master of the pond.

Though all frogs and toads require moisture to breed, some species, like leopard frogs, are less dependent on water than others. Because bullfrog tadpoles can take several seasons to mature, they require a permanent source of water. Where did Jeremiah and my biological house leopard frogs who matured and disappeared go? Maybe New Orleans is like Augusta, Georgia. John Dennis says that bullfrogs, abundant in residential areas of that city, migrate from one goldfish pond or swimming pool to another through networks of interconnecting drains that underlie the city![1]

Graceful, beautiful dragonflies and damselflies (Order Odonata) are another of the rewards bestowed on the pond-builder. They are predaceous on other insects, mostly midges and mosquitoes, and they will appear in any garden where insects abound. But since they spend their lengthy larval stage in water, a pool will be a mighty lure. Adult dragons and damsels drop their eggs directly into the water or deposit them within plant tissue, mud, sand, or submerged logs. Eggs hatch into aquatic nymphs that lurk in silt, vegetation or debris on the bottom preying on insects, tadpoles, fish and other tiny creatures. After a year or more in the larval stage, the nymph climbs partially out of the water on the stem of a water plant. Its skin splits down the middorsal line; the adult emerges, shivers as its wings fill with blood, then takes flight. If you're lucky you'll get to watch.

I've only found dried morning-after nymphal skins with lifeless legs still clutching pickerel weed stems.

Some summer days there may be fifty dragonflies patrolling my garden all at once, their crystalline wings and multi-iridescent colors sparkling in the bright sunlight. They are legacies of the neighborhood ponds.

THE POND AS A HABITAT

A body of water is a habitat, just as the soil and terrestrial habitats are. And like the others, aquatic habitats host complex webs of flora and fauna that interact to create a balance, and, where untouched by humans, to undergo succession. What is the climax stage in pond succession? The same as the climax

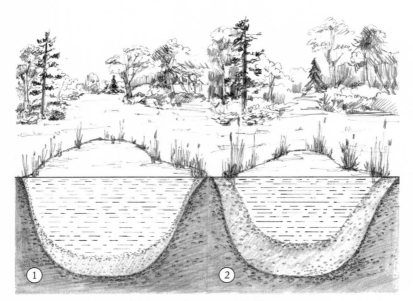

Pond succession: four stages in the filling of a pond

terrestrial stage for the region! Obviously, you'll have to perform the maintenance activities necessary to keep your backyard pond from filling in and becoming a marsh, then a swamp, then a terrestrial environment. Luckily, it doesn't happen that quickly.

Klots's *The New Field Book of Freshwater Life*[2] classifies organisms in aquatic environments as follows. See if this sounds familiar.

1) Producers: photosynthetic and chemosynthetic organisms that manufacture food, chiefly bacteria and protists (one-celled organisms such as algae, protozoans, flagellates and fungi); secondarily, higher plants.

2) Consumers: primary consumers (the plant eaters) that eat green plant material. They are herbivorous insects (corixids, the

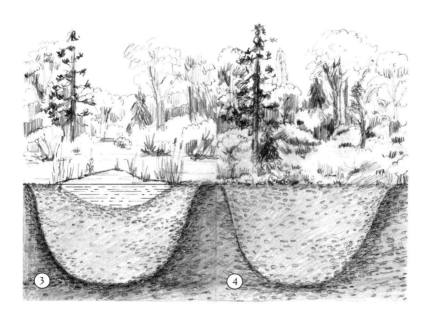

water boatmen; haliplids, the crawling water beetles; caddis fly larvae; the few aquatic pyralid moth caterpillars), crustaceans and fish. Of secondary importance are rotifers (microscopic animals that make up plankton), protists, gastropods (snails), worms, tadpoles and a few fishes.

Secondary consumers, plant eater-eaters, eat primary consumers or other secondary consumers. They are carnivorous insects, most vertebrates, and parasites.

Processors, detritus feeders, are rotifers, bryozoans or moss animalcules (tiny plant-like, colony-forming animals that form fern-like overlays on lily pads and gelatinous balls that float in pond water), tubifex worms, midge larvae, some caddis fly larvae, some mayfly and stonefly nymphs, some molluscs, and some fishes.

Scavengers feed on dead or decaying plant or animal material. They include some ciliates, many worms, crustaceans, hydrophilid or water scavenger beetles, some molluscs, and a few fishes and turtles.

3) Reducers: organisms that change organic material back to inorganic, after which it may be used again. They are bacteria and some fungi.

Will all these creatures appear in your pond? You can introduce the plants and some of the animals. But for the rest, you'll have to wait and see!

On Building and Balancing a Pond

There are many references on building ponds. I suggest you start by reading the catalogs/guides to water gardening from aquatic consultants such as Van Ness Water Gardens and Lilypons Water Gardens. They've perfected backyard systems. Even if you do not want to use their products, their books are useful resources.

When you first introduce plants, soil, fish and snails, in the species and numbers suggested by experts, the water in your pond will pass through stages of murkiness as algae levels build and change in response to levels of light and as plants and animals interact. Fish absorb oxygen in the water through their gills, excreting carbon dioxide and other wastes. Water plants absorb carbon dioxide from animal life and decaying matter, and, through the process of photosynthesis, convert it to carbohydrates needed for plant growth, releasing oxygen, a byproduct, back into the water. Algae competes with plants for oxygen. Snails, fish and other creatures eat algae. So, everything's eating everything just as in terrestrial systems. You'll know your pond is balanced when the water is clear and clean, unless yours is a "real" pond, not one defined by a liner or concrete. A pond dug in silty soil will not be clear and clean even when it is in balance.

A friend called to tell me the goldfish in his pond were all of a sudden dying. "Did your pump burn out?" I asked.

"I unplugged it. A guy at the plant place told me if I have plants in the pond it will be balanced and I won't need the pump!"

"Plug it in!" I told him. "Your pond is balancing itself right now. The fish will keep dying until there is a balance!" Obviously, he had introduced more fish than the oxygen level of the pond, even with aerating plant life, could support without mechanical aeration.

The rule of thumb, as stated in *Water Visions '93* from Van Ness Water Gardens[3] is: "A healthy, balanced pond has no more than fifteen inches of fish per square yard of surface area. That is one fifteen inch fish or two seven inch fish, but no more."

Use a recirculating pump to prevent your pond from becoming stagnant and to make water noises that attract birds and soothe beasts. With increased oxygen content of the water, you'll be able to keep more fish than would be possible in the same volume of still water.

Once you achieve a balance among flora and fauna, the less you do and the more you leave your pond to develop "naturally," the more wildlife will live there. You'll need a magnifying glass and microscope to see some of it.

Aquatic Animals

Goldfish are carps. Along with native carp and the more than two hundred species of North American minnows, they belong to the family Cyprinidae. Since an important part of fish diet is larvae of noxious mosquitoes, fish are a requirement in any pond. They also eat excess plant material, algae, aphids, other insects and larvae. Once your pond is balanced, they do not need to be fed anything else.

Goldfish are pretty, but one reason I prefer minnows is that they are too small to eat frog tadpoles. No creature seems to like the taste of toad tadpoles. Larger fish should not be introduced until plants are well rooted and the pond well established.

Snails (phylum Mollusca, class Gastropoda) are another creature necessary for balance in the artificial pond or aquarium. Pond snails belong to the family Lymnaeidae. They eat algae and scavenge organic debris and wastes. Buy them or scoop them from local lagoons.

The painted turtle (*Chrysemys picta*) is the most common species occurring in the eastern United States and the water turtle most frequently offered in the pet trade. They will probably not find their way to your urban pond on their own. In natural settings, their diet is algae, duckweed, and some arthropods like dragonfly nymphs and crawfish. In a pond, don't be surprised if they eat your fish and small frogs and take bites out of your most expensive water lilies. Unless there is a protective edge around your pond, don't count on them not to sally forth into the world. They need sunlight and terrestrial basking and resting places; a floating log or board will do. Do not introduce them to your pond until plants are well rooted.

Aquatic Plants[4]

Plants should not be allowed to cover more than one-third of the water surface of a pool. They are habitat and food for lots of wildlife, including moths that have aquatic caterpillars. Natives are much more valuable to wildlife than introductions because of the many invertebrates evolved to associate with specific plants. All those invertebrates will be food for your fish.

SUBMERGED ROOTED AQUATICS

These plants are important because of their roles in oxygenating pond water and in providing shelter and cover for tiny creatures including newly spawned fish and frog tadpoles. The following are indigenous to the eastern or southeastern United States.

Cabombaceae (Water Shield Family) Fanwort or fishgrass (*Cabomba caroliniana*).

Hydrocharitaceae (Frog's Bit Family) Eel grass, water celery or tape grass (*Vallisneria americana*) is food for water fowl. *Paraponyx* caterpillars and several species of caddis fly larvae may live in cases cut out from its leaves.

Elodea, waterweed or ditchmoss (*Elodea canadensis*=*Anacharis canadensis*).

Najadaceae (Water Nymph Family) Common water nymph, naiad or bushy pondweed (*Najas guadalupensis*).

Ceratophyllaceae (Hornwort Family) Coontail or hornwort (*Ceratophyllum demersum*).

Haloragaceae (Water Milfoil Family) Water milfoil (*Myriophyllum pinnatum*).

FLOATING ROOTED AQUATICS

These are some of the great beauties and most useful wildlife plants of the water garden.

Nelumbonaceae (Lotus Family) Yellow lotus or American lotus (*Nelumbo lutea*) was used as food by Indians who cooked the starchy rhizomes and ground seeds to use in breads. It is invasive.

Nymphaeaceae (Water Lily Family) Examples of natives, available in the trade, are white water lily or pond lily *(Nymphaea odorata)* and spatter dock or yellow pond lily *(Nuphar advena)* with flowers that are more interesting than showy. Water lilies can be invasive. Many invertebrates are associated with flowers of this family, including *Paraponyx* caterpillars, which live in cases cut from water lily leaves; brown-tail diver caterpillars (*Arzama diffusa*); black-tail diver caterpillars (*A. vulnifica*), which live in water-filled burrows in the plant; and scatophagid flies that live larval and pupal stages in the submersed parts of the plants. *Galerucella nymphaea* beetles and *Donacia* water beetles feed, mate, or lay eggs on the plants.

Polygonaceae (Buckwheat Family) Water smartweed (*Polygonum amphibium*) is food for wild ducks and other aquatic birds.

Pontederiaceae (Pickerelweed Family) Pondweeds (*Potamogeton pulcher* and other *P.* species) are eaten by birds, muskrats, beaver, and deer. Insect associates include *Paraponyx* caterpillars that live in cases cut from its leaves, *Acentropis* species caterpillars that live in dense silken webs upon its surface, *Hydrellia* species fly larvae that mine in its leaves.

Umbelliferae or Apiaceae (Parsley or Carrot Family) Penny-worts and dollar grass *(Hydrocotyle umbellata, H. verticillata)* are perennials found in wet lawns and considered by many to be weeds. Van Ness Water Gardens says that *H. umbellata* resembles a miniature lotus and offers it as an aquatic plant at $6.25 each. Check lawns in your neighborhood before buying this plant. You may be able to save some money! Umbelliferous flowers may attract the beneficial parasitic wasps.

FREE FLOATING AQUATICS

These plants float on the surface and are not anchored in soil.

Araceae (Arum Family) Water lettuce *(Pistia stratiotes)* floats freely and is easy to thin if it becomes too abundant. Many insects, including mosquitoes, lay their eggs and find shelter amidst its basal leaves. Insects and their larvae are food for pond fish.

Lemnaceae (Duckweed Family) Duckweeds are the smallest of the angiosperms, or flowering plants. Species used for natural ponds or aquaria may include *Lemna, Wolffia, Wolffiella,* and *Spirodela*, or greater duckweed, the largest. All four may be intermixed in green layers over ponds. They can be easily thinned with a dip net to allow more light for submerged aquatic plants. They are food for fish and waterfowl. There are many insect associates. *Lemna minor*, the most common duckweed, is food for larvae and adult shore flies, *Lemnaphila scotlandae.* It hosts miner-larvae of a billbug or snout beetle. Many other insects lay their eggs on aquatic plants, including duckweeds, and emerging larvae stay to feed. Larvae of a pyralid moth and a caddis fly make their cases from duckweed fronds. Snails lay their eggs on duckweed; hydras and planarians browse over their surface; bristle worms cling to the undersides.

Pontederiaceae (Pickerelweed Family) Water hyacinth (*Eichnornia crassipes*) has become a serious pest in waterways of North America since its introduction from tropical America during the nineteenth century. Its flowers are beautiful. Its tangled roots are habitat for water snakes, salamanders, eels, and many aquatic animals.

EMERGENT AQUATICS

These plants grow with their crowns under one to six inches of water but may grow up on dryer soil.

Alismataceae (Water Plantain Family) Arrowheads or bull tongue (*Sagittaria* species) bloom with delicate white, yellow-centered flowers. They are waterfowl and snapping turtle food in natural settings. Dragonflies and snails visit the flowers and may play a role in pollination. Snails eat flower petals. Noctuid caterpillars, *Plusia verrisa*, and many other species are intimately associated with *Sagittarias*.

Araceae (Arum Family) Bog torch or golden club (*Orontium aquaticum*), white arum (*Peltandra sagittaefolia*), green arum or arrow arum (*P. virginica*).

Cannaceae (Canna Family) *Canna flaccida* is native to the Southeast; *C. indica* is tropical American, naturalized in the South. Plants host larvae of the Brazilian skipper and long-tailed skipper butterflies. Hummingbirds visit the red *C. indica* and the brightly colored, nectar-filled garden hybrids, some of which are called water cannas.

Cyperaceae (Sedge Family) Spikerush (*Eleocharis montevidensis*), three-way sedge (*Dulichium arundinaceum*).

Equisetaceae (Horsetail Family) Water horsetail (*Equisetum fluviatile*).

Gramineae or Poaceae (Grass Family) Wild rice (*Zizania aquatica*), southern wild rice, *Z. miliacea*. Seeds of both are eaten by waterfowl, marsh and shore birds and songbirds.

Iridaceae (Iris Family) Grow aquatic *Iris* species including the Louisiana irises for their attractive foliage; the blooming period is brief. Flowers may attract hummingbirds. Iris hosts larvae of the iris borer moth. Noterid beetles, burrowing water beetles such as *Noteris capricornis*, tunnel into the mud at the base of aquatic iris, piercing the roots for air. Some natives are Louisiana iris hybrids, *I. fulva, I. tridenta, I. brevicaulis, I. hexagona, I. versicolor, I. virginica. I. pseudacorus* is a yellow-flowered Eurasian species, naturalized and invasive, in parts of the United States.

Amaryllidaceae (Amaryllis Family) Swamp crinum or swamp lily (*Crinum americanum*) makes beautiful white flowers.

Marantaceae (Arrowroot Family) Powdery thalia (*Thalia dealbata*).

Marsileaceae (Water Clover Family) Water clover (*Marsilea vestita*) is a fern ally that makes an attractive terrestrial ground cover. It's emerald green and looks like four-leaf clover. I grow it at the wet edge of the bricks surrounding my pond.

Pontederiaceae (Pickerelweed Family) Pickerelweed or tuckahoe (*Pontederia cordata*) is a beauty that seems to bloom its purple flowers forever, attracting bees, dragonflies, and other insects. Caterpillars of *Arzama* species moths bore into pickerel-weed stems.

Ranunculaceae (Ranunculus Family) Cowslip or marsh marigold (*Caltha palustris*).

Sparganiaceae (Bur Reed Family) Bur reed (*Sparganium americanum*) hosts noctuid caterpillars, *Nonagria laeta*, which burrow into its stems.

Typhaceae (Cattail Family) Cattail (*Typha latifolia*), narrow leaf cattail (*T. angustifolia*). *Typha* species are rich sources of food for birds and small mammals. They attract aphids (fish food) and may be mined by caterpillars of *Arzama obliqua* and *Nonagria* *oblonga* moths, which, along with *Bellura* species caterpillars, may live in burrows in the leaves. They may be webbed by cattail moth caterpillars (*Lymnaecia phragmitella*) or punctured by snout beetles, *Colandra pertinax*. Cattails are being displaced in some natural habitats by Eurasian *Phragmites* species reeds, which are beautiful but are of little value to wildlife.

WETLAND PLANTS

These plants will grow in the wet area around your pond or birdbath or other damp or wet areas of your garden.

Cyperaceae (Sedge Family) Glaucous carex (*Carex glaucescens*), giant white-top sedge or giant sedge (*Dichromena latifolia*), white top sedge or starrush (*D. colorata*). Though other sedges are wind pollinated, *Dichromena* species attract insect pollinators.

Bullrush (*Scirpus cyperinus*).

Eriocaulaceae (Pipewort Family) Pipewort (*Eriocaulon compressum*) and other *E.* species are found in wet pinelands. They are herbaceous rosettes with small white flowers that grow on stalks.

Gramineae or Poaceae (Grass Family) The cut grasses (*Leersia* species).

Juncaceae (Rush Family) The rushes (*Juncus* species).

Malvaceae (Mallow Family) Several native hibiscus grow in wet soil naturally and will tolerate wet or dryer soil in the garden. Texas star hibiscus or wild red mallow (*Hibiscus coccineus*), smooth marsh mallow (*H. militaris*), woolly mallow (*H. lasiocarpus*), large flowered mallow (*H. grandiflorus*), rose mallow (*H. moscheutos*), rose mallow (*H. palustris*). Nectar attracts hummingbirds and insects.

Melastomataceae (Melastome Family) Meadow beauty (*Rhexia virginica*) produces rose-red flowers in midsummer.

Ranunculaceae (Ranunculus Family) Swamp buttercup (*Ranunculus septentrionalis*).

Saururaceae (Lizard's Tail Family) Lizard's tail (*Saururus cernuus*). I could have paid Lilypons $7.95 a plant, but I found lizard's tail growing in a shady spot near a leaky hose faucet in a flower bed in my own garden. Flowers are tightly clustered along curved spikes in summer. It is best confined to a container set in the ground to curtail its invasiveness. Larvae of buffalo moth bore into its roots.

Scrophulariaceae (Figwort Family) Monkey flowers (*Mimulus alatus, M. ringens*) are recommended for stream-side or bog plantings. Figwort family members may host larvae of the buckeye butterfly and the chalcedony midget moth.

Xyridaceae (Yellow-eyed Grass Family) Yellow-eyed grass (*Xyris caroliniana* and other *X.* species).

The Birdbath

A well-maintained source of water can attract more species of birds than most feeders, including some species that don't visit feeders. It's always fun to watch bathing birds, too, maybe even more fun than watching them eat. The water supply for birds may be as modest a container as a garbage can lid overturned on the ground and refilled daily with a hose or an old-fashioned concrete birdbath.

Here are some criteria for success:

• The most frequently used birdbaths have a nonslip surface, are dish-shaped and shallow at the edges, and slope gradually to a depth of two to two and one-half inches. Shallow areas will be used by small birds that like to stand or wade in shallow water while drinking. The traditional cast-concrete bath on a pedestal is the ideal.

• Place the birdbath in a safe spot. Naturally, birds bathe at ground level. But, if predaceous house cats are present, the bath on a pedestal will be safer. If hungry hawks patrol your yard, place the birdbath under protective cover of trees or a patio roof. Protective shrubbery should be relatively close by to allow the bird a private preening place after its bath.

• Birdbaths must be kept clean. Algae buildup will make the bottom slippery. A much-used bath will become fouled with bird droppings and other debris. Scour the bath bottom with a forceful squirt of the garden hose each day while you refill. Scrub thoroughly with a brush several times a year.

• Running, splashing or dripping water is an even greater lure for birds than still water. Be simple—punch a hole in the bottom of a bucket suspended over the bird bath—or be elaborate—use a fountain with an electrical recirculating pump. Use a mister during peak periods of bird activity (to conserve water); hummingbirds may take fly-though baths. Either design your own systems or buy ready-made bird bathing products.

CHAPTER TEN

Attracting Wildlife with Feeders and Houses

THERE ARE FAMOUS WILDLIFE GARDENS in every region—the ones everybody knows from magazine or newspaper coverage or word of mouth—such as Leslee Reed's New Orleans garden, Jan and Cornell Tramontana's tract in River Ridge, Louisiana, Lydia Schultz's backyard in Bay St. Louis, Mississippi, and Judy Toups's in Gulfport, Bob and Martha Sargent's estate outside of Birmingham, Patty Vanossi's

Illustration: Purple martins

suburban plot in Sunrise, Florida, and lots of places in Texas. Usually, they're known for the uncommon species of birds they attract.

Why are some yards hot and others not? In addition to food and nectar plants, a variety of habitats and water supply, the really celebrated wildlife havens sport "artificial" sources of food with the natural: feeders that dispense seed, suet, nectar and fruit for birds. The advantage of feeders is that they draw wildlife in close to present a better show. Bird feeders placed outside a picture window overlooking a wildlife garden can be better than Home Box Office!

According to a survey conducted in 1985, over sixty million people fed wild birds, more than hunted and fished combined. A more recent U.S. Fish and Wildlife Service pamphlet puts the number at more than eighty-two million. A simple enough pastime, you might assume, but, except to those who think a bird is a bird is a bird, there's more to the hobby than meets the eye. Birdseed guru Aeelred Geis, now retired USF&WS biologist, elevated birdfeeding to a science. Special Scientific Report No. 233, "Relative Attractiveness of Different Foods at Wild Bird Feeders," published in 1980 and based on Geis's research, is used by hi-tech backyard birders as the basis for developing efficient feeding plans that target certain species and eliminate others.

Study continues. Geis himself is now Director of Research for Wild Bird Centers and is quoted regularly in their newsletter, *Wild Bird News*. Cornell Laboratory of Ornithology's Project FeederWatch Seed Preference Tests use data collected at backyard feeders by volunteer participants across the country. New data are revealing greater variation in regional preferences than previously suspected. You can use information from ongoing studies, as well as your own backyard observations, to customize your feeding system.

Why make birdseed such a big deal? For one thing, it costs money. If you're buying birdseed mixes that include fillers not palatable to the birds in your region, you're throwing money away, no matter how inexpensive the product. And, assuming you want to entice the biggest number of birds and widest variety of species, if you use just any old seed mix, you'll fall short of your goal. But feeding birds doesn't have to be that complicated. You can let other people do the research. The most sophisticated plan, according to Geis, is the simple one that follows.

The Basic Plan According to Geis[1]

Ingredients should be served in separate feeders placed in different niches in your backyard habitat:

• Black oil sunflower seeds (also known as perodovic sunflower or oilseed) is good for perch-feeding birds, either in the shell or as hulled "hearts and chips" to avoid mess and waste. Oilseed appeals to a large number of "desirable" species of birds, and is not appealing to starlings, house sparrows, and cowbirds. If you only want to bother with one seed, this should be the one. There are some considerations. Smaller seeds take more time for birds to eat, thus producing longer bird performances at your feeder. Accumulations of oily seed hulls on the ground will attract rodents. You can avoid this problem by using hearts and chips, but the disadvantage is that birds gobble them faster on briefer visits, resulting in a shorter showtime.

• White proso millet (*Panicum miliaceum*) works well for ground-feeding birds, preferably on a platform feeder where it is dry and protected from contamination. House sparrows and cowbirds like it, but so do some sought-after species who don't eat oilseed: rufous-sided towhee, dark-eyed junco, chipping sparrow, tree sparrow, field sparrow, song sparrow, and red-winged blackbird. To foil the bad birds, avoid making concentrated little piles of millet; use it sparingly and spread it thinly.

- Niger, the black seed we call thistle, is relished by goldfinches, pine siskins, house and purple finches and others. Starlings do not like it. Serve it in a thistle sock or thistle feeder. It is expensive, though. Goldfinches will eat hulled sunflower seed, too.

- Beef suet in a suet feeder may attract woodpeckers, nuthatches, several species of warblers, and mockingbirds. Position the feeder so that it's inaccessible to birds without gymnastic ability, like starlings. Starlings do not like hardened suet.

- Nectar feeders for hummingbirds and orioles are nice, but unless alluring plants grow in your garden or nearby, hanging them will be wasted effort. Other species known to sample nectar in hummingbird feeders: brown-headed and white-breasted nuthatches, orange-crowned warblers, and house sparrows. Orioles will use hummer feeders, also. The reason to hang one specially designed for them is to reduce competition with the littler birds.

- Water. Many backyard birders will tell you that water is more important than food in luring birds.

Other foods are less popular as a whole, or popular with fewer species of birds. These would be the ones to try if you're interested in experimenting:

- The larger gray-striped or black-striped sunflower seeds are taken by many species, though not as many as oilseed.

- Safflower seed is relatively expensive and not as popular as sunflower seed, though cardinals, doves, chickadees, titmice, and house finches will eat it. Its advantage, however, to those whose bird feeders are raided by squirrels, is that squirrels do not like it. Neither do house sparrows.

• Cracked corn is inexpensive and attractive to many ground-feeding species such as mourning doves and juncos, grackles, and several species of sparrows. Unfortunately, starlings, house sparrows, and brown-headed cowbirds like it, too. Some people spread it on the ground to divert the nuisance species from their other feeders. Quail and pheasants will eat whole kernel corn.

• Red milo, or grain sorghum, is a cheap filler in commercial birdseeds, but is of limited attraction—except, new studies reveal, to birds of the Southwest and to starlings and brown-headed cowbirds.

• Whole peanuts and kernels are attractive to blue jays, titmice, chickadees, red-winged blackbirds, and several species of sparrows, but not to starlings. Avoid peanut hearts or bits: they are starling favorites.

• Peanut butter, mixed with corn meal or cereal so it won't stick to the lining of birds' mouths, is appealing to insect-eating birds. You can imagine ways to present it to the birds: on a pine cone, spread directly on tree bark, in a specially designed "peanut butter station" offered by birdfeeding specialty stores or catalogs, or in a suet basket when prepared as a cake. The following recipe for No-Melt Suet was devised by Alabaman Martha Sargent:

1 cup crunchy peanut butter
1 cup lard
2 cups "quick cooking" oats
2 cups cornmeal
1 cup white flour
1/3 cup sugar

Melt the lard and peanut butter in a microwave or stovetop pan. Stir in the remaining ingredients. Pour the suet mixture into a square container about two inches thick. Store the suet in your freezer. These suet cakes will not melt in warm winter weather or during summer temperatures.[2]

• Canary seed is used in commercial mixes. Mourning doves and a few species of sparrows like it, but they favor other foods. Undesirable house sparrows love it.

• Red proso millet is less attractive to desirable species than white proso millet; it is favored by house sparrows and cowbirds.

• Japanese millet and German (golden) millet are much less attractive to birds generally; German millet is preferred by nuisance house sparrows.

• In Geis's studies, buckwheat was found attractive to few species other than undesirable house sparrows and cowbirds; starlings did not like it. Even though birds will glean the following seeds from fields after harvest, they preferred oilseed and white proso millet at feeders: oats, rape seed, rice, flax, and wheat. Starlings like hulled oats—a good reason not to offer it in feeders.

• Breads and other baked goods, kitchen scraps, canned and soaked dog food are popular with lots of birds, especially nuisance starlings and house sparrows. They also mold rapidly.

• Mockingbirds love raisins. Orioles will eat oranges and other sweet fruits.

• Many birds find mealworms, larvae of beetles of the genus *Tenebrio*, a real treat.

What Species Will You See at Your Feeder?

The most widespread feeder species, according to recent Project FeederWatch results[3]: dark-eyed junco, American goldfinch, blue jay, downy woodpecker, mourning dove, house finch, house sparrow, northern cardinal, black-capped chickadee, European starling, white-breasted nuthatch, American robin, tufted titmouse, common grackle, pine siskin, red-bellied woodpecker, hairy woodpecker, purple finch, white-throated sparrow, red-winged blackbird, song sparrow, northern flicker, Carolina wren, American crow, Carolina chickadee, song sparrow, evening grosbeak, brown-headed cowbird.

The most common feeder species in the southeastern United States are northern cardinal, mourning dove, tufted titmouse, American goldfinch, and Carolina chickadee.

When to Feed Birds

Contrary to popular belief, which holds the reverse to be true, natural foods for birds are most abundant in fall and less so in late spring and early summer. But birds can be fed year-round, for, according to Geis, they are not dependent on feeding by humans at any time of the year. If your feeders are empty, they'll find food somewhere else. Thank goodness! Can you imagine having to find a neighbor to keep your bird feeders full when you go away on vacation?

Selecting a Bird Feeder

To avoid waste, use feeders designed to dispense each particular type of seed. There are lots of good ones on the market. The poorly designed ones can be dangerous. Two to avoid are those made of clear plastic with feeding ports an inch or larger in diameter and wood hopper feeders with plastic walls tight to the roof. Small birds may squeeze inside almost-empty feeders of these types and become trapped.

Though suggestions abound for safe feeding of birds on the ground, a platform feeder is safest. Do you have time to scrub a patio corner where you spread seed once a week with soap and disinfectant, or rotate ground-feeding areas over periods of several days, saturating each spot with boiling water between rotations? I don't. And I don't want to boil my soil wildlife, either.

Food in platform feeders can become contaminated with bird droppings, too. Platform feeders should be cleaned and disinfected with a weak bleach solution several times a year (some sources say weekly) and other feeders at least once a year. Feeders should be cleaned out if the seeds they contain are found to be moldy, and moldy seeds thrown away. Store seed in tight cans to prevent mold.

Managing the Hummingbird Feeder

The purpose of a hummingbird feeder, as with seed dispensers for other birds, is to bring hummers in for magical close-ups. The number-one rule for attracting them is to create a yard with the right flowering plants and lots of insects and spiders. Feeders alone won't do the trick, unless your neighbors grow the right plants. The ruby-throated hummingbird is the only species that breeds in the southeastern United States. Ruby-throats winter in Mexico and Central America, but may visit feeders in various parts of the Southeast from early March, when the first migrants north hit the Louisiana coast, through the second week in October, when the last of the southbound—but for a few stragglers who hang out until mid-December—depart.

Important feeder facts follow (from *Louisiana's Hummingbirds* by Nancy L. Newfield[4]):

Visible parts of hummer feeders should be colored bright red, an irresistible color to the little birds. Feeders should have bee guards. They should be easy to clean and fill. Perches aren't essential for these miniature hover-craft, but if your feeder has them, the birds will sit and sip and you'll get a really good look!

Hang feeders out of reach of cats. If you hang more than one, put them out of sight of each other so one territorial hummer can't claim and aggressively defend them all.

Maintenance is important, as always. Change solutions every two to five days, more frequently during hot weather when solutions may spoil quickly. Feeders should be taken apart and soaked in hot water and chlorine bleach (one cup bleach to one gallon of water), rinsed and dried each time they're refilled.

The nectar in flowers pollinated and visited by hummingbirds is made up of sucrose. A feeder solution should imitate nectar: one cup of cane sugar (sucrose) dissolved in four cups of boiling water; one to three in cold weather. Never use honey, which is dextrose, corn syrup, or fructose; they're not natural hummer food and honey spoils rapidly and can cause a fatal fungus disease.

You can take your feeders down in early fall everywhere except Gulf Coast areas. Ruby-throats have passed through by then; you're not likely to see another until spring. But Gulf Coast gardens planted with winter-blooming semitropical plants may lure western species of hummers that will stake out a garden for the entire season. Black-chinned and rufous are the most common winter residents, but buff-bellied and seven other species have been sighted in Louisiana and other gulf states.

You must maintain your feeders if a freeze occurs. When flowers and insects are frozen, sugar-water nectar is hummers' only source of food. To keep it from freezing, hang a light bulb nearby or temporarily change your formula to emergency proportions: one cup of sugar to one cup of boiling water.

Bird Feeders and Houses: The Dark Side

What's this about desirable and undesirable birds at the feeder? You may welcome all birds. There's lots to admire, even in the pesty species. The birds some consider a "nuisance" are thought to be so for good reason. Maybe you won't want to feed or house them, either, once you know what I know.

House sparrows (which are really weaver finches, not sparrows) are so ubiquitous as to be the generic bird to many novices. They and starlings have become urban wildlife, just like those other adaptable imports the Norway rat, the housemouse, and the German cockroach. They are creatures of disturbance climax.

The European starling was introduced to the United States via New York City's Central Park where eighty were released in 1872 by a society whose goal was to bring to this country all species of birds mentioned in the plays of William Shakespeare. European house sparrows were first imported, also to New York City, in 1850. It was mistakenly thought they would provide biological control for some agricultural pests. Both these birds are now abundant in all American cities.

They are both cavity nesters. So are our own native chickadees, wrens, titmice, woodpeckers, eastern bluebirds and neotropical migrant purple martins, tree swallows, and great-crested flycatchers. Because of habitat destruction by humans, there are now limited cavities for nest sites. The aliens have a competitive edge over our native birds. Feisty house sparrows attack adults of native species and kill their nestlings. Starlings are no darlings, either. They have displaced several species like the eastern bluebird. Even though they prey on ground-dwelling insect pests, their beneficial activities are offset by their aggressiveness and their ever-expanding population.

Brown-headed cowbirds are native seed and insect eaters adapted to edge habitat where they parasitize the nests of other species of North American birds. A female cowbird locates a nest, watches until it lies untended, then enters, kicks out an egg and lays one of her own in its place. Some birds notice and push out the alien egg or abandon the nest, but many others don't. The cowbird hatches faster than the host and gets a headstart on its smaller nestmates. Then, because it is larger, it takes a larger share of the food from its "parents," starving out their true babies. "But this is a natural phenomenon," you might say. "Who are we to intervene?" Problems exist not because of nature's plan, but because of humans' disruption of the balance.

Birds that nest in extensive forest or forest interiors are less adept than edge species at foiling nest parasites. As people have cleared native habitat, they have fragmented forests, creating much more edge than there used to be and bringing forest interiors a lot closer to it. Cowbird populations have proliferated with the edges. Whereas fifty species are estimated to have been parasitized in precolonial times, over two hundred species are parasitized, today, most of them neotropical migrants: many beautiful species of warblers, thrushes, the yellow-billed cuckoo, and the brilliant tanagers. Because they lack the compensatory mechanisms for dealing with parasites developed by edge-dwelling birds, some species have been pushed to the brink of extinction. Even more will be affected unless something is done. The "something" in certain areas is cowbird removal or cowbird extermination programs.

We can blame deforestation in tropical wintering grounds, but experts are placing even more of the onus on us; after all, the birds breed in this country. There's even more to the story. In *National Wildlife* (October/November 1994), Les Line quotes ecologist Richard Holmes, who (with Tom Sherry of Tulane University) studied predation in pristine, unfragmented forest in New Hampshire, finding that loss of American redstart eggs and nestlings was over 70 percent in some years. "'If we're getting this level of predation in a pristine ecosystem,' says Holmes, 'imagine what can happen to nesting success in a fragmented landscape where songbirds have to cope not only with increased pressure from predators but cowbirds as well.' The problem is especially acute in rural developments with roaming house cats and with bird-feeders that boost numbers of blue jays, squirrels and cowbirds."[5]

What can I as an individual do? I can join the Nature Conservancy and Conservation International. I can create backyard habitat to host the migrants as they pass through. I can avoid feeding—or housing—cowbirds, starlings, and house sparrows.

Attracting Birds with Houses: Purple Martin, Bluebird, Other

How can I avoid housing house sparrows or starlings? Put up a sign that says "Sold!"? Wouldn't that cause desirable prospective tenants to turn away, also? Housing birds, like feeding them, is more complicated than you might think. You can avoid complications altogether if, instead of hanging bird houses, you create a garden with the vegetation layers and habitat elements where birds can build their nests. But unless there are snags in your yard, you won't attract the birds that would use houses, anyway. And there is at least one species in the eastern United States that nests nowhere else but in man-made housing.

Accounts dating back to 1831 describe the hollowed-out gourds hung by Choctaw and Chickasaw Indians as houses for purple martins, a custom that may have started hundreds of years earlier. One theory is that a pair of cavity-nesting martins may have built a nest in a long-handled dipper gourd hung by Indians near a pond for use as a drinking ladle. Amused Indians may have hung more gourds. Baby martins, imprinted on their nesting gourds, would have returned to nest in them the next year and the year after, beginning the tradition. Once you share your garden with purple martins, you'll understand why the Indians would want them to return: their wonderful gurgly sounds, which serve as a gentle early morning alarm clock; their regular annual return heralding early spring and their departure marking midsummer; their sweeping flight patterns; their soap-operatic community drama close enough to watch. Purple martins of the eastern United States now nest only in man-made apartment houses or in artificial or real gourds hung in clusters Indian fashion and situated within one hundred feet of human homes. And it's a good thing they do, for the virgin forests with hollow trees the martins once used for nesting sites are gone.

Beautiful eastern bluebirds are the only cavity-nesting members of the thrush family. A symbol of happiness, they used to be common in open woodlands, meadows, and grasslands in the eastern United States. Their numbers have declined almost 90 percent over the past sixty years, partly because of reduction of habitat and nesting cavities, and also because extremely aggressive alien house sparrows and starlings have taken over many of the remaining natural nesting sites. Dr. T. E. Musselman originated the bluebird trail concept in the 1930s; he mounted a total of 102 birdhouses on wooden fence posts along forty-three miles of rural roads. Due to his efforts, populations of eastern bluebirds around his home in Quincy, Illinois, were reestablished. His model has been copied by bluebird lovers in other places with the same happy outcomes.

There are secrets of success with birdhouses. And there is a case for saying that if you aren't going to do it right, don't do it at all. First, I'll tell the secrets!

Birds will not nest in any old house, and any old bird will not nest in a house—unless, of course, you mean any old house sparrow and starling. We've already discussed the reasons for not helping those guys out! The indigenous birds most likely to use backyard birdhouses in the southeast United States are some species that naturally nest in cavities: Carolina wrens, bluebirds, titmice, nuthatches, chickadees, purple martins, and great-crested flycatchers. They're called secondary nesters because they use existing holes, including old woodpecker nests. For woodpeckers, as primary nesters, excavating a nesting cavity is part of breeding behavior. But one source suggests that certain species—including flickers and red-headed woodpeckers—may "excavate" a nest box filled with sawdust, and downy woodpeckers may roost in birdhouses during winter. Some shelf nesters, such as robins, barn and cliff swallows, and eastern phoebes, may be induced to use a properly built house. Birds like owls, ducks, and kestrals may use specially constructed platforms or large nest boxes. The first step in your plan, however, is to determine which of the birds that will use birdhouses nest in your area. To find out, review field guides, visit your local nature and science center, contact your local Audubon Society or ornithology society. You're not going to attract birds that aren't there!

The second step is to buy or build a birdhouse that meets the specific requirements—that is, it duplicates significant elements of the natural nesting cavity—of the bird you want to attract. The critical factors, which vary from species to species, are the dimensions of the floor of the inner cavity, the depth of the cavity, the diameter of the entrance and its height above the birdhouse floor. How will you find the important numbers? For years, books and articles detailed dimensions derived from the same source: a U. S. Department of Agriculture paper based on field studies and published around 1920, a report on bird housing equivalent to Geis's report on bird feeding. Recent studies on nesting habits have been conducted by the U. S. Forestry Service. New nest box dimensions are listed in the free publication *Homes for Birds* (see Sources and Resources). Donald and Lillian Stokes offer some new perspectives in their book, *The Complete Birdhouse Book*. Even if you're buying a ready-made bird house, you should measure openings and dimensions and compare them with data from one of these sources to maximize chances that the house will suit the species you seek and minimize access to undesirable species and predators.

Whether you buy or build your birdhouses, look for design features that provide ventilation and insulation against heat and protection from predators. Do not use perches; they are not present before natural cavities, and, when installed on birdhouses, they make it possible for the undesirable, aggressive house sparrows to defend the birdhouse at the entrance. Light-admitting holes in house walls are important so that when the bird sticks its head through the entrance and blocks the light, it can still see well enough to inspect for predators.

Step three is to mount the house in the appropriate niche in a suitable habitat. If there is no water, cover, or sources of natural food for adult and baby birds nearby, or if other specific needs are not met, birds (other than house sparrows) are not very likely to use your birdhouse. The apartment-type house used by colonies of purple martins must be situated ten to twenty feet above the ground but in a clearing allowing at least twenty-five feet of swooping, diving, and circling space. But individual bluebird houses must be mounted three to six feet above the ground and twenty-five feet (some sources say seventy-five) apart to accommodate those birds' territorial requirements. In every case, metal guards and baffles, or other forms of protection from predators, are important. Even if you do everything right, you may wait two to three years for birds to decide to use a house. They must first decide that it is part of the natural scene. Be patient.

Step four is ongoing: maintain the birdhouse. Repair and clean it just before nesting season each year. Discard old nesting material after each nesting cycle for two reasons: (1) debris and droppings left in a nest may harbor avian mites, lice, and parasites; (2) nest building is an important part of courtship behavior. It is equally important to monitor nesting boxes for the presence of house sparrows and starlings. Discourage them by removing their nesting material and eggs, if it's gone that far. You may have to do this repeatedly, for they can be pretty persistent. But you must win the battle, for if you allow the aliens to nest in your house, you're not only *not* helping native birds, you are harming them by encouraging an increase of their enemies. The ultimate solution, which I, for one, would have difficulty enacting, is to "eliminate or destroy" adult house sparrows and starlings. The federal and state laws that protect wild birds, their nests and eggs, do not apply to the introduced species. Starling/house sparrow nest-box traps and books such as *How to Control House Sparrows* are available from the Purple Martin Conservation Association (see Sources and Resources).

I can personally attest to the pleasures of observing nesting purple martins. Seven years ago we constructed a house according to the plan in *Homes for Birds*, mounted it in time for the return of the martins to Louisiana in February, and on March 1 were rewarded with tenants who have since returned yearly. My immediate neighbors had paved the way by hosting colonies of martins; my birds were undoubtedly offspring of theirs. Since eastern martins are completely dependent on man-made housing and eastern bluebirds may continue their decline without help from human friends, do build houses for these species.

Providing birdhouses for other cavity nesters can be fun, but unless you, as landlord, accept certain responsibilities in their maintenance, artificial nesting cavities do more harm than good. The most important factor in attracting birds is proper habitat, whether or not you hang a birdhouse. Habitat should be the wildlife gardener's focus.

Feeding and Housing Other Wildlife

BEES

There are lots of species of wild bees, most of them solitary, like leaf-cutting bees, carpenter bees, and miner bees. Bumblebees and honeybees, the bees you are most likely to see in your garden, are social. Bees are important pollinators of flowers. One source quotes a botanist as saying: "Without bees to pollinate their flowers, one hundred thousand species of plants or more would perish from the earth."[6] With lots of bees in your garden, your plants will produce more fruit, more seed, and more food for other wildlife! That makes them pretty essential.

Honeybees, the most important pollinator of agricultural crops, are considered a domesticated animal because most of them live in man-made hives. They were introduced to North America by the pilgrims; Indians called them "white man's flies." Domesticated honeybees become even more important with habitat destruction, for numbers of wild or feral honeybees and other species of bees are decreasing. I never thought about keeping bees until I read the first paragraph in Sue Hubbell's *A Book of Bees:* "For a long, long time—for nearly forty years—I never had any bees. I can't think why. Everyone should have two or three hives of bees. Bees are easier to keep than a dog or a cat. They are more interesting than gerbils. They can be kept anywhere. A well-known New York City publisher keeps bees on the terrace of his Upper East Side penthouse, where they happily work the flowers in Central Park.

"I have had bees now for fifteen years, and my life is the better for it. . . ."[7]

Review Sources and Resources for additional information on beekeeping. The best place to start is the cooperative extension service in your county/parish.

I am going to The Nature Company tomorrow to buy a "bee condo" to attract native orchard or mason bees (*Osmia lignaria*), a glossy black species present in most North American gardens (according to catalog copy) and said to be an even better pollinator of flower and fruit trees than honeybees![8]

Butterflies

Gary Noel Ross, the first scientist to document trans-gulf migration by monarch butterflies, discovered that during March and October, enormous numbers of monarchs make pit stops on bright yellow offshore rigs in the Gulf of Mexico.[9] They love the color yellow, probably because goldenrod is yellow and they love goldenrod. It was just a matter of time before someone would capitalize on this knowledge and design a yellow nectar feeder to lure butterflies. It should work, but, as always, the flowers and larval host plants must be present or there won't be butterflies to come to the feeder!

Butterfly hibernation boxes provide a predator-proof shelter for butterflies that overwinter; in the southeastern United States that can include the cloudless sulphur, hop merchant, question mark, mourning cloak, and red admiral. Hang or mount your hibernation box in the shade. Supply a natural butterfly hotel, too: a log pile or Spanish moss.

BATS

Provide bats a place of honor in your garden with a bat house. Either buy one or build one yourself; in either case, the design should be based on ones developed by Bat Conservation International. Their new manual, *The Bat House Builder's Handbook*, describes the different requirements—crevice widths, box depths, roosting temperatures, and nearness to trees—of the dozen species of North American bats that will use bat houses.[10] In general, bat houses should be hung ten to fifteen feet above the ground and should face east or southeast. If you live in a hot climate, hang your bat house in the shade. Houses mounted on the side of buildings seem to be most successful at luring residents, but bat attracting is still a developing art. As with birdhouses, bat houses may be unoccupied for a year or forever, or they may be used from the very first night they are installed. Lure bats with an outside night-light mounted at least twenty feet high on a pole or tree to draw clouds of bugs.

Read *America's Neighborhood Bats* by Merlin Tuttle, head of Bat Conservation International. If you are like me, this book will quiet your fears and help you develop an appreciation, even a fascination, with bats. The examples of bat abuse will probably anger you; you may even become bat champion of your neighborhood!

Some of the species of bats found in the southeastern United States include southeastern myotis (*Myotis austroriparius*), eastern pipistrelle (*Pipistrellus subflavus*), big brown bat (*Eptesicus fuscus*), red bat (*Lasiurus borealis*), seminole bat (*Lasiurus seminolus*), Brazilian free-tailed bat (*Tadarida brasiliensis*).

Squirrels

What a love-hate relationship people seem to have with tree squirrels! "Squirrelly" is certainly not a complimentary term. But we seem to be divided on whether squirrels are greedy and destructive or clever and resourceful. Your philosophy will be reflected in your choice of approaches to feeding them in your wildlife garden. If you feed birds, the chances are very great that squirrels will find their way to your garden, also. Species found in gardens of the southeastern United States include gray squirrels (*Sciurus carolinensis*) and fox squirrels (*Sciurus niger*). Fox squirrels sometimes eat bird eggs!

If you enjoy tree squirrels, or if you begrudgingly feed them to divert them from your bird feeders, use dried corn or peanuts as choice lures. They also like any sunflower, in or out of the shell. If you do not want them sharing seed with birds, you can buy "squirrel-proof" feeders of various designs, with baffles and special mounting poles. Place your bird feeders up high or in the center of the yard away from any prominence that may serve as a launching pad for squirrels. But be ready to admire them when they thwart all your efforts.

Their manners leave much to be desired. They once chewed my tubular sunflower seed feeder in half to get the seeds. Even worse, I was told by a friend, the squirrels in Houma, Louisiana, hide behind tombs in cemeteries until funeral services are over, then run out and eat the flowers in the floral offerings, especially the carnations. "They like the juice. It's a terrible thing!" she says.

CHAPTER ELEVEN

The Urban Interface

Cats

I'M NOT SAYING A WORD ABOUT CATS! They're too touchy a subject. But just listen to what other people have said:

"The 'tabby' that sits curled up on your couch is not a *natural predator* and has never been in the natural food chain in the western hemisphere."

Migratory Songbird Conservation,
a U. S. Fish and Wildlife Service pamphlet

Illustration: Gray squirrel

"Although cats may play a useful role by eliminating sick or injured birds from the population, many become such skillfull predators that they also threaten healthy birds."

Wild Bird News, vol. VII, no. 3 (Summer 1993)

"We have little control over such predators as hawks and shrikes, other than limiting the ease in which they can prey on the birds we feed. Besides, raptors have a rightful place in nature.

"We can lessen the impact of cats, though. One of the most logical solutions is to keep cats inside. Unfortunately, this is not a popular attitude. . . . "

Craig Orr, "Feeding Birds Safely," in *WildBird* Magazine (November 1989)

"Estimates of the numbers of birds killed each year in the United States by house cats range from 50 million to 1.5 billion, an enormous drain on bird populations. . . . Lizards and frogs, also voracious consumers of garden insects, are also killed by house cats in even greater numbers."

J. V. Remsen, Jr., in *Attracting Birds to Southern Gardens*

"If you live in an urban or suburban setting, you should be aware that protecting and maintaining a variety of wildlife in the garden is not always easy. Domestic cats that roam from yard to yard are likely to prey on lizards, snakes and toads, and they also hunt down larger insects, such as black ground beetles, that are very important predators of pests."

Common-Sense Pest Control

"Cats.—These pets are one of the greatest obstacles in efforts toward increasing bird life in urban or suburban communities. . . . Vagrant cats often obtain much of their food during spring and summer from bird life and had best be eliminated from areas where birds are being encouraged. In thickly settled regions, live traps can be used effectively."

Out-of-print U. S. Fish and Wildlife Service booklet *Homes for Birds*
(Conservation Bulletin 14; revised 1979)

"If you are unwilling to eliminate free-roaming cats, do not attract birds to your yard by putting out feeders, nest boxes and baths. Eliminating free-roaming cats is the best way you can 'protect' your backyard birds from cat predation."

Backyard Bird Problems,
a U. S. Fish and Wildlife Service pamphlet

Strong opinions! Many wildlife lovers are cat lovers, too. What can we do? The people who made the comments above have the following suggestions:

Try putting a collar and bell on your cat. The bell will warn birds—unless the cat is lying patiently still, waiting to attack. And he probably is. Some cats become adept in removing collars. Declawing cats is not effective, either.

Cooperate with SPCA programs to spay and neuter cats, in an effort to eliminate strays and free-roaming cats. I have friends in Baton Rouge—other friends call their home the Stay and Spay—who take any strays that roam into their yard for a visit to the vet to be altered.

Keep your own cats indoors.

Dogs

Dogs are a threat to birds, too, especially to nestlings in spring and summer. We are less aware of their activity because they kill swiftly and do not parade around showing off their prey. As Craig Orr says, "They get into more obvious mischief than cats." But we are more likely to control our dogs than our cats.

Plate Glass Windows

Thud! I hate it when a bird flies into the large window over-looking my back yard. I first learned to identify yellow-rumped warblers as window kill. And finding ruby-throated humming-birds on the deck makes me wonder if the pleasure of seeing the birds up close is worth the pain of seeing them dead on impact. Project Feederwatch studies support the estimate proposed in 1990: between 100 and 900 million birds die in window strikes yearly.[1] Most deaths occurred when draperies were open and when the sun was not shining on the window. Though hawk silhouettes are avidly advertised, several sources state they are not much help in preventing bird-window collisions. Some suggestions:

1) Place feeders very close to the window. Birds must slow down to land on the feeder. If startled, they cannot attain a high enough speed to hurt themselves if they do fly into the glass.

2) Conversely, if too many strikes occur at a particular window, you may want to move feeders away from that window.

3) If your hummingbird garden, lush with blooming plants, is reflected in the window, definitely maintain a feeder at that window so hummers will fly to it, not to the "other garden" in the reflection.

4) Install windows with an inward tilt to reduce reflection.

5) Place a window guard—a grid of black and white adhesive strips—over as much of the window as you are willing to ob-scure. For more subtle protection, try black or green plastic mesh bird netting—designed to keep birds from fruit trees—mounted on frames installed about a foot away from your deadliest win-dows.

The Animals You Don't Want

The native rats and mice that may be attracted to your wildlife garden in the southeastern United States include marsh rice rats (*Oryzomys palustris*), harvest mice (*Reithrodontomys* species), cotton and white-footed mice (*Peromyscus* species), golden mice (*Ochrotomys nuttalli*), cotton rats (*Sigmodon hispidus*), and eastern wood rats, also known as "pack rats" or "trade rats" (*Neotoma floridana*). The mice are sweet little creatures! George Lowery, in *The Mammals of Louisiana,* says of the fulvous harvest mouse: "Dainty and otherwise attractive in appearance, it is always a source of delight."[2] Native mice eat weed seeds, grain, and green vegetation. Some may eat insects and crustaceans. The cotton rat causes some damage to farm crops and vegetable gardens, but it is also a major food source for hawks and owls, foxes, coyotes, bobcats, skunks, and weasels. Lowery describes the eastern wood rat as "scrupulously clean and well-groomed and almost wholly vegetarian."[3] The native rodents do not pose health threats and are fun to watch.

On the other hand, the introduced Norway rats (*Rattus norvegicus*) and roof rats (*Rattus rattus*), says Lowery, "are responsible for inestimable human misery."[4] They damage crops, contaminate large quantities of foods and stored grains, and carry diseases to which humans are susceptible. The preferred food of these rats is human garbage, especially grain in the form of bread. They will not eat raw or cooked vegetables.

The house mouse (*Mus musculus*) contaminates large amounts of food with its urine and feces, gnaws clothing, furniture, and upholstery, and spreads diseases like typhus.

The alien rats and mice live in buildings and are adapted to urban areas. Native mice sometimes try to enter suburban or rural homes in fall when the weather chills. Here is how you can host the natives in your garden without having them as house-guests and without encouraging the foreigners:

- Mouse-proof your house to exclude any mouse visitors. Do not build your brush pile habitat close to the base of your house.
- Stop feeding rats. Use rat-proof garbage cans for garbage. Make sure they are tightly closed at all times.
- Do not leave pet food out overnight. Put limited amounts of seed in bird feeders accessible to rats. Use hulled sunflower seeds to avoid ground buildup of the oil-soaked hulls that will attract rodents.
- Make sure any pet food, bird and even grass seeds that are stored in sheds and outbuildings are in rat-proof containers.
- Do not plant date palms, Algerian ivy (*Hedera canariensis*) or other plants rats live in or feed on.

Just as there are articles and books on attracting wild creatures to your property, there is plenty of information on how to keep them away! I like Rhonda Hart's *Bugs, Slugs & Other Thugs*. Obviously, living with some wildlife, mammals especially—deer, raccoons, squirrels, and rabbits—could have its down side. The exclusionary measures taken to deny house mice and Norway and roof rats access to your house and to exclude pigeons from your attic should work for squirrels, raccoons, and bats. Rat-proofing garbage and seeds stored in outbuildings should deter raccoons. I know that deer are a problem in some parts of the Northeast; there are many creative suggestions for discouraging them.

I would be so pleased to find any of the above animals, as well as chipmunks, ground squirrels, moles, voles, woodchucks, opossums, skunks, and any of the native mice and rats in my yard, that the tone of a recent home improvement article I read just didn't compute! One of the suggestions was interesting: use rock and roll music, especially heavy metal, to expel raccoons. Position a speaker near the lair and turn it on full blast!

I wonder what kind of music would *attract* raccoons?

Human Neighbors

A fastidious business associate invited me to stop by her new apartment to discuss some work issues, but other issues dominated the conversation. She had rented the ground level of a two-story residence. Her landlord lived upstairs. What she originally thought was a good deal had turned into a nightmare! On the phone, she described her situation. "My front entrance is in his side yard. It's a jungle! His grass needs cutting, and he's got all these wild plants growing up everywhere. He says they're rare species. I say they're weeds!

"He had this pile of old leaves he said was a compost heap right by my doorway. It cost me a fortune to haul them away. Then he complained I'd dug up one of his rare plants. He raked some more leaves, put them in bags, and left them sitting there in full view. And that grass! I know they must have weed ordinances around here! I could call and report him!"

What did I find when I got there? An example of the clash of cultures that's becoming less uncommon as more people turn to natural landscaping. I followed stepping stones in a healthy growth of St. Augustine grass, not manicured but barely ankle deep. They led through a side gate toward the entrance to my friend's abode. There was a fine old oak tree (*Quercus virginiana*) in the front yard and pecans (*Carya illinoensis*) and a black cherry (*Prunus serotina*) in the rear. Yaupons (*Ilex vomitoria*) lined the edge of the property on the left. The hedge of growth surrounding the house included old garden plants—"old lady plants"—

some known to become invasive but also known to attract hummingbirds. The stalks of cashmere bouquet (*Clerodendrum bungei*) and firespike (*Odontonema strictum*) that migrated out into the lawn had been allowed to stand. I saw oak-leaf hydrangea (*Hydrangea quercifolia*) with persistent brown flowers left from spring bloom, clumps of red-flowering *Canna indica* and sultan's turban (*Malvaviscus arborea* var. *drummondii*), some rusty-red-blossomed shrimp plants (*Justicia brandegeana*), and the red parrot lily (*Alstroemeria pulchella*) naturalized in New Orleans gardens. He needs some help, more native plants, I thought, but he's got the right idea! It was an embryonic wildlife garden.

Most of us would know better than to start a compost heap in view of the entrance to a neighbor's or tenant's home, or to stack bags of garden debris on someone's front lawn. That's asking for trouble. This guy was pretty inconsiderate. But when my friend shouted "weed ordinance," my hackles rose. What would she think of my garden? I don't have a lawn at all!

I live in an old neighborhood of nontraditional gardens. But, in a place where all the gardens are uniform, with sheared lawns, clipped hedges and beds of petunias, a fully developed wildlife garden is going to stand out. Things are changing, through efforts such as the National Wildlife Federation Backyard Wildlife Habitat Program and others by nongame divisions of state departments of wildlife and fisheries such as the Texas Wildscapes Program. It's still a good idea to make the transformation from traditional to natural landscaping slowly. Check local ordinances, first. Make sure your neighbors understand what you're doing. Be considerate of traditional neighbors by choosing plants that do not infringe on their gardens; i.e., do not plant suckering shrubs at the property line. Explain to neighbors that "wild" does not mean "neglected," that establishing a natural landscape by encouraging native or otherwise chosen species and limiting invaders can be very hard work until your natives are established. Explain that, because of all the destruction of native habitats, natural yards are critical habitat links for birds and other wildlife.

As a wildlife gardener, you must design for wildlife and for people at the same time. You must accept the challenge of creating the disorder that will appeal to wildlife while achieving an aesthetically pleasing garden. This is a new way to garden. There are few answers and much room for innovation!

You may look to the English gardeners' treatment of their perennial borders or to books like *Nature's Design* by Carol Smyser. Structure is the secret to organizing the lack of order. Lay boundaries of plants or basking rocks or decaying logs to demarcate pathways or encircle beds and to contain brambles and brushy growth. Erect trellises to direct twining, clinging vines. Place a sculpted concrete birdbath or other garden furniture to add a touch of symmetry where there's none. Give your imagination free rein. Let the garden be your own interpretation of characteristic natural features of your region.

Liz and Tony Bennett of Harlingen, Texas, recently won a fight to maintain their nontraditional garden of native plants. Their rewards? A green heron in their backyard and acknowledgment by Texas Wildscapes Program. But battles are being waged elsewhere. In Tulsa, Oklahoma, on June 4, 1994, Evelyn Connors was cited with violating a weed ordinance at the very moment five hundred visitors departed after taking a "natural habitat" tour of her property![5] It's as if native gardening were un-American! But what's so American about lawns and garden plants from the Orient?

I think one of the nice things about growing indigenous plants and luring native wildlife to naturally landscaped gardens is that in doing so, we pay homage to our country, to our state, and to our own ecological region. When I visited Manaus, Brazil, in 1991, I looked forward to seeing gardens of *Tibouchina* and yesterday, today, and tomorrow (*Brunfelsia* species)—beautiful Brazilian plants. But what I found was oriental hibiscus and the same magenta Madagascar periwinkle heavily grown in southern United States gardens. Daylilies, originally from Asia and Europe, were the cover flower for the May 1991 issue of the garden magazine *Sitios & Jardins*. I wondered: do gardens look the same the world over? Isn't that a shame!

If native vegetation is used in landscaping in such a way as to create habitats teeming with a diversity of indigenous creatures, the individuality and unique beauty of any particular place in the world would be expressed. We would grow our own gardens— with our own wildlife—and no one else's. In the words of Sara Stein, we could "Grow America!"[6] Even better, I could grow southeastern Louisiana. Zev MacGregor could grow San Francisco, California. Madeline Jean Delaney could grow North Ferrisburgh, Vermont. Amanda and Valerie Keim could grow Mesa, Arizona. Travis Bennett could grow Harlingen, Texas.

Shortcuts to a Wildlife Garden

Flowers by Season of Bloom

Choose flowers for your garden from each of the following families and groups for each season. This list, by no means complete, includes the most significant nectar and pollen plants for butterflies, bees, and beneficial insects and the most important seed producers. For birds to benefit from seed production, plants must be left in place after they finish blooming and until they dry and turn brown.

SPRING-BLOOMING FLOWERS

Asclepiadaceae (Milkweed Family)

Asclepias curassavica, bloodflower; *A. humistrata*, sandhill milkweed; *A. lanceolata* red milkweed; *A. quadrifolia*, four-leaved milkweed; *A. rubra*, red milkweed; *A. tuberosa*, butterfly weed; *A. variegata*, white milkweed; *A. viridis*, spider milkweed

Compositae or Asteraceae (Sunflower or Composite Family)

Achillea millefolium, white yarrow
Ageratum houstonianum, ageratum, floss flower
Bellis perennis, English daisy
Calendula officinalis, calendula, pot marigold
Centaurea cyanus, cornflower, bachelor's button; *C. moschata*, sweet
    sultan

Chrysanthemum frutescens, marguerite; *C. X superbum*, shasta daisy
Chrysogonum virginianum, golden star
Coreopsis lanceolata, tickseed; *C. tinctoria*, painted coreopsis, calliopsis
Echinacea purpurea, purple coneflower
Erigeron philadelphicus, daisy fleabane
Eupatorium coelestinum, mistflower, wild ageratum (sometimes blooms in
    April)
Gaillardia pulchella, firewheel, Indian blanket; *G. X grandiflora*,
    blanketflower
Hieracium venosum, rattlesnake weed, poor-Robin's-plantain
Rudbeckia hirta, black-eyed Susan; *R. amplexicaulis*, clasping leaf cone
    flower; *R. fulgida*, bracted coneflower
Sanvitalia procumbens, creeping zinnia
Senecio glabellus, butterweed, yellowtop
Spilanthes americana, creeping spot flower
Stokesia laevis, Stoke's aster, stokesia

Cruciferae (Mustard Family)

Barbarea vulgaris, winter cress, yellow rocket
Brassica species, wild mustards, ornamental cabbages, flowering kale
Cardamine bulbosa, spring cress
Cheiranthus species, wallflower
Erysimum species, wallflower
Iberis amara, rocket candytuft; *I. umbellata*, globe candytuft
Lobularia maritima, sweet alyssum
Matthiola incana, stock
Tropaeolum majus, nasturtium

Labiatae or Lamiaceae (Mint Family)

Conradina species, wild rosemary
Monarda citriodora, lemon bee balm; *M. fistulosa*, wild bergamot or bee
    balm
Prunella vulgaris, self-heal, heal-all

Pycnanthemum species, mountain mints

Rosemarinum officinalis, rosemary

Salvia coccinea, Texas sage, scarlet sage, tropical sage; *S. greggii*, autumn
   sage; *S. lyrata*, lyre-leaved sage, cancerweed; *S. miniata*, Belize sage

Thymus species, the thymes

Polygonaceae (Buckwheat Family)

Polygonum species, the knotweeds and smartweeds

P. lapathifolium, dock-leaved smartweed; *P. capitatum*, knotweed

Rumex crispus, curly dock; *R. hastatulus*, wild sorrel

Umbelliferae or Apiaceae (Parsley or Carrot Family)

Ammi majus, bishop's flower

Anethum graveolens, dill

Angelica archangelica, angelica, archangel, wild parsnip

Daucus carotus, Queen Anne's lace; *D. pusillus*, rattlesnake weed

Petroselinum crispum, parsley

Zizia aptera, golden parsnip, heart-leaved Alexander; *Z. aurea*, golden
   Alexander; *Z. trifoliata*

Leguminosae or Fabaceae (Pea-Legume Family)

Baptisia species, wild or false indigo

Erythrina herbacea, mamou, coral bean

Lathyrus latifolius, everlasting pea, perennial pea

Lupinus perennis, wild lupine; *L. subcarnosus*, Texas bluebonnet

Thermopsis caroliniana, Carolina lupine

Trifolium incarnatum, crimson clover; *T. pratense*, red clover; *T. repens*,
   white clover

OTHER SPRING-FLOWERING PLANTS

Agapanthus species, lily of the Nile, agapanthus

Alcea rosea, hollyhock (plant in fall for spring bloom in areas with hot
   summers)

Alstroemeria species, Peruvian lily

Amsonia tabernaemontana, blue star

Anchusa capensis, bugloss, cape forget-me-not

Antirrhinum majus, snapdragon

Aquilegia species and hybrids, columbine

Callirhoe papaver, poppy mallow

Camassia scilloides, wild hyacinth, eastern camas

Commelina species, dayflower

Consolida orientalis, larkspur, rabbit ears

Cynoglossum amabile, Chinese forget-me-not

Delphinium carolinianum, *D. tricorne*, *D. exaltatum*, *D. virescens*, native
   larkspurs

D. grandiflorum, Siberian larkspur

Dianthus species, pinks

Digitalis purpurea, foxglove

Euphorbia species, flowering spurge, wild poinsettia, milkweed

Filipendula species, meadowsweets, queen-of-the-pasture

Fragaria virginiana, common or wild strawberry

Gaura lindheimeri, gaura

Geranium species, cranesbills, wild geraniums

Hemerocallis species, daylily

Hibiscus coccineus, scarlet rose mallow, Texas star hibiscus; *H. moscheutos*,
   rose mallow; *H. militaris*, halberd-leaved rose mallow; *H. lasiocarpos*,
   woolly rose mallow

Ipomopsis rubra, standing cypress, scarlet gilia

Lathyrus odoratus, sweet pea

Linaria species, toadflax

Lithospermum carolinense, puccoon; *L. canescens*, hoary puccoon, Indian
   paint

Malva sylvestris, zebrina

Mitchella repens, partridgeberry

Myosotis sylvatica, garden forget-me-not

Nigella damascena, love-in-a-mist

Oenothera fruticosa, sundrops; *O. speciosa*, showy, pink, Mexican primrose
Opuntia species, prickly pear cactus
Penstemon digitalis, P. species, beardtongues
Phlox carolina, P. *glaberrima*, P. *maculata*, tall phlox
P. *divaricata*, blue phlox; P. *drummondii*, annual phlox
Ranunculus bulbosus, buttercup
Ruellia species, wild petunia
Russelia equisetiformis, coral plant, fountain plant
Saponaria ocymoides, S. *officinalis* soapworts
Silene virginica, fire pink; S. *caroliniana*, wild pink; S. *subcilliata*, scarlet
   catchfly
Sisyrinchium capillare, blue-eyed grass
Spigelia marilandica, Indian pink, pinkroot
Stellaria pubera, giant chickweed
Tradescantia virginiana, spiderwort
Verbena bonariensis, purple-top; V. *canadensis*, rose vervain, rose verbena;
   V. *peruviana*, Peruvian verbena; V. *rigida*, tuber vervain; V. X *hybrida*,
   garden verbena
Viola cornuta, viola; V. *tricolor*, Johnny-jump-up; V. species violets and
   pansies

Summer-Blooming Flowers

Amaranthaceae (Amaranth Family)

Amaranthus caudatus, love-lies-bleeding; *A. tricolor*, Joseph's coat
Celosia cristata, cockscomb
Gomphrena globosa, globe amaranth

Asclepiadaceae (Milkweed Family)

Asclepias curassavica, bloodflower; *A. humistrata*, sandhill milkweed; *A.
   lanceolata*, red milkweed; *A. rubra*, red milkweed; *A. syriaca*, common milkweed; *A. tuberosa*, butterfly weed; *A. variegata*, white
   milkweed; *A. viridis*, spider milkweed

Chenopodiaceae (Goosefoot Family)

Kochia scoparia var. *trichophylla*, summer cypress

Compositae or Asteraceae (Sunflower or Composite Family)

Achillea millefolium, white yarrow; *A.* species, yarrow

Artemisia species, wormwood

Bidens aristosa, beggar ticks, sticktight, sunflower

Centaurea cyanus, cornflower

Chrysanthemum frutescens, marguerite; *C. leucanthemum*, oxeye daisy

Chrysogonum virginianum, golden star

Cichorium intybus, common chicory

Coreopsis lanceolata, tickseed; *C. tinctoria*, painted coreopsis, calliopsis; *C.* species, coreopsis

Cosmos species, cosmos

Echinacea purpurea, purple coneflower; *E. vernus*, Robin's-plaintain

Eupatorium coelestinum, mistflower, wild ageratum; *E. fistulosum*, joe-pye weed; *E. rugosum*, white snakeroot

Gaillardia pulchella, firewheel, Indian blanket; *G. X grandiflora*, blanketflower, gaillardia

Helenium autumnale, sneezeweed

Helianthus species, sunflowers

Heliopsis helianthoides, oxeye

Heterotheca subaxillaris, camphorweed

Hieracium venosum, rattlesnake weed, poor-Robin's-plantain

Lactuca species, wild lettuces

Liatris species, blazing star, gayfeather

Ratibida columnifera and *R. pinnata*, Mexican hat

Rudbeckia fulgida, bracted coneflower; *R. fulgida* Goldsturm, bracted coneflower; *R. hirta*, black-eyed Susan; *R. hirta* Gloriosa Daisy, black-eyed Susan; *R. laciniata*, cutleaf coneflower; *R. maxima*, giant coneflower

Spilanthes americana, creeping spot flower

Stokesia laevis, Stoke's aster, stokesia
Tanacetum vulgare, tansy
Verbesina species, crownbeards
Vernonia species, ironweed

Cruciferae (Mustard Family)

Barbarea vulgaris, winter cress, yellow rocket
Cheiranthus species, wallflower
Erysimum species, wallflower

Labiatae or Lamiaceae (Mint Family)

Agastache species, hyssops
Lavandula angustifolia, English lavender
Leonotis leonurus, lion's ear
Mentha species, spearmint, peppermint, etc.
Monarda didyma, bee balm, bergamot; *M. citriodora*, lemon bee balm;
  M. fistulosa, wild bergamot, bee balm; *M. punctata*, dotted mint,
  horsemint
Physostegia virginica, obedient plant, false dragonhead
Pycnanthemum incanum, other *P.* species, mountain mints
Salvia azurea grandiflora, prairie sage; *S. azurea* var. *azurea*, blue sage; *S.
  coccinea*, Texas sage, scarlet sage, tropical sage; *S. elegans*, pineapple
  sage; *S. farinacea*, mealy-cup sage; *S. guaranitica*, anise sage; *S.
  greggii*, autumn sage; *S. miniata*, Belize sage; *S. splendens*, scarlet sage
Scutellaria moiciniana, Costa Rican red skullcap, *S.* species, other
  skullcaps
Teucrium canadense, American germander, wood sage
Thymus species, the thymes

Leguminosae, or Fabaceae (Pea-Legume Family)

Cassia fasciculata, partridge pea
Lathyrus latifolius, everlasting pea, perennial pea
Lespedeza species, bush clovers

Polygonaceae (Buckwheat Family)

Eriogonum species, wild buckwheats
Polygonum species, knotweeds and smartweeds; *P. lapathifolium*, dock-leaved smartweed; *P. capitatum*, knotweed
Rumex crispus, curly dock; *R. hastatulus*, wild sorrel

Umbelliferae or Apiaceae (Parsley or Carrot Family)

Anethum graveolens, dill
Ammi majus, bishop's flower
Angelica archangelica, angelica, archangel, wild parsnip; *A. venenosa*, hairy angelica
Daucus carota, Queen Anne's lace; *D. pusillus*, rattlesnake weed
Foeniculum vulgare, fennel
Petroselinum crispum, parsley

Other Summer-Flowering Plants

Agapanthus species, lily of the Nile, agapanthus
Alcea rosea, hollyhock
Allium cernuum, wild onion
Alstroemeria species, Peruvian lily
Apocynum species, dogbanes
Borago officinalis, borage
Buddleia species, butterfly bush
Callirhoe papaver, poppy mallow
Canna species, canna
Capsicum annuum, ornamental peppers
Catharanthus roseus, *Vinca roseus*, Madagascar periwinkle
Centranthus ruber, red valerian or Jupiter's-beard
Cleome species cleome, spider flower
Commelina species, dayflower

Diodia virginiana, buttonweed

Euphorbia species, flowering spurge, wild poinsettia, milkweed

Filipendula species, meadowsweets, queen-of-the-pasture

Gaura lindheimeri, gaura

Heliotropium arborescens, heliotrope

Hemerocallis species, daylily

Hibiscus coccineus, scarlet rose, Texas star hibiscus; *H. lasiocarpos*, woolly rose mallow; *H. militaris*, halberd-leaved rose mallow; *H. moscheutos*, rose mallow

Hymenocallis species, spider lily

Impatiens balsamina, garden balsam, lady's slippers; *I. capensis*, jewel weed, spotted touch-me-not; *I. wallerana*, impatiens, sultana

Justicia brandegeana, shrimp plant

Kosteletzkya virginica, salt marsh mallow

Lobelia cardinalis, cardinal flower; *L. syphilitica*, blue lobelia

Mimulus alatas, monkeyflower

Mitchella repens, partridgeberry

Nicotiana alata, flowering tobacco, *N.* species

Oenothera biennis, evening primrose; *O. fruticosa*, sundrops; *O.* speciosa, showy, Mexican, pink evening primrose

Opuntia species, prickly pear cactus

Pentas lanceolata, Egyptian star-cluster

Petunia X hybrida, petunia

Phlox carolina, *P. glaberrima*, *P. maculata*, tall phloxes; *P. paniculata*, perennial phlox, summer phlox; *P. drummondii*, annual phlox

Ruellia species, wild petunia

Russelia equisetiformis, coral plant, fountain plant

Ruta graveolens, rue

Saponaria officinalis, soapwort

Scabiosa atropurpurea, pincushion flower

Sedum spectabile, showy sedum; *S. virginica*, fire pink; *S. caroliniana*, wild pink; *S. subcilliata*, scarlet catchfly

Stellaria pubera, giant chickweed
Symphytum officinale, comfrey, healing herb, boneset
Torenia fournieri, torenia, wishbone flower
Verbascum species, mullein
Verbena rigida, tuber vervain; *V. tenuisecta*, moss verbena
Veronicastrum virginicum, Culver's root

Fall-Blooming Flowers

Amaranthaceae (Amaranth Family)

Amaranthus caudatus, love-lies-bleeding; *A. tricolor*, Joseph's coat
Celosia cristata, cockscomb
Gomphrena globosa, globe amaranth

Asclepiadaceae (Milkweed Family)

Asclepias curassavica, bloodflower; *A. lanceolata*, red milkweed; *A. rubra*,
red milkweed; *A. viridis*, spider milkweed

Chenopodiaceae (Goosefoot Family)

Kochia scoparia var. *trichophylla*, summer cypress

Compositae or Asteraceae (Sunflower or Composite Family)

Ageratum houstonianum, ageratum, flossflower
Artemisia species, wormwood
Aster species, aster
Bidens aristosa, beggar ticks, sticktight, sunflower
Centaurea cynanus, cornflower
Chrysanthemum hybrids, annual chrysanthemum; *C. X morifolium*,
garden chrysanthemum; *C. nipponicum*, Nippon daisy, Nippon oxeye
daisy; *C. parthenium* or *Matricaria capensis*, feverfew
Cichorium intybus, common chicory
Coreopsis tinctoria, calliopsis
Cosmos species, cosmos

Diodia virginiana, buttonweed

Eupatorium coelestinum, mistflower, wild ageratum; *E. fistulosum*, joe-pye weed; *E. rugosum*, white snakeroot

Gaillardia pulchella, firewheel, Indian blanket

Helianthus species, sunflower; *H. angustifolius*, swamp sunflower

Heterotheca subaxillaris, camphorweed

Lactuca species, wild lettuces

Liatris species, blazing star, gayfeather

Ratibida columnifera and *R. pinnata*, Mexican hat

Rudbeckia laciniata, cutleaf coneflower, other *R.* species

Solidago species, goldenrod

Spilanthes americana, creeping spot flower

Stokesia laevis, Stoke's aster, stokesia

Tagetes species, marigold

Tithonia rotundifolia, Mexican sunflower

Verbesina species, crownbeards

Vernonia species, ironweed

Zinnia species, zinnia

Cruciferae (Mustard Family)

Tropaeolum species, nasturtium

Labiatae or Lamiaceae (Mint Family)

Agastache species, hyssops

Leonotis leonurus, lion's ear

Monarda didyma, bee balm, bergamot; *M. fistulosa*, wild bergamot, bee balm; *M. punctata*, dotted mint, horsemint

Perilla frutescens, perilla

Physostegia virginica, obedient plant, false dragonhead

Pycnanthemum incanum, other *P.* species, mountain mints

Salvia azurea grandiflora, prairie sage; *S. azurea* var. *azurea*, blue sage; *S. coccinea*, Texas sage, scarlet sage, tropical sage; *S. elegans*, pineapple sage; *S. guaranitica*, anise sage; *S. greggii*, autumn sage; *S. iodantha*,

Mexican fuchsia sage (blooms through winter in frostfree areas); *S. leucantha*, Mexican bush sage; *S. madrensis*, forsythia sage (blooms into winter in frostfree areas); *S. miniata*, Belize sage; *S. regla*, mountain sage; *S. splendens*, scarlet sage
Scutellaria moiciniana, Costa Rican red skullcap, *S.* species, skullcaps
Teucrium canadense, American germander, wood sage
Thymus species, the thymes

Leguminosae or Fabaceae (Pea-Legume Family)

Cassia fasciculata, partridge pea
Lathyrus latifolius, everlasting pea, perennial pea
Lespedeza species, bush clovers

Polygonaceae (Buckwheat Family)

Eriogonum species, wild buckwheats
Polygonum species, knotweeds and smartweeds; *P. lapathifolium*, dock-leaved smartweed; *P. capitatum*, knotweed
Rumex crispus, curly dock

Umbelliferae or Apiaceae (Parsley or Carrot Family)

Anethum graveolens, dill
Angelica archangelica, angelica, archangel, wild parsnip
Daucus carota, Queen Anne's lace
Foeniculum vulgare, fennel
Petroselinum crispum, parsley

OTHER FALL-FLOWERING PLANTS

Apocynum species, dogbanes
Buddleia species, butterfly bush
Canna species, canna
Capsicum annuum, ornamental peppers
Catharanthus roseus, Vinca roseus, Madagascar periwinkle
Cleome species, cleome, spider flower

Commelina species, dayflower
Euphorbia species, flowering spurge, wild poinsettia, milkweed
Gaura lindheimeri, gaura
Heliotropium arborescens, heliotrope
Hemerocallis species, daylily
Hibiscus coccineus, scarlet rose mallow, Texas star hibiscus; *H. militaris*, halberd-leaved rose mallow; *H. moscheutos*, rose mallow
Impatiens balsamina, garden balsam, lady's slippers; *I. capensis*, jewel weed, spotted touch-me-not; *I. wallerana*, impatiens, sultana
Justicia brandegeana, shrimp plant
Kosteletzkya virginica, salt marsh mallow
Lobelia cardinalis, cardinal flower; *L. syphilitica*, blue lobelia
Nicotiana alata, flowering tobacco; *N.* species, flowering tobaccos
Oenothera biennis, evening primrose; *O.* speciosa, showy, Mexican, pink evening primrose (occasional fall bloom)
Pentas lanceolata, Egyptian star-cluster
Petunia X hybrida, petunia
Phlox carolina, *P. glaberrima*, *P. maculata*, tall phloxes; *P. paniculata*, perennial phlox, summer phlox
Ruellia species, wild petunia
Russelia equisetiformis, Mexican, coral plant, fountain plant
Ruta graveolens, rue
Saponaria officinalis, soapwort
Scabiosa atropurpurea, pincushion flower
Torenia fournieri, torenia, wishbone flower
Verbena rigida, tuber vervain

Plants for the Hummingbird Garden

NATIVE TO THE SOUTHEAST UNITED STATES

Aesculus pavia, red buckeye
Aquilegia canadensis, wild columbine
Bignonia capreolata, cross vine
Campsis radicans, trumpet vine, trumpet creeper

Cirsium species, thistles
Erythrina herbacea, eastern coralbean, cardinal spear, or mamou
Hibiscus coccineus, scarlet rose mallow, Texas star hibiscus
Ipomopsis rubra, standing cypress, scarlet gilia
Impatiens capensis, jewelweed, spotted touch-me-not
Iris fulva, copper iris
Liriodendron tulipifera, tulip tree, tulip poplar, yellow poplar
Lobelia cardinalis, cardinal flower; *L. syphilitica*, blue lobelia
Lonicera sempervirens, coral honeysuckle
Monarda fistulosa, wild bee balm
Phlox divaricata, blue phlox; *P.* species, tall phlox, perennial phlox,
    summer phlox
Rhododendron species, rhododendrons and azaleas, including but not
    limited to *R. canescens*, wild azalea; *R. maximum*, great laurel; *R.*
    catawbiense, catawba rhododendron, mountain rosebay; *R. viscosum*,
    summer or swamp azalea
Salvia coccinea, tropical, scarlet, or Texas sage
Spigelia marilandica, Indian pink

HUMMINGBIRD-ATTRACTING PLANTS USED TO PROMOTE CONTINUOUS BLOOM, WINTER BLOOM IN SOUTHEASTERN HUMMINGBIRD GARDENS

Abutilon pictum, flowering maple, Chinese bellflower
Citrus species, citrus
Cuphea ignea, Mexican cigarflower; *Cuphea micropetala*, Mexican cigar
    plant
Eriobotrya japonica, Japanese plum, loquat
Ipomoea coccinea, red morning glory
Ipomoea quamoclit, cypress vine or cardinal climber
Justicia gutatta, shrimp plant
Malvaviscus arboreus or *grandiflorus*, giant turk's cap; *M. arboreus* var.
    drummondii, sultan's turban

Manettia cordifolia, firecracker vine
Odontonema strictum, firespike, hummingbird plant
Russellia equisetiformis, fountain plant
Salvia species, almost any
Tecomaria capensis, cape honeysuckle

OTHER EXOTIC PLANTS ATTRACTIVE TO HUMMINGBIRDS

Abelia X grandiflora, glossy abelia
Agave species, agave
Albizia julibrissin, mimosa, silk tree
Alcea rosea, hollyhock
Aloe species, aloe
Alstroemeria species, Peruvian lily
Bougainvillea hybrids, bougainvillea
Buddleia species, butterfly bush
Callistemon citrinus, C. rigidus, bottlebrush
Canna species, canna
Cleome species, cleome, spider flower
Clerodendrum philippinum, cashmere bouquet, glory bower; *C. paniculatum*, or *C. speciosissimum*, giant salvia, java shrub, pagoda flower
Erythrina crista-galli, coral tree, cry-baby tree
Gladiolus X hortulanus, garden gladiolus
Hemerocallis (reds and oranges), daylily
Hibiscus rosa-sinensis, Chinese hibiscus; *H. syriacus*, althaea, rose-of-Sharon (single flowers)
Impatiens balsamina, garden balsam; *I. hybrids*, impatiens hybrids
Iris hybrids and species, iris
Kniphofia uvaria, red-hot-poker, tritoma
Lantana camara, ham and eggs

Leonotis leonurus, lion's ear
Lonicera species, honeysuckles
Mirabilis jalapa, four-o'clock
Musa species, banana
Nicotiana glauca, tree tobacco; *N.* species, flowering tobacco
Pentas lanceolata, pentas, Egyptian star-cluster
Phaseolus coccineus, scarlet runner bean
Schlumbergera bridgesii, Christmas cactus
Strelitzia reginae, bird-of-paradise
Weigela hybrids, cardinal shrub, others
Wisteria sinensis, wisteria, Chinese wisteria

Butterfly Larvae Host Plants

Acacia farnesiana, sweet acacia, Huisache	silver-spotted skipper
Alcea rosea, hollyhock	checkered skipper
Amaranthus species	common sooty wing
Ambrosia species, ragweeds	common sooty wing
Amorpha fruticosa, Indigo bush, false indigo, lead plant	silver-spotted skipper mottled dusky wing
Aquilegia species, columbine	columbine dusky wing
Apocynum species, dogbanes	monarch
Aristolochia species, Dutchman's pipe	pipevine swallowtail polydamas swallowtail
Artemesia absinthium, wormwood	painted lady
Asarum species, ginger	pipevine swallowtail
Asclepias species, milkweeds	monarch queen
Asimina species, pawpaw or false-banana	zebra swallowtail
Aster species, asters	pearl crescent American painted lady
Baptisia species, false indigos	mottled dusky wing frosted elfin eastern tailed blue

Bidens pilosa, shepherd's-needle	dwarf yellow sulphur
Borago species, borage	American painted lady
	painted lady
Canna species	Brazilian skipper
	long-tailed skipper
Carex species, sedges	dun skipper
Carpinus caroliniana, hornbeam, ironwood	red-spotted purple
	tiger swallowtail
Carya species, hickory and pecans	banded hairstreak
Cassia species	cloudless sulphur
	orange-barred sulphur
	Mexican sulphur
	little sulphur
Cassia species, partridge pea, cassias	cloudless sulphur
	little sulphur
	alfalfa
	sleepy orange
Ceanothus americanus, New Jersey tea	Pacuvius dusky wing
	spring azure
	brown elfin
Celtis species, hackberries	hackberry
	Empress Flora
	tawny emperor
	snout
	question mark
	mourning cloak
Cercis canadensis, redbud, Judas tree	Henry's elfin
Cirsium species, thistles	painted lady
Citrus species	giant swallowtail
	eastern black swallowtail
Cleome species, spider flower	checkered white
	great southern white
Cornus species, dogwoods	spring azure

Crataegus species, hawthorns

Cruciferae (Mustard Family)

Cynoglossum species, forget-me-not
Erigeron species, fleabane
Fraxinus species, ashes
Gaylussacia species, huckleberries
Gleditsia species, locusts

Helianthus species, sunflowers

Helenium autumnale, Helen's flower,
   sneezeweed
Hypericum species, St.-John's-worts
Juglans species, walnuts
Lathyrus latifolius, everlasting
   or perennial pea
Leguminosae, many legumes

Lespedeza species, bush clovers

Lindera benzoin, spicebush

Liriodendron tulipfera, tulip tree,
   yellow poplar
Lupinis perennis, wild lupine

Malva species, mallows
Malva sylvestris, zebrina

striped hairstreak
northern hairstreak
red-spotted purple
Pteridae family butterflies
(whites and sulphurs)
gray hairstreak
checkered white
tiger swallowtail
Henry's elfin
dreamy dusky wing
Zarucco dusky wing
painted lady
gorgone checkerspot

dwarf yellow sulphur
gray hairstreak
banded hairstreak

eastern tailed blue
gray hairstreak
Zarucco dusky wing
eastern tailed blue
silver-spotted skipper
northern cloudy wing
palamedes swallowtail
spicebush swallowtail

tiger swallowtail
frosted elfin
eastern tailed blue
checkered skipper
checkered skipper

Magnolia virginia, sweetbay magnolia — palamedes swallowtail
Medicago sativa, alfalfa — funereal dusky wing
alfalfa or orange sulphur
common sooty wing

Monarda punctata, dotted mint, horsemint
Myosotis species, forget-me-not — American painted lady
painted lady

Myrica species, bayberry or wax myrtle — red-banded hairstreak
Passiflora species, passionflower vine — gulf fritillary
variegated fritillary
zebra

Persea species, bays — palamedes swallowtail
spicebush swallowtail

Phaseolus species, beans — eastern tailed blue
long-tailed skippers

Polygonum species, knotweeds — pipevine swallowtail
Populus species, cottonwoods, poplars — tiger swallowtail
red-spotted purple
viceroy
mourning cloak

Prunus americana, wild plum — Henry's elfin
Prunus serotina, wild cherry — tiger swallowtail
coral hairstreak
red-spotted purple

Prunus species — coral hairstreak
striped hairstreak

Ptelea trifoliata, common hoptree — giant swallowtail
eastern black swallowtail

Quercus species, oaks — white M hairstreak
Edward's hairstreak
banded hairstreak
striped hairstreak
southern hairstreak

Robinia pseudoacacia, black locust

Ruta graveolens, rue

Ruellia species, wild petunias

Rumex species, sorrels, dock
Sabal palmetto
Sassafras albidum, sassafras
Serenoa repens, saw palmetto
Salix species, willows

gray hairstreak
sleepy dusky wing
dreamy dusky wing
Zarucco dusky wing
giant swallowtail
eastern black swallowtail
buckeye
Cuban crescentspot
Texan crescentspot
American copper
monk
spicebush swallowtail
palmetto arpo skipper
tiger swallowtail
red-spotted purple
viceroy
mourning cloak
striped hairstreak
faunus angle wing (green comma)
spring azure

Scrophulariaceae (Figwort Family)
    members including:
    Veronicastrum virginicum, Culver's
    root, *Mimulus*, monkeyflowers,
    Penstemon species, penstemons, *Linaria*
    species, toadflax, wild snapdragon,
    Antirrhinum species, snapdragons,
    Torenia Fournieri, wishbone flower,
    bluewings
Sedum species, stonecrops, sedums
Senecio species, ragworts, butterweed
Stellaria pubera, giant chickweed
Symplocos tinctoria, sweetleaf
    or horse sugar

buckeye
variegated fritillary
painted lady
dwarf yellow sulphur

king's hairstreak

Tagetes species, marigolds | dwarf yellow sulphur
Tilia species, basswood | tiger swallowtail
| question mark
Trifolium species, clovers | clouded sulphur
| eastern tailed blue
| northern cloudy wing
| dogface
Trifolium incarnatum, crimson clover | cloudless sulphur
| little sulphur
| sleepy orange
| alfalfa
Ulmus species, elms | comma
| question mark
| mourning cloak

Umbelliferae (Parsley or Carrot Family) | black swallowtail
Urtica species, nettles | comma
| American painted lady
| red admiral

Vaccinium species, blueberries,
  deerberries | striped hairstreak
| Henry's elfin
| spring azure

Verbena species | buckeye
Verbesina species, crownbeards | spring azure
Viburnum species, viburnum | spring azure
Viola species, violets and pansies | variegated fritillary
Wisteria species, wisteria | Zarucco dusky wing
| long-tailed skipper
| silver-spotted skipper

Zanthoxylum clava-herculis,
  Hercules'-club, prickly
  ash, or toothache-tree | eastern black swallowtail
| giant swallowtail

Native Berry-Producing Shrubs by Season of Fruiting

SUMMER

Amelanchier species	serviceberry
Prunus species	black cherry, wild plums
Rhamnus species	buckthorns
Rubus species	blackberries, dewberries, etc.
Sambucus species	elderberries
Vaccinium species	blueberries, huckleberries

FALL

Callicarpa species	beautyberry
Cornus species	dogwoods
Malus species	crab apples and apples
Viburnum species	arrowwood, blackhaw, rusty blackhaw, etc. (not all species bear fruit; select carefully)

PERSISTING INTO WINTER

Aronia species	chokeberries
Crataegus species	hawthorns
Ilex species	hollies
Myrica species	bayberries or wax myrtles
Prunus caroliniana	cherry laurel
Rosa species, natives with numerous small hips such as	
R. *palustris*	swamp rose
R. *virginiana*	Virginia rose

Trees High in Spring Sap

Acer species	maples
Betula species	birches
Malus species	apples

Best Nesting Trees for Birds

Four groups selected from Cornell Laboratory of Ornithology nest card records by John Dennis (*The Wildlife Gardener*). Data was collected nationwide and in Canada.

Group I (harbored at least twenty or more nesting species known to nest near houses): elm, hackberry, hawthorn, maple, oak, pine, red cedar, willow

Group II (harbored between fifteen and nineteen nesting species): ash, blackberry, black locust, box elder, cottonwood, juniper

Group III (harbored between ten and fourteen nesting species): American elm, arborvitae, cherry, crab apple, dogwood, mulberry, pear, plum, poplar, privet, red maple, red oak, rose, sweet gum, sycamore

Group IV (plants known to be useful to nesting birds but not rated according to number of users): alder, birch, black willow, elderberry, English ivy, flowering dogwood, flowering plum, ginkgo, grape, hickory, holly, honey locust, honeysuckle, linden, live oak, pyracantha, silver maple, sugar maple, sumac, willow oak.

Invasive Alien Plants

The following are a few of the most notorious introduced plants which have become invasive in parts of the eastern or southeastern United States. My source is *American Horticulturist* News Edition (March, 1995): 6-12.

Acer platanoides, Norway maple
Ailanthus altissima, tree-of-heaven

Casuarina species, Australian pine
Celastrus orbiculatus, oriental bittersweet
Coronilla varia, crown vetch
Eichhornia crassipes, water hyacinth
Elaeagnus angustifolia, Russian olive
Ligustrum ovalifolium, California privet
Ligustrum japonicum, Japanese privet
Ligustrum sinense, Chinese privet
Lonicera japonica, Japanese honeysuckle
Lygodium japonicum, Japanese climbing fern
Lythrum salicaria, purple loosestrife
Nandina domestica, heavenly bamboo
Pueraria lobata, kudzu vine
Rosa multiflora, multiflora rose
Sapium sebiferum, Chinese tallow tree
Schinus terebinthifolius, Brazilian pepper

Notes

CHAPTER TWO

1. Bill Fontenot, "Notes On Backyard Wildlife Habitat Enrichment Techniques," *L.O.S. News, The Newsletter of the Louisiana Ornithological Society* (April 2, 1992), 11.

2. Paul Hamel, *The Land Manager's Guide to the Birds of the South* (Chapel Hill, NC: The Nature Conservancy, Southeastern Region, 1992), 2.

CHAPTER THREE

1. National Wildlife Federation, *Backyard Wildlife Habitat* (Washington, DC: National Wildlife Federation), 6.

2. Edward O. Wilson, *The Diversity of Life* (Cambridge, MA: The Belknap Press of Harvard University Press, 1992), 346–47.

3. Lamson Scribner, *Ornamental and Useful Plants of Maine*, 1874. Quoted by Steven Foster, "Echinaceas, the Purple Coneflowers," *American Horticulturist* (August 1985): 14.

4. Sally Wasowski, *Requiem for a Lawnmower and Other Essays on Easy Gardening with Native Plants* (Dallas: Taylor Publishing Company, 1992), 13.

5. Mark Plotkin, "The Outlook for New Agricultural and Industrial Products from the Tropics," in *Biodiversity*, ed. E.O. Wilson (Washington, DC: National Academy Press, 1988), 106.

6. Marcia Bonta, "Restoring Our Tallgrass Prairies," *American Horticulturist* (October 1991): 10–18.

7. Dorothy J. Allard, *Southeastern United States Ecological Community Classification*, Interim Report Version 1.2 (Chapel Hill, NC: The Nature Conservancy, Southeast Regional Office, November 1990).

8. Charles Wharton, *The Natural Environments of Georgia* (Atlanta: Georgia Department of Natural Resources, 1978), 158.

References within quotation:

E. P. Odum, *Fundamentals of Ecology*, 3rd ed. (Philadelphia: W. B. Saunders Co., 1971), 574.

D. W. Johnson and E. P. Odum, "Breeding Bird Populations in Relation to Plant Succession on the Piedmont of Georgia," *Ecology* 37 (1956): 50–62.

9. Walter Conrad Muenscher, *Weeds* (Ithaca and London: Cornell University Press, 1980).

10. Latimore Smith, *The Natural Communities of Louisiana* (Baton Rouge, LA: Louisiana Natural Heritage Program, 1988), 1.

11. Wharton, 8.

12. Bonta.

13. Smith, 15.

14. *Ibid.*, 1.

15. William R. Fontenot, *Native Gardening in the South: A Personal Guide for Understanding, Appreciating, and Using the Indigenous Plants of Dixie* (Carencro, LA: A Prairie Basse Publication, 1992), 7-10.

16. Smith.

17. Fontenot, *Native Gardening*, 7.

CHAPTER FIVE

1. Rhonda M. Hart, *Bugs, Slugs & Other Thugs: Controlling Garden Pests Organically* (Pownal, VT: Storey Communications, Inc., 1991).

2. Chief sources of information on beneficial wildlife:

Donald J. Borror and Richard E. White, *A Field Guide to the Insects* (Boston: Houghton Mifflin Company, 1970).

Hart, *Bugs, Slugs, & Other Thugs*.

William Olkowski, Sheila Daar, and Helga Olkowski, *Common-*

Sense Pest Control (Newtown, CT: The Taunton Press, 1991).

Miranda Smith and Anna Carr, *Rodale's Garden Insect, Disease & Weed Identification Guide* (Emmaus, PA: Rodale Press, 1988).

Chapter Six

1. Chris Maser, *Forest Primeval: The Natural History of an Ancient Forest* (San Francisco: Sierra Club Books, 1994).

2. Peter Steinhart, "Soil, the Miracle We Take For Granted," *National Wildlife* (February-March 1985): 15–22.

3. Wharton, 158.

Reference within quotation:

D. K. Kuo, *Changes in Soil Organisms Associated with Forest Communities in the Georgia Piedmont* (Ph.D. dissertation, University of Georgia, Athens, 1965).

4. Quoted by Richard Conniff, "On the Lowly Worm We Earthlings Pin Our Loftiest Dreams," *Smithsonian* (July 1993): 86–95.

5. Olkowski, Daar, and Olkowski, 530.

6. *Ibid.*

7. Scott Shalaway, "Ghost Trees Come Alive," *Birder's World* (August, 1993): 52–55.

8. Scott Shalaway, "Birdscaping," *WildBird* (June 1992): 62.

Chapter Seven

1. Wasowski, *Requiem for a Lawnmower*, 28.

2. Borror and White, *Field Guide to the Insects*.

3. T. T. Kozlowski, "Carbohydrate Sources and Sinks in Woody Plants," *The Botanical Review* 58 (April-June 1992), 166–67.

4. Charles V. Covell, Jr., *A Field Guide to the Moths of Eastern North· America* (Boston: Houghton Mifflin Co., 1984), 358.

5. Olkowski, Daar, and Olkowski, 613.

6. Chief sources of wildlife associates of trees and shrubs:

Janine M. Benyus, *The Field Guide to Wildlife Habitats of the Eastern United States* (New York: Simon & Schuster, Inc., 1989).

Borror and White, *Field Guide to the Insects*.

Covell, *Field Guide to the Moths*.

Alexander B. Klots, *A Field Guide to the Butterflies of North America East of the Great Plains* (Boston: Houghton Mifflin Co., 1951).

Elbert Little, *The Audubon Society Field Guide to North American Trees* (New York: Alfred A. Knopf, 1980).

George A. Petrides, *A Field Guide to Trees and Shrubs* (Boston: Houghton Mifflin Co., 1986).

Robert Michael Pyle, *The Audubon Society Field Guide to North American Butterflies* (New York: Alfred A. Knopf, 1981).

Donald Wyman, *Wyman's Gardening Encyclopedia* (New York: Macmillan Publishing Co., Inc., 1977).

7. Wasowski, *Requiem for a Lawnmower*, 124–25.

8. Wyman, 195.

9. Fontenot, *Native Gardening*, 66.

10. Petrides, *Field Guide to Trees and Shrubs*, 126.

11. Olkowski, Daar, and Olkowski, 632.

12. Fontenot, *Native Gardening*, 82.

13. Sally Wasowski, *Gardening with Native Plants of the South* (Dallas: Taylor Publishing Co., 1994), 105.

Chapter Eight

1. Olkowski, Daarm, and Olkowski.

2. Janet Marinelli, "Where to Get Native Plants: Five Commandments for Conservation-Minded Gardeners," *The Environmental Gardener* (Brooklyn Botanical Gardens, Inc., 1992), 93.

3. Chief sources of wildlife associates of flowers, ferns, grasses:

Borror and White, *Field Guide to the Insects*.

Covell, *Field Guide to Moths*.

Alexander B. Klots, *A Field Guide to the Butterflies of North America, East of the Great Plains* (Boston: Houghton Mifflin Co., 1951).

Pyle, *Audubon Society Field Guide*.

Donald and Lillian Stokes, *The Butterfly Book: An Easy Guide to*

Butterfly Gardening, Identification, and Behavior (Boston: Little, Brown and Company, 1989).

Xerces Society/Smithsonian Institution, *Butterfly Gardening, Creating Summer Magic in Your Garden* (San Francisco: Sierra Club Books, 1990).

4. John V. Dennis, *The Wildlife Gardener* (New York: Alfred A. Knopf, 1985), 162.

5. Fontenot, *Native Gardening*, 93.

6. Craig Tufts, *The Backyard Naturalist* (Washington, DC: National Wildlife Federation, 1988), 10.

7. Allen Lacy, *The Garden in Autumn* (New York: Atlantic Monthly Press, 1990), 126.

8. Wasowski, *Requiem for a Lawnmower*, 130.

9. Fontenot, *Native Gardening*, 86.

10. Lacy, 53–54.

11. Fontenot, *Native Gardening*, 92.

12. Wilbur H. Duncan and Leonard E. Foote, *Wildflowers of the Southeastern United States* (Athens: University of Georgia Press, 1975), 116.

13. Samuel B. Jones, Jr., and Leonard E. Foote, *Gardening with Native Wild Flowers* (Portland, OR: Timber Press, 1990), 120–38.

14. Wasowski, *Gardening with Native Plants*, 173.

15. Charles M. Allen, *Cultivable Native Grasses (Poaceae)*, reprinted in Fontenot, *Native Gardening*, 98–99.

16. Chief sources of recommendations of native grasses, rushes, and sedges in the garden and of information on specific growing requirements:

Allen, *Cultivable Native Grasses (Poaceae)*, reprinted in Fontenot, 97–99.

Jones and Foote, *Gardening with Native Wild Flowers*, 112.

Wasowski, *Gardening with Native Plants*, 171.

Chapter Nine

1. John V. Dennis, *The Wildlife Gardener* (New York: Alfred A. Knopf, 1985), 228.

2. Elsie B. Klots, *The New Field Book of Freshwater Life* (New York: F. P. Putnam's Sons, 1966).

3. Van Ness Water Gardens, *Water Visions '93* (Catalog of Van Ness Water Gardens, 2640 North Euclid Avenue, Upland, CA 91786-1199).

4. Chief source of information about aquatic plants:
Jones and Foote, *Gardening with Native Wild Flowers*, 147–68.
Chief sources of animal associates of aquatic plants:
Borror and White, *Field Guide to the Insects*.
Covell, *Field Guide to the Moths*.
Klots, *New Field Book of Freshwater Life*.

Chapter Ten

1. John V. O'Neill, "Birdseed Expert," *Birdwatcher's Digest* (May–June 1989): 47–51.

2. Scott Shalaway and Linda Shalaway, "Winter Feeding in the Sunbelt," *WildBird* (February 1992): 51.

3. Project Feederwatch results from:
Patricia Barnes-Svarney, "Watching For Science," *WildBird* (April 1989): 49–51.
Carol Bishop, "Feeder Favorites," *WildBird* (February 1991): 53.
Diane L. Tessaglia and Kenneth V. Rosenberg, "Project Feederwatch: Annual Report 1993-94," *Birdscope* (Autumn 1994): 1–6.

4. Nancy L. Newfield, *Louisiana's Hummingbirds* (Baton Rouge, LA: Louisiana Department of Wildlife and Fisheries, Louisiana Natural Heritage Program, 1992).

5. Les Line, "Tale of Two Warblers," *National Wildlife* (October–November 1994): 19.

6. Anne Ophelia Dowden, *The Clover & the Bee: A Book of Pollination* (New York: Thomas Y. Crowell, 1990), 23.

7. Sue Hubbell, *A Book of Bees . . . and How to Keep Them* (New York: Ballantine Books, 1988), 3.

8. Bee condos for orchard-mason bees are available from:

The Nature Company stores or catalog. Home office: 750 Hearst Avenue, Berkeley, CA 94710; 1(800)227-1114

Duncraft Specialties for Birdfeeding, Penacook, NH 03303-9020; 603-224-0200.

9. Gary Noel Ross, "The Trans-Gulf Express," *Louisiana Conservationist* (September–October 1993): 15–17.

10. To obtain a copy of *The Bat House Builder's Handbook*, send a donation to: Bat Conservation International, P.O. Box 162603, Austin, TX 78716.

Chapter Eleven

1. E. H. Dunn, "Bird Mortality from Striking Residential Windows in Winter," *Journal of Field Ornithology*, 64 (1993): 302–9.

2. George Lowery, *The Mammals of Louisiana and Its Adjacent Waters* (Baton Rouge, LA: Louisiana State University Press, 1974), 235.

3. *Ibid.*, 258.

4. *Ibid.*, 284-89.

5. "City Tells Gardener to Cut it Out or Else," *New Orleans Times-Picayune* (June 9, 1994): A-16.

6. Sara Stein, *Noah's Garden: Restoring the Ecology of Our Own Back Yards* (Boston: Houghton Mifflin Co., 1993).

The following books, periodicals, and articles include the ones I used in preparation of this book and others I recommend for backyard naturalists.

Basic Background for Wildlife Gardeners

Free pamphlets: *Attract Birds. Homes for Birds. Backyard Bird Problems. Migratory Songbird Conservation. Will We Lose Our Songbirds? Not if We Can Help It!—Partners in Flight.* Order by mail: Department of the Interior, Fish and Wildlife Service, Publications Unit, 130 Webb Building, 4401 North Fairfax Drive, Arlington, VA 22203. Phone (703) 358-1711 or FAX (703) 358-2283. Ask for a current publications list for other titles.

Free pamphlets: Call the cooperative extension in your county/parish for literature on gardening topics, beekeeping, more.

Olkowski, William, Sheila Daar, and Helga Olkowski. *Common-Sense Pest Control.* Newtown, CT: The Taunton Press, 1991.

Phillips, Harry R. *Growing and Propagating Wild Flowers.* Chapel Hill: University of North Carolina Press, 1985.

Reilly, Ann. *Park's Success With Seeds.* Park Seed Company, Cokesbury Road, Greenwood, SC 29647-0001. Photographs of seedlings are especially valuable.

Free catalog: Wild Seed, Inc., 1101 Campo Rosa Road, P. O. Box 308, Eagle Lake, TX 77434. Drawings of wildflower seedlings are very helpful.

Stein, Sara. *Noah's Garden, Restoring the Ecology of our own Back Yards.* New York: Houghton Mifflin Co., 1993.

Tufts, Craig. *The Backyard Naturalist.* Washington: National Wildlife Federation, 1993.

Wasowski, Sally. *Requiem for a Lawnmower and Other Essays on Easy Gardening with Native Plants*. Dallas, TX: Taylor Publishing Company, 1992.

For All Wildlife Gardeners

Barton, Barbara J. *Gardening By Mail, A Source Book*. Boston: Houghton Mifflin Co., 1995.

Bonta, Marcia. "Restoring Our Tallgrass Prairies." *American Horticulturist* (October 1991): 10–18.

Brittingham, Margaret, and John V. Dennis. "Winter Bird Feeding." *WildBird* (February 1993): 51–55.

Brooklyn Botanical Garden. 1000 Washington Avenue, Brooklyn, NY 11225-1099. Phone 718-941-4044, ext. 272. Plants and Gardens handbooks: *The Environmental Gardener. Gardening for Wildlife. Gardening with Wildflowers. Gardening with Wildflowers and Native Plants. Going Native: Biodiversity in Our Own Backyards. Herbs and Their Ornamental Uses. Hollies: A Gardener's Guide. Low-Maintenance Gardening. Natural Insect Control: The Ecological Gardener's Guide to Foiling Pests. The Natural Lawn and Alternatives. Perennials: A Gardener's Guide. Propagation. Soils. Water Gardens.*

Burchard, Hank. "Guide to Gourmet Bird Feeding." *National Wildlife* (December–January 1985): 37–39.

Clausen, Ruth R., and Nicolas Ekstrom. *Perennials for American Gardens*. New York: Random House, 1989.

Clench, Mary Heimerdinger, Ph.D. *Beginner's Guide to Attracting Birds to Your Backyard*. Lincolnwood, IL: Publications International, Ltd., 1991.

Conniff, Richard. "On the Lowly Worm We Earthlings Pin Our Loftiest Dreams." *Smithsonian* (July 1993): 86W95.

Cornell University, Staff of the L. H. Bailey Hortorium. *Hortus Third, A Concise Dictionary of Plants Cultivated in the United States and Canada*. New York: Macmillan Publishing Company, 1976.

Dennis, John V. *A Complete Guide to Bird Feeding*. New York: Alfred A. Knopf, 1994.

————.*The Wildlife Gardener*. New York: Alfred A. Knopf, 1985.

Dennis, John V., and Mathew Tekulsky. *How to Attract Hummingbirds & Butterflies*. San Ramon, CA: Ortho Books, 1991.

Deno, Norman C. *Seed Germination, Theory and Practice*. 1993. Can be ordered for $20, postage paid, from Norman C. Deno, 139 Lenor Drive, State College, PA 16801.

Dufresne, Richard. *A World of Salvias*. Flyer.

————.*Herb Placards and Horticultural Information for 104 New and Underutilized Varieties* (salvias, agastaches and others). June 22, 1990. Richard F. Dufresne, 313 Spur Road, Greensboro, NC 27406. Phone 919-674-3105.

Ernst, Ruth Shaw. *The Naturalist's Garden, How to Garden with Plants That Attract Birds, Butterflies, and Other Wildlife*. Old Saybrook, CT: The Globe Pequot Press, 1993.

Foster, Steven. "Echinaceas, the Purple Coneflowers." *American Horticulturist* (August 1985): 14–17.

Harrison, George H. "Boom Times for Backyard Habitat." *National Wildlife* (October–November 1983): 35–39.

Hart, Rhonda Massingham Hart. *Bugs, Slugs & Other Thugs: Controlling Garden Pests Organically*. Pownal, VT: Storey Communications, Inc., 1991.

Hill, James R. III. "The First American Birdhouses: How Native Americans Began the Tradition of Attracting Purple Martins." *WildBird, Birding at Its Best* (March 1993): 50–51.

Hubble, Sue. *A Book of Bees . . . and How to Keep Them*. New York: Ballantine Books, 1988.

————.*Broadsides From the Other Orders: A Book of Bugs*. New York: Random House, 1993.

Jackson, Jerome A. "Attracting Birds: Take a Walk on the Wild Side." *Guide to Attracting Birds: A Supplement to Birder's World*.

Johnsgard, Paul A. *The Hummingbirds of North America*. Washington, DC: Smithsonian Institution Press, 1983.

Johnson, Lady Bird, and Carlton B. Lees. *Wildflowers across America*. New York: National Wildflower Research Center, Abbeville Press, 1988.

Jones, Adam. "When Less Is More, Selective Feeding Can Affect the Bird Species at your Feeder." *WildBird* (July 1990): pp. 24–27.

Kozlowski, T. T. "Carbohydrate Sources and Sinks in Woody Plants." *The Botanical Review* 58, no. 2 (April–June 1992): 166–67. Published quarterly by the New York Botanical Garden.

Krueger, Harry. "Bluebirds: This May Be a Way to Help Keep Sparrows Out of Nest Boxes." *Nature Society News* 26, no. 11 (November 1991): 12. Article includes plan for Joe Huber's trap-in-a-box sparrow trap.

Lacy, Allen. *The Garden in Autumn*. New York: The Atlantic Monthly Press, 1990.

————.*Gardening with Groundcovers and Vines*. New York: Harper-Collins Publishers, 1993.

Lawren, Bill. "Singing the Blues for Songbirds." *National Wildlife* (August–September 1992): 5–11.

Lilypons Water Gardens, P. O. Box 188, Brookshire, TX 77423. Water plants, tadpoles, pool supplies. Catalog $5.00. Lists references on ponds and water gardening.

Lipske, Mike. "Defending the Right to Be Wild." *National Wildlife* (October–November 1985): 18–19.

Manry, David. "Con-Artist Extraordinaire." *WildBird* (September 1992): 62–65. Article about cowbirds.

Martin, Tovah. "The Sage of Salvias." *American Horticulturist* (October 1992): 20–25. Article about Richard Dufresne.

Maser, Chris. *Forest Primeval: The Natural History of an Ancient Forest*. San Francisco: Sierra Club Books, 1994.

McKinley, Michael. *How to Attract Birds*. San Francisco: Ortho Books, 1983.

Newfield, Nancy L., and Barbara Nielsen. *Hummingbird Gardening*. Shelburne, VT: Chapters Publishing Ltd., forthcoming 1996.

O'Neill, John V. "Birdseed Expert." *Bird Watcher's Digest* (May–June 1989): 47–51. Article about Aelred Geis.

Orr, Craig. "Feeding Birds Safely." *WildBird* (November 1989): 40–43.

Patterson, Marion J. "Natural Landscaping for Your Birding Garden." *WildBird* (March 1990): 46–51.

Plotkin, Mark J. *Tales of a Shaman's Apprentice: An Ethnobotanist Searches for New Medicines in the Amazon Rain Forest.* New York: Viking-Penguin, 1993.

Pyle, Robert Michael. *Handbook for Butterfly Watchers.* New York: Houghton Mifflin Co., 1992.

Rosenberg, Kenneth V., and Andr A. Dhondt. "Seed Preferences: East versus West." *Birdscope: News and Views from Sapsucker Woods, Cornell Lab of Ornithology* (Winter 1995): 1–3.

Ross, Gary Noel. *Everything You Ever Wanted to Know About Butterflies: 100+ Questions and Answers.* To order, send $13.95 ($11.95 + $2.00 postage and handling) to: Gary Noel Ross, 6095 Stratford Ave., Baton Rouge, LA 70808. Phone 504-927-8179.

Shalaway, Scott. "Attracting Birds, Ghost Trees Come Alive." *Birder's World* (August 1993): 52–55. Article about snags.

———, and Linda Shalaway. "Winter Feeding in the Sunbelt." *WildBird* (February 1992): 48–53.

Skutch, Alexander F. *The Life of the Hummingbird.* New York: Crown Publishers, Inc., 1973.

Smith, Miranda, and Anna Carr. *Rodale's Garden Insect, Disease & Weed Identification Guide.* Emmaus, PA: Rodale Press, 1988.

Smyser, Carol A., and the Editors of Rodale Press Books. *Nature's Design: A Practical Guide to Natural Landscaping.* Emmaus, PA: Rodale Press, 1982.

Stein, Sara B. *My Weeds: A Gardener's Botany.* New York: Harper & Row, Publishers, 1988.

Steinhart, Peter. "Soil, the Miracle We Take For Granted." *National Wildlife* (February–March 1985): 15–22.

Stokes, Donald, and Lillian Stokes. *The Hummingbird Book: The Complete Guide to Attracting, Identifying, and Enjoying Hummingbirds.* Boston: Little, Brown and Co., 1989.

———.*The Complete Birdhouse Book.* Boston: Little, Brown and Co., 1990.

———."The Scoop on Bird Seed." *WildBird* (May 1990): 40–45.

————.*The Bluebird Book*. Boston: Little, Brown and Co., 1991.

————.*The Butterfly Book: An Easy Guide to Butterfly Gardening, Identification, and Behavior*. Boston: Little, Brown and Co., 1992.

Terborgh, John. *Essays on the Biology and Conservation of Birds That Migrate to the American Tropics*. Princeton, NJ: Princeton University Press, 1989.

Tessaglia, Diane L., and Kenneth V. Rosenberg. "Project Feeder Watch: Annual Report 1993–94." *Birdscope: News and Views from Sapsucker Woods, Cornell Lab of Ornithology* (Autumn 1994): 1–6.

Tuttle, Merlin D. *America's Neighborhood Bats*. Austin: University of Texas Press, 1988.

Water Visions '93, The Complete Guide to Water Gardening. Catalog of Van Ness Water Gardens, 2640 North Euclid Avenue, Upland, CA 91786-1199. $6.00. Lists references on ponds and water gardening.

Wilson, Edward O. *Biophilia, the Human Bond with Other Species*. Cambridge, MA: The Belknap Press of Harvard University Press, 1984.

————.*The Diversity of Life*. Cambridge, MA: The Belknap Press of Harvard University Press, 1992.

Wilson, William H. W. *Landscaping with Wildflowers & Native Plants*. San Francisco: Ortho Books, 1984.

Xerces Society/Smithsonian Institution. *Butterfly Gardening: Creating Summer Magic in Your Garden*. San Francisco: Sierra Club Books, 1990.

For Wildlife Gardeners in the East/Southeast

Allen, Charles M. *Grasses of Louisiana*. Eunice, LA: Cajun Prairie Habitat Preservation Society, 1992.

Benyus, Janine M. *The Field Guide to Wildlife Habitats of the Eastern United States*. New York: Simon & Schuster, Inc., 1989.

Blake, Ed. "Goldenrod, *Solidago*." *Mississippi Gardens* (September–October 1993): 28–30.

Brzuszek, Robert F. *Native Trees for Urban Landscapes in the Gulf South*. Picayune, MS: The Crosby Arboretum, 1993.

Cerulean, Susan, Celeste Botha, and Donna Legare. *Planting a Refuge for Wildlife: How to Create a Backyard Habitat for Florida's Birds and Beasts.* Available free from: Nongame Wildlife Program, Florida Game and Fresh Water Fish Commission, 620 South Meridian Street, Tallahassee, FL 32399-1600.

Dundee, Harold A., and Douglas A. Rossman. *The Amphibians and Reptiles of Louisiana.* Baton Rouge and London: Louisiana State University Press, 1989.

Eleuterius, Lionel N. *Tidal Marsh Plants.* Gretna, LA: Pelican Publishing Company, 1990.

Fontenot, William R. *Native Gardening in the South: A Personal Guide for Understanding, Appreciating, and Using the Indigenous Plants of Dixie.* Carencro, LA: A Prairie Basse Publication, 1992. To order, send $16.00 (LA. residents add $1.20) to: Prairie Basse, Rt 2 Box 491-F, Carencro, LA 70520.

————."Notes On Backyard Wildlife Habitat Enrichment Techniques." *L.O.S. News, The Newsletter of the Louisiana Ornithological Society*, No. 146 (April 2, 1992): 3, 10.

Foote, Leonard E., and Samuel B. Jones, Jr. *Native Shrubs and Woody Vines of the Southeast: Landscaping Uses and Identification.* Portland, OR: Timber Press, 1989.

Jones, Samuel B., Jr., and Leonard E. Foote. *Gardening with Native Wild Flowers.* Portland, OR: Timber Press, 1990.

Kale, Herbert W. II, and David S. Maehr. *Florida's Birds: A Handbook and Reference.* Sarasota, FL: Pineapple Press, 1990.

Lowery, George H., Jr. *Louisiana Birds.* Baton Rouge, LA: Louisiana Press, 1974.

————.*The Mammals of Louisiana and Its Adjacent Waters.* Baton Rouge, LA: Louisiana State University Press, 1974.

Newfield, Nancy L. *Louisiana's Hummingbirds.* Baton Rouge, LA: Louisiana Department of Wildlife & Fisheries, Louisiana Natural Heritage Program, 1992.

Odenwald, Neil G., and James R. Turner. *Identification, Selection, and Use of Southern Plants for Landscape Design.* Baton Rouge: Claitor's Publishing Division, 1987.

Pope, Thomas, Charles Fryling, Jr., and Neil Odenwald. *Attracting Birds to Southern Gardens*. Dallas, TX: Taylor Publishing Company, 1993.

Ross, Gary Noel. *Gardening for Butterflies in Louisiana*. Baton Rouge, LA: Louisiana Department of Wildlife & Fisheries, Louisiana Natural Heritage Program, 1994.

————. "The Trans-Gulf Express." *Louisiana Conservationist* (September-October 1993): 15-17. Article about the migration of monarch butterflies.

Rushing, Felder. *Gardening Southern Style*. Jackson and London: University Press of Mississippi, 1987.

Toups, Judith A., and Jerome A. Jackson. *Birds and Birding on the Mississippi Coast*. Jackson and London: University Press of Mississippi, 1987.

Wasowski, Sally. *Gardening with Native Plants of the South*. Dallas, TX: Taylor Publishing Company, 1994.

Wrensch, Ruth D. *The Essence of Herbs: Growing Herbs in the Southeast*. Jackson and London: University Press of Mississippi, 1982.

Field Guides/Identification

Audubon Society Field Guides: *Butterflies. Insects and Spiders. Mammals. Mushrooms. Reptiles and Amphibians. Trees. Wildflowers.*

Borror, Donald J., and Richard E. White. *A Field Guide to the Insects*. Boston: Houghton Mifflin Co., 1970.

Brown, Clair A. *Wildflowers of Louisiana and Adjoining States*. Baton Rouge: Louisiana State University Press, 1980.

Covell, Charles V., Jr. *A Field Guide to the Moths of Eastern North America*. Boston: Houghton Mifflin Co., 1984.

Duncan, Wilbur H., and Leonard E. Foote. *Wildflowers of the Southeastern United States*. Athens: University of Georgia Press, 1975.

Golden Guides. *Butterflies and Moths. Flowers. Insect Pests. Insects. Mushrooms. Pond Life. Reptiles and Amphibians. Spiders and their Kin. Trees. Weeds.*

Klots, Alexander B. *A Field Guide to the Butterflies of North America East of the Great Plains.* Boston: Houghton Mifflin Co., 1951.

Klots, Elsie B. *The New Field Book of Freshwater Life.* New York: G. P. Putnam's Sons, 1966.

Little, Elbert L. *The Audubon Society Field Guide to North American Trees.* New York: Alfred A. Knopf, 1980.

Mitchell, Robert T., and Herbert S. Zim. *Butterflies and Moths.* New York: Golden Press, 1987.

Muenscher, Walter Conrad. *Weeds.* Ithaca and London: Cornell University Press, 1980.

National Geographic Society. *Field Guide to the Birds of North America.* Washington, DC: National Geographic Society, 1987.

Peterson, Roger Tory. *A Field Guide to the Birds East of the Rockies.* Boston: Houghton Mifflin, Co., 1980.

Petrides, George A. *A Field Guide to Trees and Shrubs.* Boston: Houghton Mifflin Co., 1986.

Pyle, Robert Michael. *The Audubon Society Field Guide to North American Butterflies.* New York: Alfred A. Knopf, 1981.

Robbins, Chandler S., Bertel Bruun, and Herbert S. Zim. *Birds of North America.* New York: Golden Press, 1966.

Timme, S. Lee. *Wildflowers of Mississippi.* Jackson and London: University Press of Mississippi, 1989.

The Wild Model: Some Sources for Southeastern Regions

Alabama Natural Heritage Section, Preliminary List of Natural Communities of Alabama (February 1993). Natural Heritage Section, Department of Conservation and Natural Resources, State Lands Division, 64 North Union Street, Montgomery, AL 36130.

Florida Natural Areas Inventory - Natural Communities (July 1992). Florida Natural Areas Inventory, 1018 Thomasville Road, Suite 200-C, Tallahassee, FL 32303.

Hamel, Paul B. *Land Manager's Guide to the Birds of the South.* Available for $20.00 postage paid from: The Nature Conservancy,

Southeastern Region, P.O. Box 2267, Chapel Hill, NC 27515-2267.

Mississippi Natural Heritage Program Ecological Communities (January 1994). Mississippi Department of Wildlife, Fisheries and Parks, 111 North Jefferson Street, Jackson, MS 39202.

Smith, Latimore M. *The Natural Communities of Louisiana* (December 1988). Louisiana Natural Heritage Program, Louisiana Department of Wildlife and Fisheries, P.O. Box 98000, Baton Rouge, LA 70898.

Texas Wildscapes. Nongame and Urban Program, Texas Parks and Wildlife Department, 4200 Smith School Road, Austin, TX 78744, 800-792-1112.

Wharton, Charles H. *The Natural Environments of Georgia.* Atlanta, GA: Geologic and Water Resources Division and Resource Planning Section, Office of Planning and Research, Georgia Department of Natural Resources, 1978. To order, send a check for $6.00 (Georgia residents, $6.25) to: Georgia Geologic Survey, 19 M. L. King Drive S.W., Room 400, Atlanta, GA 30334. Request Bulletin 114, *The Natural Environments of Georgia*.

Organizations/Activities/Publications

American Birding Association. P.O. Box 6599, Colorado Springs, CO 80934. Phone 800-634-7736 or FAX 800-590-2473. Magazine *Birding* is for serious birders. ABA Sales *Annotated Catalog and Pricelist* is a highly useful resource for any backyard naturalist: checklists of birds, "rare bird alert" phone numbers, books on birds, wildlife, wild places specific to each state.

American Horticultural Society, 7931 East Boulevard Drive, Alexandria, VA 22308. Phone 703-768-5700. Members receive *American Horticulturist* six times a year, *American Horticulturist* news edition six times a year. Many articles on native plants. Guide to pronunciation of botanical names used in each edition is very helpful. Seed Exchange Program annual catalog is published in the news edition.

Bat Conservation International, P.O. Box 162603, Austin, TX 78716. Catalog lists educational publications and programs, books about bats, bat houses, other items. Members receive the quarterly publication, *Bats*.

The Bio Integral Resource Center (BIRC), P. O. Box 7414, Berkeley, CA 94707. Phone 415-524-2567. The ultimate source on integrated pest management, least toxic methods for managing insect, weed, disease and rodent pests. Publication: *Common Sense Pest Control Quarterly.*

Bird Watcher's Digest. Pardson Corporation, P. O. Box 110, Marietta, OH 45750-9977. Bimonthly. Practical articles, ads for birdseed, supplies, other resources.

Birder's World: The Magazine Exploring Wild Birds and Birding. 44 E. 8th Street, Suite 410, Holland, MI 49423. Bimonthly. Practical articles, ads for birdseed, supplies, other resources.

Conservation International. 1015 18th Street, NW, Suite 1000, Washington, DC 20036. Phone 202-429-5660 or FAX 202-887-5188. Membership benefits: periodic members' reports to keep you informed on CI's work with people and communities near the earth's richest and most threatened ecosystem—the "hot spots" of biodiversity. CI builds on local initiative and enthusiasm to help local people protect forests and other critical habitats around the world, including wintering habitat for our native songbirds.

Cornell Laboratory of Ornithology, 159 Sapsucker Woods Road, Ithaca, NY 14850. Sponsors Project Feeder Watch and conducts seed preference tests. Members receive quarterly magazine, *Living Bird, For the Study and Conservation of Birds*; catalog for The Crow's Nest Birding Shop, which sells wildlife feeders, field guides and other natural history books, bird and butterfly videos, tapes of songbirds, frog and toad calls. Write for information or call 1-800-843-BIRD.

Horticulture, The Magazine of American Gardening. P. O. Box 53879, Boulder, CO 80321. Monthly.

Louisiana Conservationist. Department of Wildlife and Fisheries, P. O. Box 98000, Baton Rouge, LA 70898. Bimonthly.

Mississippi Gardens. Mississippi Gardens, Inc. P. O. Box 7856, Jackson, MS 39284. Bimonthly.

National Audubon Society P. O. Box 52529, Boulder, CO 80322.
Members receive bimonthly magazine, *Audubon*. Write for information about local Audubon societies and Christmas bird counts in
your region.

National Gardening Association, 180 Flynn Avenue, Burlington, VT
05401. Phone 802-863-1308. Members receive *National Gardening,
The Gardener's Newsmagazine*, monthly. Seed search service.

National Wildflower Research Center, 2600 FM 973 North, Austin,
TX 78725. Phone 512-929-3600. Members receive newsletter and
other benefits.

National Wildlife Federation. 8925 Leesburg Pike, Vienna, VA, 22184.
Subscription to bimonthly magazine, *National Wildlife*, comes with
membership. Write or call 1-800-432-6564, to find out how to have
your backyard certified by NWF's Backyard Wildlife Habitat
Program. Part of the kit you'll receive is Craig Tufts's *The Backyard
Naturalist*. Write NWF for the name and address of the affiliate in
your state. Your local wildlife federation conducts grassroots activities and takes the lead in state and local issues in conservation and
may also have a newsletter and projects related to wildlife and native
plants in your area.

The Nature Conservancy, 1815 N. Lynn St., Arlington, VA 22209.
Phone 703-841-5300. Bimonthly magazine, *Nature Conservancy*.
Mission is to preserve plants, animals and natural communities that
represent the diversity of life on earth by protecting the lands and
waters they need to survive. Your local chapter can direct you to
preserves in your region and models for your garden.

The Nature Society, Purple Martin Junction, Griggsville, IL 62340.
Monthly newsletter, *Nature Society News*, stars purple martins and
bluebirds, but covers hummingbirds and other species, too. Each
issue is full of practical information, photos and diagrams such as
plans for burrowing owl nest tunnels and house sparrow traps.

North American Bluebird Society, Box 6295, Silver Spring, MD
20916-6295. Members receive quarterly journal, *Sialia*. Send self-
addressed stamped envelope for catalog of houses, supplies, books.

North American Butterfly Association, 4 Delaware Road, Morristown, NJ 07960. Phone 201-285-0907. Membership benefits: *American Butterflies* (magazine), *The Anglewing* (newsletter), 4th of July butterfly counts.

Purple Martin Conservation Association, Edinboro University of Pennsylvania, Edinboro, PA 16444. Membership benefits: quarterly issues of *Purple Martin Update*, a magazine full of statistics, illustrations, and practical information on martins; "Martin Market Place" catalog, source of starling/house sparrow traps; *How To Control House Sparrows* by Don Grussing; and many other products.

WildBird Magazine. P. O. Box 52898, Boulder, CO 80322-2892. Monthly. Practical articles, ads for birdseed, supplies, other resources.

Wild Bird Centers' free newsletter, *Wild Bird News*, contains useful information on luring, feeding, and housing all kinds of backyard wildlife and articles by Dr. Aelred Geis, birdseed guru and Director of Research for Wild Bird Centers of America, Inc. Call 800-WILD-BIRD to find the store nearest you and get on the mailing list.

Xerces Society, 10 SW Ash Street, Portland, OR 97204. Phone 503-222-2788. The only conservation organization devoted solely to the protection of invertebrates. Sponsors 4th of July butterfly counts. Members receive *Wings: Essays on Invertebrate Conservation*, a biannual magazine.

Plant and Seed Sources

How can I suggest you grow native plants from local sources and then offer a list of plant and seed companies with national orientations? That would be inconsistent. So, I recommend that you begin your search for native plants locally:

1) Collect seeds of native wildflowers within a fifty-mile radius of your garden; propagate them yourself.

2) Buy plants from local nurseries that have propagated plants themselves or whose suppliers of nursery-propagated natives are close by. How do you know where plants come from? Ask. What if no local

nurseries offer natives? Ask them to order natives. They'll find sources if they perceive there is a demand.

3) To locate regional sources of plant material:

a) Contact your state or region's native plant society, nature and science center, botanical garden, or arboretum. To find those, start with the phone book. Another reference is Barbara J. Barton's *Gardening By Mail, A Source Book* (Boston: Houghton Mifflin Co., 1995). Updated yearly, this volume can direct you to all of the above—plants, other supplies, botanical gardens, arboretums, societies—in every state.

b) To receive a list of "Recommended Sources for Native Propagated Plants and Seeds" for the Southeast, send a self-addressed, stamped envelope to: North Carolina Botanical Garden, University of North Carolina, CB # 3375 Totten Center Chapel Hill, NC 27599-3375. Phone 919-962-0522.

For the Northeast, order *Sources of Propagated Native Plants and Wildflowers* from the New England Wildflower Society, Garden in the Woods, 180 Hemenway Road, Framingham, MA 01701-2699. Phone 617-237-4924.

For western sources, write to Native Plant Society of New Mexico, P. O. Box 5917, Santa Fe, NM 87502.

4) Nonregional sources of seeds of native and other plants:

The American Horticultural Society Seed Exchange Program. Seeds contributed by members, horticultural societies and seed companies are available to members for a minimal donation. The annual seed catalogue is published in the news edition of the *American Horticulturist* magazine.

Boothe Hill Greenhouse, 23B Boothe Hill, Chapel Hill, NC 27514. Phone 919-967-4091. Plants and seeds or propagated native plants. Send self-addressed stamped envelope for catalog.

Clyde Robin Seed Company, P. O. Box 2366, Castro Valley, CA 94546. Write for wildflower catalog.

Flowerplace Plant Farm, P. O. Box 4865, Meridian MS 39304. Phone 1-800-482-5686. Plants. Catalog is $3.00—and worth it!

J. L. Hudson, Seedsman, Star Route 2, Box 337, La Honda, CA, 94020. Send $1.00 for "The 1995 Ethnobotanical Catalog of Seeds." Seeds you'll find almost nowhere else, including *Chenopodiums*, *Amaranths*, *Urticas*, *Capsicums*, *Manfreda virginica*, *Phytolacca*, and many more.

Native Seed/SEARCH, 2509 North Campbell Avenue #325, Tucson, AZ 85719. Phone 602-327-9123.

Park Seed Company, Cokesbury Road, Greenwood, SC 29647-0001. Seeds and plants.

Seeds for Change, P. O. Box 15700, Santa Fe, NM 87506-5700. This catalog is a sourcebook, too. It offers seeds of *Chenopodiums*, *Amaranths*, *Spilanthes*, *Urtica*, *Monardas*, *Capsicums*, and many more.

Sunnybrook Farms, 9448 Mayfield Road, P. O. Box 6, Chesterland, OH 44026. Write for catalog. Source of perennials and herbs including a nice selection of salvias.

Thompson & Morgan, P. O. Box 1308, Jackson, NJ 08527. Seeds.

Wild Seed, Inc., 1101 Campo Rosa Road, P. O. Box 308, Eagle Lake, TX 77434. Offers individual wildflower seeds in small quantities.

Index